ADDRESSING
COMMUNITY
PROBLEMS

The Claremont Symposium on Applied Social Psychology

This series of volumes highlights important new developments on the leading edge of applied social psychology. Each volume concentrates on one area in which social psychological knowledge is being applied to the resolution of social problems. Within that area, a distinguished group of authorities present chapters summarizing recent theoretical views and empirical findings, including the results of their own research and applied activities. An introductory chapter integrates this material, pointing out common themes and varied areas of practical applications. Thus each volume brings together trenchant new social psychological ideas, research results, and fruitful applications bearing on an area of current social interest. The volumes will be of value not only to practitioners and researchers but also to students and lay people interested in this vital and expanding area of psychology.

Books in the Series

Interpersonal Processes, *Stuart Oskamp and Shirlynn Spacapan, Editors*

The Social Psychology of Health, *Shirlynn Spacapan and Stuart Oskamp, Editors*

The Social Psychology of Aging, *Shirlynn Spacapan and Stuart Oskamp, Editors*

People's Reactions to Technology, *Stuart Oskamp and Shirlynn Spacapan, Editors*

Helping and Being Helped, *Shirlynn Spacapan and Stuart Oskamp, Editors*

Gender Issues in Contemporary Society, *Stuart Oskamp and Mark Costanzo, Editors*

Violence and the Law, *Mark Costanzo and Stuart Oskamp, Editors*

Diversity in Organizations, *Martin M. Chemers, Stuart Oskamp, and Mark Constanzo, Editors*

Understanding and Preventing HIV Risk Behavior, *Stuart Oskamp and Suzanne C. Thompson, Editors*

Cross-Cultural Work Groups, *Cherlyn Skromme Granrose and Stuart Oskamp, Editors*

Addressing Community Problems, *Ximena B. Arriaga and Stuart Oskamp, Editors*

ADDRESSING COMMUNITY PROBLEMS

Psychological Research and Interventions

XIMENA B. ARRIAGA
STUART OSKAMP

editors

The Claremont Symposium on
Applied Social Psychology

SAGE Publications
International Educational and Professional Publisher
Thousand Oaks London New Delhi

For information:

SAGE Publications, Inc.
2455 Teller Road
Thousand Oaks, California 91320
E-mail: order@sagepub.com

SAGE Publications Ltd.
6 Bonhill Street
London EC2A 4PU
United Kingdom

SAGE Publications India Pvt. Ltd.
M-32 Market
Greater Kailash I
New Delhi 110 048 India

Printed in the United States of America

Library of Congress Cataloging-in-Publication Data

Main entry under title:

Addressing community problems: Research and intervention / by Ximena B. Arriaga and Stuart Oskamp, Editors.
     p. cm.
     Includes bibliographical references and index. ISBN 0-7619-1077-8 (cloth: acid-free paper) ISBN 0-7619-1078-6 (pbk.: acid-free paper)
      1. Community life—United States. 2. Social problems—United States. 3. Community organizations—United States. 4. Social psychology—United States. 5. United States—Social conditions. I. Arriaga, Ximena B. II. Oskamp, Stuart.
HM131 .A313 1998
307'.0973—ddc21   98-19701

This book is printed on acid-free paper.

98 99 00 01 02 03 04 7 6 5 4 3 2 1

Acquiring Editor:	Jim Nageotte
Editorial Assistant:	Heidi Van Middlesworth
Production Editor:	Sherrise M. Purdum
Production Assistant:	Lynn Miata
Typesetter/Designer:	Danielle Dillahunt

Contents

1

Addressing Community Problems
An Introduction

STUART OSKAMP

XIMENA B. ARRIAGA

P roblems in community life are among the most distressing and troublesome aspects of modern society, yet psychology as a field gives them relatively little attention. The great bulk of psychological practice and research is directed at individual psychological problems and at difficulties in dyadic relationships. Community problems, however, arguably are broader and more important because to a large degree they affect us all—young and old, rich and poor, male and female, majority and minority group members. For instance, among the most serious community problems, we are all directly or indirectly injured by crime and delinquency, prejudice and discrimination, poverty and unemployment, drug and alcohol abuse, and epidemics of illness and disease. These problems afflict us not only in the communities where we live but also where we work and where we spend our leisure time.

Psychology should and does have a contribution to make in solving such community problems. The official view of that contribution is stated by the bylaws of the American Psychological Association (APA, 1992, p. 1), which define *psychology* as "a science and profession and as a means of promoting human welfare" and include as one of its goals "the application of research findings to the promotion of the public welfare." Unofficially, many branches of psychology pay less attention to advancing human welfare, but community psychology and applied social psychology focus much of their effort in that area.

The goal of this volume is to bring together recent psychological analyses and research findings about various community problems that applied psychologists have been addressing productively. Rather than focus on a single problem area, the volume covers a broad range of community troubles that represent some of the most serious ills of modern industrial societies.

These ills include homelessness, racism and prejudice, violence in the broader community as well as in personal relationships, substance abuse, workplace stress, and unemployment. By focusing on issues affecting the community, this volume enables us to identify some common themes in both the approaches and the findings in these apparently disparate areas. It also brings together research findings with programs and suggestions for interventions, combining the analytic approach of scientific research with the activist tradition of applied social science.

In this chapter, we highlight current community problems plaguing our society and evaluate the applied social science response. By outlining the approach taken by each of the authors to address some challenges that communities face, we hope to underscore the ways these chapters individually and collectively make a significant contribution to documenting, understanding, and ameliorating social troubles.

Seriousness of Current Community Problems

Anywhere one turns in the United States and in most other countries, the tragic evidence of community distress is easy to find. For example, about one third of a million U.S. residents are homeless on any given day, and it is estimated that about 3% of the U.S. population has been homeless over the past 5 years (Shinn & Tsemberis, this volume, Chapter 3). Severe mental illness afflicts 3% of our citizens, and 20% have some degree of mental disorder in a given year (National Advisory Mental Health Council, 1993). Eighteen million American adults have a serious problem with alcohol abuse during a typical year, and health services for alcoholics cost $15 billion per year (Timko, this volume, Chapter 6).

Health care expenses are estimated to consume 16% of the U.S. gross national product, and yet at any given time about one quarter of U.S. residents have no health insurance and consequently no regular access to routine medical care (Oskamp & Schultz, 1998). More than one million U.S. residents are estimated to be infected with HIV, which means that they will suffer and die from AIDS in the future (Mann, Tarantola, & Netter, 1992), and AIDS is already the leading cause of death for U.S. adults between the ages of 25 and 44 (National Center for Health Statistics, 1994).

Each year, more than one million U.S. children see their families break up in divorce, and millions more suffer the debilitating effects of family conflict. Because of the high divorce rate, over 30% of American children currently live with one parent or no biological parent, and 25% will live with a stepparent at some time before reaching adulthood (Mason & Mauldon, 1996). About one fifth of American children drop out of school before graduation from high school (Parker & Asher, 1987), and two million children each year suffer child abuse (American Association for Protecting Children, 1987).

Racism, discrimination, and prejudice affect the lives of almost all minority citizens, even those who are affluent or well educated or both. The stress they cause for their targets can damage physical and mental health (Jackson & Volckens, this volume, Chapter 2). The media often amplify this impact by spreading and perpetuating oppressive stereotypes and by highlighting cultural conflicts (Rappaport, this volume, Chapter 9). Minorities, even more than the dominant majority population, are threatened by the prevalence of community crime, drug use, and violence. About 35 million Americans are victimized by crime each year (National Crime Survey, 1991). Carrying a deadly knife or gun is becoming ever more common, and gun homicide rates have increased greatly (Zimmerman, Steinman, & Rowe, this volume, Chapter 4). Violence in dating and marital relationships has also displayed a marked increase and may be experienced by one quarter of U.S. adolescents (Foshee, this volume, Chapter 5).

Underlying these community problems are worldwide demographic and economic trends such as rapidly increasing population, urbanization, and industrialization. These forces have led to many profound changes in people's residential patterns and working conditions. Many U.S. companies have shifted production facilities overseas, markedly affecting employment opportunities both here and abroad. Global competition and economic recessions have frequently led to mass unemployment, job-losses, organizational downsizing, and increases in temporary and short-term jobs. These stresses affect not only the workers' health and mental health but also family structure and roles and community-wide processes such as the membership and effectiveness of local groups (Price, Friedland, Choi, & Caplan, this volume, Chapter 8). Even for those who remain employed, problems and changes in working conditions produce serious job or health problems for half of the U.S. workforce (Donaldson, Gooler, & Weiss, this volume, Chapter 7).

Meanwhile, the gap between rich and poor is growing all over the world. The buying power of the average American's income has been falling while the salaries of many corporate CEOs have been rising sharply into the tens of millions of dollars. In the United States, 1% of the population owns 40% of the national wealth (Jason, 1997), and such disparities from equality contribute greatly to social tensions and the community problems that are discussed in this volume.

Psychological Contributions Regarding Community Problems

Given the prevalence and immediacy of community problems, it is not surprising that attempts to address them have come from several disciplines in addition to psychology. In particular, sociology and economics have attempted to analyze the background and structure of community problems, political science and public administration have focused on policies to prevent or alleviate them, and social work has tried to implement policies and programs to combat them.

Psychology historically has shown an interest in conducting research aimed at ameliorating social problems. Kurt Lewin's "action research" exemplifies how scholarly research can, and should, have practical implications. Echoing Lewin's call for action research, others have advocated "public affairs psychology" (cf. Brayfield & Lipsey, 1976) or "social issue psychology" directed toward issues of practical concern in the public domain (Berger, 1994; Lipsey, 1987). An example is presented in the following quotation:

> A psychology that serves its science but not its society does not participate
> in the reality it claims to study. A psychology that serves its society but

not its science does not test what it claims to know nor use its experience effectively to expand its knowledge. A psychology that serves its science *and* its society, however, is an instrument of both reflection and reform—it seeks to understand what goes on in this human world, and to test and improve that understanding, but it also reaches out to try to make that world better and in some, perhaps modest way, improve the human condition. (Lipsey, 1987, p. 8)

The application of action-oriented psychological research to community problems is most apparent in the areas of applied social psychology and community psychology. These areas have contributed theory, research methods, and policy analyses directed at understanding and resolving community troubles.

Three rather different streams of psychological writing have focused on community problems. One stream builds on empirical research findings to develop theories and policy perspectives. It is epitomized by texts on community psychology (e.g., Levine & Perkins, 1997; Orford, 1992) and on applied social psychology (e.g., Oskamp & Schultz, 1998) and is illustrated in many issues of relevant journals such as the *Journal of Social Issues* and *Social Problems*. These contributions emphasize research findings and general principles concerning stressful situations in society, how groups and individuals react to, and cope with, them (e.g., Zander, 1990), as well as empirical evaluations of interventions intended to improve community conditions. A second and somewhat different stream of psychological writing emphasizes the *values* that characterize various groups in our society and how these values can augment or damage people's sense of community and their feelings of separation from, or oneness with, their environment (e.g., Jason, 1997). This genre seeks to understand the ills of modern society and to pre-scribe value-based approaches that will help overcome them. Finally, a third stream of writing in psychology and social work follows an activist tradition, presenting experience-based advice about how to organize community groups, build coalitions and alliances, define tactical goals, and accomplish them. Authors in this tradition focus on empowerment of disadvantaged groups (Mondros & Wilson, 1994) or write handbooks for activists (Shaw, 1996).

This volume profits from all three streams of psychological writing about community problems. Primarily, its chapters are research based, presenting empirical findings and conclusions from programs of re-search on particular problem areas. Yet, all the chapters also are founded on a strong value position concerning what constitutes a community problem, and they aim to present recommendations about desirable solutions for them. Finally, the theme of empowering formerly excluded groups in society runs through many of the chapters.

Summary of Chapters in This Volume

Each chapter in this volume tackles one or more pressing community problems. Part 1, on discrimination and violence, examines the antecedents and consequences of negative intergroup and interpersonal relations. The model advanced in Chapter 2, by James Jackson and Julie Volckens, adopts a social-structural viewpoint, positing that community problems such as economic recessions produce stress within dominant (more powerful) and subordinate groups, which in turn leads to increases in racism; and racism and stress in turn produce declines in psychological and physical health. Their perspective is unique in at least two ways. First, although many models of racism suggest that the targets of prejudice experience negative outcomes, this model suggests that racist beliefs are also unhealthy for those who hold them; second, this model examines racism from a broader community context, rather than from an interpersonal context.

Chapter 3, by Marybeth Shinn and Sam Tsemberis, examines the success of various programs to end homelessness. As is the case for subordinate groups described in the previous chapter, homeless families and individuals are often assumed to comprise a homogenous group and, as a group, are not well understood by the general population. Just as stereotypic beliefs about a group can lead to inappropriate behaviors, the authors demonstrate how inaccurate beliefs about the needs of homeless individuals and families often lead to inappropriate forms of assistance. Specifically, they present preciously rare data on the effectiveness of programs that make housing assistance contingent on completing health-related and other treatments. Their results are not intuitive and are likely to be important in shaping the community resources that will become available for homeless people in the future.

Two chapters examine violence among adolescents, both adopting the perspective that such violence is a central community problem. In

Chapter 4, Marc Zimmerman, Kenneth Steinman, and Karen Rowe begin by reviewing the disconcerting statistics documenting the high rates at which adolescents carry weapons to school, or know of someone killed by a weapon, or are themselves victims of violence. In the light of the tremendous risks that youths face, this analysis is particularly compelling. Rather than simply list factors predictive of violence, Zimmerman et al. compare different models that specify the process by which adolescents avoid violence: They suggest that positive factors, such as parental support, may compensate for the high-risk factors that confront adolescents; in combination, these factors may offset each other. But it may also be the case that the presence of positive, "protective" factors "guard" against the influence of other risk factors, such as violent peers, and that the absence of protective factors increases the impact of risk factors. Zimmerman et al. review their own findings in relation to these two alternative models.

Taking a different approach to the analysis of violence, Vangie Foshee, in Chapter 5, provides direct evidence that schools and communities have an important role in preventing and minimizing dating violence. She describes a rigorous study that employed a true experimental and longitudinal design to assess the immediate and long-term impact of Safe Dates, a dating violence prevention program. This chapter provides a detailed account of the organization and coordination involved in mobilizing teachers, parents, students, school administrators, police departments, community agencies—in short, an entire community—to enact a large-scale intervention. Moreover, the intervention was noteworthy in its dual aims of primary and secondary prevention—that is, in attempting to prevent the onset *and* repeated occurrence of dating violence.

Part 2 of this volume, on health and work, focuses more directly on health problems and how work-related programs can prevent such problems. In the first chapter of this section, Chapter 6 by Christine Timko, it becomes clear how many community problems stem from poor individual health. Timko describes the various problems experienced by individuals who are dependent on alcohol—problems such as criminal behavior, violent behavior, and work neglect resulting in unemployment. Because severe alcoholism has been shown to be strongly related to various community ills, an important applied issue is to understand the factors that facilitate alcoholics' return to a healthier lifestyle. Timko describes a longitudinal study that attempted to (a) identify factors that make individuals more inclined to enter treatment and (b) compare various types of treatment in their effectiveness at restoring a healthy lifestyle.

Among individuals who are generally healthy, however, one of the most effective places to encourage health promotion and disease prevention practices is in the work setting. Stewart Donaldson, Laura Gooler, and Rachel Weiss have spearheaded an evaluation of programs that promote health and well-being in the workplace and the community. Chapter 7, by Donaldson et al., describes these programs, which vary widely in their aims and foci. Two programs are oriented toward raising awareness of work and health issues in California. For instance, they identify ways that workplaces are changing and affecting levels of well-being, and they analyze health care coverage and health promotion programs in the California workplace. The chapter also describes two community interventions: (a) The Winning New Jobs program combats adverse health consequences of unemployment and (b) the Computers in Our Future program provides computer skills to young adults in lower-income communities, thereby directly improving education and employment opportunities and indirectly improving the well-being of their families and communities. In addition to describing each program, Donaldson et al. provide a summary of the early findings.

In Chapter 8, Richard Price, Daniel Friedland, Jin Nam Choi, and Robert Caplan provide a detailed description of the JOBS program—a community-based organized support system for coping with the potentially disruptive and detrimental effects of job-loss or job transitions. These authors describe (a) the global economic changes that make such a program necessary, (b) the theoretical underpinnings of the program, and (c) the substantial empirical support for its effectiveness. Importantly, this chapter includes an extensive discussion of how to implement the JOBS program and, more generally, how innovations such as JOBS require mutual adaptation between a host organization or community and the structure of the innovation itself. The authors cogently argue that such programs work best in specific organizations or communities when a theory of the intervention guides the process of mutual adaptation.

In the final section, Part 3 on empowering communities, Julian Rappaport examines how narratives—stories, shared beliefs, and representations of collective identity—can be employed to communicate a community's desired image. A community that suffers from the types of problems described in the other chapters undoubtedly also has other, more desirable characteristics by which members of that community may wish to be perceived. Given that our individual identities are strongly influenced by the ways our own groups and communities are depicted, social scientists can be of assistance to those in communities that are "stuck" with a personally oppressive image. Specifically, Rappaport reminds us that, by documenting and disseminating the favorable aspects of communities and their organizations—"the visions of ordinary people, and the strengths and abilities they possess"—we can each be instruments of social change.

Emerging Themes

Across the contributions in this volume, common themes can be identified. First, several authors emphasize the heterogeneity of the target groups that their research is attempting to help. Among homeless individuals, the characteristics and needs of families are quite different from those of single adults (Shinn & Tsemberis, Chapter 3). Survey studies of ethnic minority groups show a great variety in their beliefs, attitudes, and behavioral patterns, even within a single ethnic group such as African Americans (Jackson & Volckens, Chapter 2). Among violent youths, distinct differences exist between those who get into trouble for fighting and those who engage in violent assaults (Zimmerman et al., Chapter 4). Problem drinkers can be divided into groups, both in terms of the severity of their drinking problems and their difficulties in everyday functioning, and in terms of the treatment modes they choose (Timko, Chapter 6).

Second, many problem individuals suffer from more than one kind of disabling condition, and that fact makes them especially vulnerable. Many homeless individuals, though by no means all, also have diagnosed mental illnesses (Shinn & Tsemberis, Chapter 3). Workplace problems often contribute to poor physical and mental health, and they are exacerbated by lack of health insurance (Donaldson et al., Chapter 7). Losing one's job can contribute to emotional distress, individual mental illness, and breakdowns in family structure and functioning (Price et al., Chapter 8). Similarly, drinking problems can contribute to impaired workplace performance (e.g., increased absenteeism, decreased productivity), greater workplace injuries, and loss of employment, as well as to child abuse, criminal behavior, and homelessness (Timko, Chapter 6). Thus, these problems often occur simultaneously, suggesting that an efficient community response might be to centralize resources and services that can provide help for concomitant problems.

Third, structural factors in society are largely responsible for many of the problems displayed by individuals; that is, they are community-level dysfunctions caused by community stressors, and treating them as individual-level problems overlooks these structural factors. For instance, prejudice and racism in our society lower the well-being of all members of disadvantaged ethnic minority groups (Jackson & Volckens, Chapter 2). Economic, political, and social decision making combine to create a shortage of affordable housing, which is the primary factor causing homelessness (Shinn & Tsemberis, Chapter 3). Stressful working conditions, and especially unemployment, contribute to poor physical and mental health (Donaldson et al., Chapter 7; Price et al., Chapter 8). Problems such as youth violence need to be attacked on many levels, including the provision of relevant human service agencies and the training of teachers and community workers (Foshee, Chapter 5).

Related to that point is the importance of contextual factors in social problems. On the one hand, the social context of poverty, limited community resources, and cultural norms and values that tolerate violence is a powerful influence on the occurrence of youth violence; on the other hand, family structures that provide parental support can help diminish it (Zimmerman et al., Chapter 4). Cultural narratives and stereotypes can oppress subordinate groups in society, or they can improve these groups' self-esteem and promote positive social change (Rappaport, Chapter 9). The workplace context is particularly powerful in influencing workers' mental and physical health (Donaldson et al., Chapter 7). When an intervention is planned to combat a community problem, the intervention needs to be adapted to the particular organizational and cultural context in which it will be used (Price et al., Chapter 8).

Yet, individual differences are also important factors affecting problem behaviors. Childhood patterns are a risk factor for later violence, but many aggressive youths do not become later violent offenders (Zimmerman et al., Chapter 4). Experiencing dating violence, as a victim or as a perpetrator, frequently leads to repetition of these patterns in later relationships (Foshee, Chapter5). Demographic factors, however, such as socioeconomic status, are poor predictors of interpersonal violence (Zimmerman et al., Chapter 4), and homelessness is often not the result of substance abuse or mental illness (Shinn & Tsemberis, Chapter 3).

Another point on which these chapters agree is the importance of theory in understanding and ameliorating social problems. In several areas, conflicting theories have empirical support, and it becomes crucial to determine under what conditions each theory applies. For instance, in the area of intergroup conflict, various theories view prejudice and discrimination as the result of individual pathology, or of realistic group competition for scarce resources, or of ideological and symbolic differences in values (Jackson & Volckens, Chapter 2). Violence may be viewed as a result of learning and modeling experiences in childhood, but resiliency theory can be used to explain compensating or protective factors that counter these learned patterns (Zimmerman et al., Chapter 4). In planning interventions, theory-driven research is of special importance because theories specify the mediating processes and moderating conditions through which social problems can be diminished (Price et al., Chapter 8). For example, in attempting to disseminate an intervention to new settings and agencies, different theoretical approaches use different paradigms and specify different indices for measuring success (Price et al., Chapter 8). One theoretical concept on which many authors agree is the role of individual and social stress in producing community problems (e.g., Jackson & Volckens, Chapter 2; Timko, Chapter 6).

The authors in this volume highlight interventions that have successfully attacked particular community problems. For instance, Jackson and Volckens (Chapter 2) cite several types of programs that have reduced intergroup conflict, such as training White participants to become allies of Blacks in advocating for equality. Price et al. (Chapter 8) summarize past research that has demonstrated the value of their JOBS program in aiding job-losers to seek reemployment and to cope with their stressful situations. Foshee (Chapter 5) describes her evaluation of a successful countywide program for reducing dating abuse. Shinn and Tsemberis (Chapter 3) report on a highly successful New York City program for placing and stabilizing homeless individuals in adequate housing. Rappaport (Chapter 9) summarizes the 20-year history of a strong grassroots organization that has achieved better health care for community residents. In addition, Rappaport, Shinn and Tsemberis, and others stress the importance of assisting disadvantaged groups and individuals by empowering them to seek and find their own solutions to community problems.

In such efforts to accomplish desirable social changes, many traditional approaches may be ineffectual or even detrimental. For example,

Shinn and Tsemberis (Chapter 3) point out that homeless individuals often resist placement in agency settings that combine housing and treatment programs in a step-by-step "continuum of care," where progress toward more independent living arrangements is dependent on meeting treatment goals such as remaining abstinent from drugs for a specified time period. In addition to being too restrictive for many clients, such programs produce additional stress with each transition to a new living arrangement, and they may also make clients dependent on the services they provide. Similarly, Foshee (Chapter 5) notes that available community services are rarely used by adolescents, who prefer to seek help from peers and family members. An analogous finding is reported by Donaldson et al. (Chapter 7), who observe that traditional workplace health programs are usually used by only a tiny percentage of the eligible employees, and often not the ones who need them most.

Consistent with such reports of difficulties in accomplishing treatment goals, several programs described here have reported mixed results for their interventions. For instance, the dating abuse program evaluated by Foshee (Chapter 5) found notable reductions in perpetration of abuse by program participants but nonsignificant changes in victimization reports, which apparently reflected continuing levels of abuse by many program *non*participants. In the area of alcohol abuse, Timko (Chapter 6) found less drinking for individuals in several different treatment modalities than for untreated control subjects, but the groups did not differ in their scores on social functioning, including employment. Moreover, even the control group displayed less drinking and lowered stress levels over a 3-year period, showing that some individuals can achieve "spontaneous improvement." Similarly, Shinn and Tsemberis (Chapter 3) point out that many individuals are able to move out of homelessness without any formal programmatic assistance.

An important consideration in comparing the value of different social programs is their cost-effectiveness in relation to their demonstrated benefits. In this regard, Shinn and Tsemberis (Chapter 3) emphasize that independent-living models of providing housing for homeless individuals not only achieve greater stability of remaining housed but also are much less expensive than traditional continuum-of-care models, which provide many ancillary services on a 24-hour basis. Similarly, Timko (Chapter 6) notes that the degree of a person's participation in Alcoholics Anonymous (AA) is related to lower drinking levels and that the costs for AA programs are substantially less than for outpatient or inpatient treatment of alcoholics.

A related point about the costs of social service programs, which may make expenditures for the disadvantaged seem more acceptable, is that affluent groups in our society also receive huge government subsidies in the form of tax credits for home mortgage payments, capital gains on investments, and so on (Shinn & Tsemberis, Chapter 3). In this regard, the recent new "workfare" requirements for people receiving welfare payments and the accompanying stringent limits on the total years of welfare aid may change many living patterns for disadvantaged groups in the community, and these changes may occur in ways that are as yet unanticipated.

Finally, a methodological dimension on which the programs described in this volume vary is the level of interaction between investigators and the individuals being investigated. On one end of the spectrum, some investigators actively seek input from those who are studied, as in the JOBS program described by Price et al. (Chapter 8) or the evaluations conducted by Donaldson et al. (Chapter 7). These investigators have adopted a strategy of working with program directors and employees in defining program goals. This strategy avoids alienating the individuals implementing the programs and, consequently, minimizes potential threats to the program's effectiveness. On the other end of the spectrum are studies such as Foshee's (Chapter 5), which involve deliberate efforts to standardize communications with participants and to minimize special communications between participants and community agencies that are related to the study. In an experimental study, failure to take these measures could create confounds and undermine the research design. Each approach is appropriate, depending on the research aims.

All the chapters address issues from perspectives that directly or indirectly define the community as the unit of analysis. As noted earlier, it is common for the problems described to occur together, such as homelessness, violence, workplace problems, and drinking problems. Often, resources that could be used to address these problems are planned and distributed by community-level groups, such as organizations and local governmental agencies. Often, the solutions that work in one community have less success in another. Thus, it becomes imperative to treat the community as the unit of analysis—to examine each of these problems in the light of its impact on the community, to understand how each problem may create risk conditions for other problems, and to create interventions tailored for specific groups rather than for specific problems without consideration of the social context.

Need for More Research

For these and many other reasons, more research on community problems and treatment programs is needed. As mentioned at the outset of this chapter, psychologists have conducted relatively little research on community problems, and much more will certainly be needed in the uncharted future. The extent of both new and long-standing problems that affect community life will need to be assessed, and the success of proposed programs for ameliorating community problems will need to be evaluated. Much of this research will have to be longitudinal to observe changes in individual participants in social programs and to separate these changes from concurrent shifts in the surrounding social and economic conditions.

Three basic types of research designs can be useful here. First, *descriptive research* can clarify the extent of perceived community problems and the empirical relationships between potential causal and resultant variables (e.g., Jackson & Volckens, Chapter 2; Zimmerman et al., Chapter 4). Second, studies of *naturalistic interventions* can show their impact in real-life situations but without the possibility of controlling concurrent variables that may have confounding effects (e.g., Timko, Chapter 6). Third, *experimentally created interventions,* with greater degrees of control over important related conditions, can show more precisely what effects a particular intervention can produce (e.g., Foshee, Chapter 5; Shinn & Tsemberis, Chapter 3). In addition, theory-driven research can pinpoint the components of social programs that are most effective and the mediating processes and moderating conditions that contribute to program success (e.g., Donaldson et al., Chapter 7; Price et al., Chapter 8).

Research methods used by the authors in this volume provide heuristic examples of methods that will be useful in future research. A basic method is the survey of community conditions and/or personal reactions to them, obtained either from a written questionnaire or from a personal interview (e.g., Jackson & Volckens, Chapter 2; Shinn & Tsemberis, Chapter 3). Surveys may be one-time events or a series of cross-sectional studies to show overall changes in conditions. More informative, as well as much more difficult to carry out effectively, however, are longitudinal surveys of the same panel of respondents (e.g., Foshee, Chapter 5). Some authors conducted longitudinal surveys over periods as long as 4 years (Shinn & Tsemberis, Chapter 3; Zimmerman et al., Chapter 4) or 8 years (Timko, Chapter 6). Such studies typically require very careful prior construction of measuring instruments (e.g., Foshee, Chapter 5) and use of sophisticated data analysis methods, such as factor analysis (Zimmerman et al., Chapter 4), multiple regression or path analysis (Jackson & Volckens, Chapter 2), and analysis of covariance to remove the effect of prior demographic or dispositional variables (Timko, Chapter 6).

Another basic research method is careful observation of social conditions and media portrayals of community problems and attempted solutions (e.g., Rappaport, Chapter 9). Observations and survey data are usually combined in evaluation research, which is crucial in determining the value of interventions aimed at resolving community problems. Excellent examples of evaluations of social programs are contained in the chapters by Foshee (Chapter 5) on date abuse prevention and by Timko (Chapter 6) on alcohol abuse treatment. Finally, Price et al. (Chapter 8) and Donaldson et al. (Chapter 7) go beyond evaluation research to study the diffusion of innovations such as particular social programs aimed at reducing the problems stemming from job-loss or unhealthy workplaces.

These chapters provide good models for the research that is so much needed on ways of reducing community problems and of empowering people to improve their own quality of life.

Acknowledgments

We acknowledge the assistance of those who made the symposium and this volume possible. We are grateful for the financial contributions from Claremont Graduate University (CGU) and the other Claremont Colleges in support of the Claremont Symposium on Applied Social Psychology last year. We sincerely thank all those whose efforts helped make for a successful conference, including the CGU student assistants (Sally Augustin, Sharrilyn Hurin, Inga James, Diana Kyle, Andrew Lohmann, Elena Reigadas, Kris Simmers, and Alison Stolkin) and especially the authors of the chapters in this volume. We also appreciate the help we received from Gloria Leffer and B. J. Reich in preparing for the conference, and the assistance of Amber Garcia and Christopher Agnew in preparing this volume. The efforts of these contributors were indispensable to making the current volume possible; for this, we express our heartfelt gratitude .

References

American Association for Protecting Children. (1987). *National estimates of child abuse and neglect reports, 1976-1986.* Denver: American Humane Association.

American Psychological Association (APA). (1992, November). *Bylaws.* Washington, DC: Author.

Berger, D. E. (1994, August). *Marketplace opportunities for psychologists: Niches.* Paper presented at the American Psychological Association meeting, Los Angeles.

Brayfield, A. H., & Lipsey, M. W. (1976). Public affairs psychology. In P. J. Woods (Ed.), *Career opportunities for psychologists: Expanding and emerging areas.* Washington, DC: American Psychological Association.

Jason, L. A. (1997). *Community building: Values for a sustainable future.* New York: Praeger.

Levine, M., & Perkins, D. V. (1997). *Principles of community psychology: Perspectives and applications* (2nd ed.). New York: Oxford University Press.

Lipsey, M. W. (1987, April). *Graduate training in applied psychology.* Paper presented at the Western Psychological Association meeting, Long Beach, California.

Mann, J. M., Tarantola, D. J. M., & Netter, T. W. (1992). *AIDS in the world: A global report.* Cambridge, MA: Harvard University Press.

Mason, M. A., & Mauldon, J. (1996). The new stepfamily requires a new national policy. *Journal of Social Issues, 52,* 11-27.

Mondros, J. B., & Wilson, S. M. (1994). *Organizing for power and empowerment.* New York: Columbia University Press.

National Advisory Mental Health Council. (1993). *Health care reform for Americans with severe mental illnesses.* Bethesda, MD: National Institute of Mental Health.

National Center for Health Statistics. (1994). *Annual summary of births, marriages, divorces, and deaths: United States, 1993.* Hyattsville, MD: U.S. Public Health Service.

National Crime Survey. (1991, March 24). *National Crime Survey preliminary press release.* Washington, DC: National Institutes of Health.

Orford, J. (1992). *Community psychology: Theory and practice.* Chichester, UK: Wiley.

Oskamp, S., & Schultz, P. W. (1998). *Applied social psychology* (2nd ed.). Upper Saddle River, NJ: Prentice Hall.

Parker, J. G., & Asher, S. R. (1987). Peer relations and later adjustment: Are low-accepted children at risk? *Psychological Bulletin, 102,* 357-389.

Shaw, R. (1996). *The activist's handbook: A primer for the 1990s and beyond.* Berkeley: University of California Press.

Zander, A. (1990). *Effective social action by community groups.* San Francisco: Jossey-Bass.

PART I

DISCRIMINATION
AND VIOLENCE

2

Community Stressors and Racism
Structural and Individual
Perspectives on Racial Bias

JAMES S. JACKSON
JULIE VOLCKENS

The purpose of this chapter is to examine the nature of intergroup conflict from a community-level perspective. We suggest that ameliorative individual-change approaches, though perhaps helpful to individuals, do not address structural and institutional factors related to group disadvantages. Specifically, we propose that it is time for social scientists to recognize the intermingling of macrolevel community stressors, individual and group stress, racial and ethnic conflict, and racism and to bring together these concepts in one theoretical framework for addressing some root causes of intergroup strife. If we are correct in our hypothesis that much intergroup hostility and conflict is rooted in macroeconomic events and institutionalized relations among unequal and hierarchically organized social groups (Greenberg, Simon, Pyszczynski, Solomon, & Chatel, 1992; Jones, 1997), then the individual-change models for reducing intergroup conflict that predominate in the social sciences will need revision to address what are essentially community-level problems (Bowser, 1995).

For the last 20 years, we have been involved in a program of study designed to enhance understanding of the nature of African Americans' reactions to their unequal status in the United States (Jackson, 1991).

This work has investigated how structural disadvantages in the environment are translated into social, physical, and psychological outcomes. Coverage of this program of work has been widespread, including research on health, religion, political behavior, social supports, perceptions of discrimination, family structure and roles, mental health and mental disorder, and aging and human development. Findings of this research have had a notable influence on the way we construct and implement social science research on racial and ethnic minorities.

On the basis of our results concerning African Americans from the National Survey of Black Americans (NSBA), we became more and more interested in the individual perceptions, reactions, and feelings of dominant group members about low-power out-groups in diverse national and cultural settings (e.g., Pettigrew et al., 1997). We have concluded that valid and generalizable models of dominant group attitudes, prejudice, and racism and subordinate group responses will emerge only from this type of cross-national research.

In the following pages, we explore the role of community stressors and perceived economic stress on dominant group prejudice and on subordinate group economic stress and well-being outcomes. The *reverberation theory of stress and racism* (Jackson & Inglehart, 1995) conceptualizes stress and racism as mutually interrelated phenomena and points to their combined reciprocal relationship with social, psychological, and physical health outcomes (see Figure 2.1). We close the chapter with a brief review of some recent models and approaches for reducing racism and intergroup conflict, noting their almost exclusive focus on individual-change processes.

The escalating importance of race and racism as significant societal problems is not in dispute. Incidents of anti-Semitism, acts of racism, and continued blocked opportunities for sizable numbers of people of color in our society are notable. Some uglier manifestations of these societal problems have spilled over onto college campuses. The history of the United States is pervaded with community-level violence, from the earliest slave revolts prior to the Civil War, through the community violence directed against African Americans in the South and the North following Reconstruction and during the Jim Crow era, to the more recent urban unrest of the 1960s and 1990s (Pincus & Ehrlich, 1994).

As for the future, the diversification of America is continuing at a rapid pace. Higher birth rates of "minorities" and the influx of immigrants guarantee that, in a few decades, the majority of Americans will be people of color, and current characterizations of minority and major-

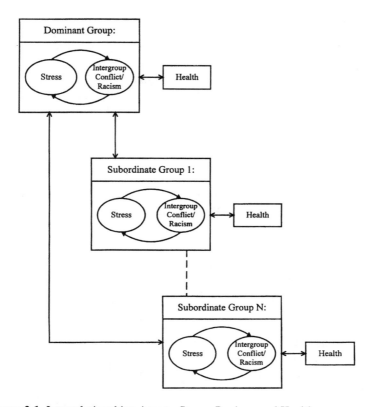

Figure 2.1. Interrelationships Among Stress, Racism, and Health

ity groups will have to be revised. The continuing conflict among historically contentious groups in the United States and the growth of new ethnic and racial diversity guarantee increased intergroup strife unless intervention is effective.

We believe that individual-change models are not effective approaches to reducing the structural, macrolevel, community factors related to intergroup conflict. Thus, it is crucial to explore the relationships among community stressors, intergroup conflict/racism, and physical and psychological health within racially and ethnically hierarchically structured societies (see Figure 2.1). The model presented in Figure 2.2 (p. 29) suggests that (a) personal as well as community-level stressors influence members of dominant as well as subordinate groups in a society;

(b) this stress contributes directly to increased intergroup conflict/ racism in these groups, which in turn increases the stress level experienced by these different groups; and (c) this stress influences social, psychological, and physical health outcomes of group members in all hierarchial positions. Data from two national and one regional probability study conducted in the United States and data from four West European countries are used in a preliminary test of this proposed framework.

Racism in the United States and Western Europe

Recent studies in the United States have found a decrease in prejudice or racial intolerance over the years but no increase in support for policies of assistance (e.g., Schuman, Steeh, & Bobo, 1985). Some researchers have argued that this is a result of racism taking a new form today, becoming subtler and more intertwined with conservative value orientations (Sears, 1987). Others have taken exception to this view (e.g., Sniderman & Piazza, 1993; Sniderman & Tetlock, 1986), arguing that conservative ideology is not necessarily related to racism or discrimination. Other researchers have argued that real and perceived group conflict exerts a significant influence on support for governmental policies designed to assist out-groups and on specific governmental actions designed to overcome discrimination (e.g., Bobo, 1983). None of these studies, to our knowledge, have investigated these issues outside the United States, and few have ventured outside the confines of White-Black superordinate and subordinate relationships (Bobo, Johnson, Oliver, Sidanius, & Zubrinsky, 1992, is one exception).

We hold that it is not possible to understand the nature of inequality, racism, and injustice within the United States outside its larger global manifestations (Jackson, Kirby, Barnes, & Shepard, 1993). Of particular concern is the nature of ethnic and racial conflict. A recent United Nations report noted that 33 separate ethnic conflicts occurred or were continuing in the early 1990s. The 1993 World Refugee Survey estimated that between 18 million and 22 million refugees and asylum seekers required international protection because they were unable or unwilling to repatriate out of fear or persecution and violence in their homelands (United Nations Economic and Social Council, 1993).

Another, even more dramatic marker is that, since 1968, approximately 2.3 million people around the world have been killed in what the United Nations designates as ethnic conflicts—in Africa, South Asia, Pacific Asia, Central and South America, the Middle East, and Europe (United Nations Economic and Social Council, 1993). Ongoing ethnic wars in the former Soviet Republics and Yugoslavia, along with anti-Semitic tensions in Poland and other East European countries, demonstrate the power of ethnic group boundaries in contributing to armed conflict, bloodshed, and human atrocities. The enduring and virulent religious conflicts in the Middle East and Northern Ireland reinforce the fact that neither simple nor short-term solutions are readily available.

Prejudice and Racism

Literally dozens of theories concerned with prejudice and discrimination have been published in the last half century. They have variously emphasized historical, sociocultural, situational, or psychodynamic factors. Many have suggested ways to categorize the factors (Insko, Nacoste, & Moe, 1983; Kinder, 1986). Some of the oldest theories of prejudice can be subsumed under personality or individual-difference models. In these models (Allport, 1954), frustration and deprivation within individuals, if uncontrolled, are likely to be discharged against ethnic minorities. For the most part, these theories (e.g., Adorno, Frenkel-Brunswik, Levinson, & Sanford, 1950; Altemeyer, 1988; Dollard, Doob, Miller, Mowrer, & Sears, 1939) view problems of prejudice and discrimination as residing within the person.

A second set of theories identifies value, belief, and ideological differences between in- and out-groups as motivations for out-group rejection behaviors (Insko et al., 1983; Kinder, 1986; Rokeach, 1979; Sears & Kinder, 1985; Weigel & Howes, 1985). Many models within this category have been viewed as antagonistic (Pettigrew, 1985; Weigel & Howes, 1985). An underlying theme, however, is an emphasis on perceived or actual ideological differences and a de-emphasis on irrational motives (e.g., prejudice) as proximate causal factors in negative out-group behaviors.

A third group of theories of intergroup conflict can be loosely labeled as social-conflict theories. These models hold that actual conflict in group interests leads the dominant group to engage in negative out-group behaviors toward the subordinate group(s) (Bobo, 1983, 1988b; Giles & Evans, 1985; Jackman & Muha, 1984). These models are closely tied to Marxist analyses, as well as to ethnic theories of social movements (Nielsen, 1985; Olzak, 1992). These theories also encompass some concerns regarding out-group threats to personal and familial interests (Weigel & Howes, 1985).

A fourth set of theories argues that perceived individual threat based on interpersonal anxiety leads to out-group rejection (e.g., Stephan & Stephan, 1985). Finally, a fifth category, based on evolutionary principles and the concept of *inclusive fitness,* suggests that racial and ethnic conflicts are extensions of kinship-preference sentiments (Hamilton, 1971; Wilson, 1978).

These various theoretical approaches can be classified within three major areas: (a) person-centered prejudice models of out-group rejection; (b) social, economic, and political real-group conflict models; and (c) models of value-, belief-, and ideology-congruity and symbolic racism. The underlying theme in all of these models is conflict and perceptions of threat, although the kind of perceived threat posited in different models differs dramatically. In prejudice-type theories, conflicts are internal and become cathected on external objects, resulting in out-group rejection and conflict. According to these models, the perceived threat is related to issues about personal integrity. In the individual/group real-conflict models, perceptions of conflict and threat are tied to the groups' social, economic, or political statuses, and these form the basis of out-group rejection behaviors. Finally, in the value-conflict models, out-group rejection results from perceived differences between one's own group and the out-group in their extent of adherence to cherished values, beliefs, or ideologies, leading to a perceived threat to one's own ideological position. In each case, conflict and threat provide the motivation for overt out-group reactions—threat to self-identity (Allport, 1954), threat to group identity (Milner, 1981; Tajfel & Turner, 1979), or threat to position dominance (Blumer, 1958; Bobo, 1988a; Giles & Evans, 1985; Nielsen, 1985; Sidanius, Pratto, & Bobo, 1996; Yinger, 1985). Walter Stephan and his colleagues have reached a similar conclusion about underlying threats (Stephan & Stephan, 1985; Stephan, Ybarra, & Bachman, 1997; Ybarra & Stephan, 1994).

Threat, Stress, and Racism

The multitude of approaches to explaining intergroup conflict is impressive, and we do not attempt to suggest one single organizing framework for these different models. On the one hand, a strong argument can be made that all theories of intergroup conflict have some accuracy, depending on historical circumstances, cultural considerations, and economic, social, and political contexts, all of which may highlight the operation of factors unique to each theory. Thus, under circumstances of constrained resources, real-group conflict may be operative. Under conditions of rich resources and a relatively tight hierarchy among groups, social identity may be a more operative factor. Under conditions in which long-term ethnic and racial divisions and conflict demarcate the hierarchy, socialization theories, symbolic concerns, and basic value differences may provide a more parsimonious explanation of group conflict.

On the other hand, we suggest that—regardless of the theoretical account—threat and psychological stress, especially to the hierarchically dominant group and individuals, account for the proximate immediate orientations, feelings about, and actions toward individuals in the group(s) lower in the hierarchy (Jackson & Inglehart, 1995; Pettigrew et al., 1997).

We propose that this concept of *perceived threat* is theoretically related to the concept of *stress*. Scientific differences in the definition of stress, however, may be even larger than the differences pointed out earlier among intergroup theorists. Different definitions and approaches to the theoretical nature of social stress and to ways of assessing it are numerous in the literature. One common definition has applied the term *stress* to any situation in which environmental demands, internal demands, or both tax or exceed the adaptive resources of an individual, social system, or tissue system (Cohen, Kessler, & Underwood-Gordon, 1995). In this view, stress is neither an environmental condition nor an individual response, but rather an environment-person transaction. Cohen et al. (1995) point to the important psychological dimensions of the stress response. They suggest, concerning the psychological dimensions of stress, that a feeling of threat arises when the demands imposed on an individual are perceived to exceed her or his felt ability to cope with these demands. Perceiving members of other social groups as a threat can be stress-provoking and, as suggested later, can be negative for one's psychological and mental health.

We suggest that basic beliefs, attitudes, and values of individuals will feed into the subjective appraisal process (Smith & Ellsworth, 1985). We also propose, however, that situational/structural factors will shape the subjective appraisal of social situations. For example, political, social, and economic changes in the "real world" might lead to high rates of unemployment and to inflation, crime, and violence. These are structural factors that clearly cause stress, both on a community level and an individual level, and this stress might prime and enhance negative appraisals of social situations.

Reactions to affirmative action programs provide one timely example of the relationship between real and perceived threat. Blacks constitute about 12% of the total U.S. population and an even lower proportion of the group who are adult, able-bodied, and capable of work. If all of these individuals were given positions solely on the basis of affirmative action principles, it is not clear (given the relative size of this small population and the large size of the economy) whether this would pose a significant risk of not having available jobs for others. Plous (1996) has estimated that significantly less than 1% of Whites would be affected if affirmative action was applied widely to all unemployed, job-qualified African Americans. Yet, the perception of threat to employment for individuals higher in the hierarchy (Whites) is certainly related to opposition to affirmative action and to stated fears of either loss of opportunity or blocked opportunities for advancement in careers and jobs. This example points to the importance of perceptual processes and to the psychological nature of threats to individuals' hierarchial positions (Blumer, 1958).

In summary, whatever the theoretical account of intergroup strife, threat is at the crux of the story, and stress follows threat. Whatever definition one may use for prejudice, racism, and discrimination, they are certainly hostile, aggressive, and mean-spirited beliefs and acts— just the type of behaviors we might expect from groups and individuals who are psychologically stressed. In fact, recent research by Krause (1994) and by Thoits (1991) points out the importance of stressors in salient life roles, such as the economic provider role used in the empirical examples in this chapter. This stressor → threat → stress → racism chain and its effects on personal well-being are at the core of our arguments about the relationship among community-level, macrostressors, and group and individual intergroup conflict (Jackson & Inglehart, 1995).

Stress, Racism, and Health

Subordinate Group Perspectives

We use African Americans as an exemplar of subordinate groups for purposes of explicating the proposed model, although we recognize that many other groups in all parts of the world share similar subordinate statuses. A substantial proportion of the U.S. African American population live in environments where they likely are exposed to a relatively large number of stressors (Jackson et al., 1996). Low socioeconomic status is related to a stressful lifestyle that may include poor nutrition, poor education, crime, traffic hazards, substandard and overcrowded housing, low-paying jobs, unemployment and underemployment, and lack of health insurance and access to basic health services. It is frequently suggested that these factors contribute to the development of a wide range of health problems in Black communities.

It has also been suggested that racism adversely affects the health status of African Americans. Researchers have uniformly noted that racism and discrimination are important factors in understanding African Americans' social, economic, and health statuses, and they sometimes suggest that it may account for particular patterns of association (Essed, 1991). Few empirical attempts have been made, however, to assess racism or racial discrimination and to explore its consequences for the psychological well-being of African American children, adolescents, and adults (Jackson et al., 1996). Recent research has revealed strong relationships of verbal racial abuse to both psychological and physical health outcomes among African Americans (e.g., McNeilly et al., 1996). Other empirical research suggests that the low positions of African Americans on social, economic, and political status hierarchies may be linked with negative physical, social, and psychological outcomes, perhaps mediated by racism and discrimination (Jackson et al., 1996; Jones, 1997).

Dominant Group Perspectives

As noted above, individual, cultural, and institutional racisms can be interpreted as stressors for the targets of this discrimination and can thus negatively affect life outcomes, such as health (Jones, 1997). Under-standing the effects of racism and intergroup conflict on the dominant group's stress level and health status, however, has been a neglected topic. Psychologically unhealthful conditions, such as an authoritarian personality (Adorno et al., 1950), frustration (Dollard et al., 1939), or low self-esteem (Crocker, Thompson, McGraw, & Ingerman, 1987), have often been viewed as causes of prejudiced reactions. In many accounts (e.g., Adorno et al., 1950), however, prejudiced reactions have been interpreted as serving a positive function for the racist. Some positive outcomes have been linked with bigoted positions, including functional, material, social, and psychological benefits (e.g., Katz, 1960). For example, it has been argued that, by scapegoating a certain out-group member, an individual might be able to reestablish his or her inner peace (Duckitt, 1992). Thus, the relationship between expressions of racism and psychological health in the dominant group was tradition-ally seen as positive, although not exclusively so (Jackson & Inglehart, 1995). A wide range of possible negative consequences for bigoted behavior has been excluded from empirical investigation. Conse-quently, an important area for initiating changes in social policies has been overlooked (Jackson & Inglehart, 1995).

We suggest that reducing intergroup conflict and racist behavior will be beneficial for *all* groups and individuals in socially and economically hierarchically ordered societies. For the dominant group members—regardless of any positive tangible, social, or psychological gain—we propose that detrimental health effects accompany big-oted behavior; that is, being a bigot may be "dangerous to one's health." For instance, hostility is one crucial component of racism and bigotry, and much research has demonstrated a strong negative relationship between a person's degree of hostility and favorable health outcomes (Cohen et al., 1995; Jackson & Inglehart, 1995). Hostility and anger are often evoked in stressful situations, leading, we believe, to increased racist and bigoted behaviors on the part of individuals higher in the status hierarchy.

In summary, we see a need to explore the ways all groups and individuals in a racially (or ethnically or religiously) stratified soci-ety suffer because of racism and to study how stressors and stress affect racism and are affected by it and how health outcomes relate to stress and racism among both dominant and subordinate group members.

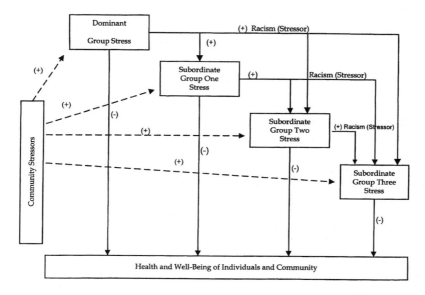

Figure 2.2. Hypothesized Relationships Among Community Stressors, Racism, and Health for Dominant and Subordinate Groups

The Reverberation Model of Stress, Racism, and Health

Figure 2.2 represents a hypothetical community, including one dominant group and several subordinate groups (e.g., the former South Africa, the United States). In this case, we argue that community stressors, such as unemployment and related macrosocial and economic conditions, affect members of all hierarchically organized racial and ethnic groups. In addition, we suggest that this increased stress leads the dominant group to act in ways (e.g., discrimination) that cause further stress in subordinate groups. We propose that the original stressful conditions and the racism displayed toward each successively lower subordinate group will lead to increased stress. Thus, Subordinate Group 3 has four sources of stress in this model: the original community stressor (e.g., unemployment, poor economic conditions) and the racism directed toward Group 3 by the dominant group and by Subordinate Groups 1 and 2. Stress and racism then reverberate in the community, lowering well-being and possibly increasing subsequent stress levels.

We propose that community-level stressors (e.g., unemployment, downturns in macroeconomic conditions) will influence the perceptions of both dominant and subordinate group members. Among dominant group members, stress contributes to the lowering of psychological well-being and leads to increased racist sentiments toward subordinate groups. Among subordinate groups, these same negative macroeconomic conditions will contribute to the experience of stress, which in turn will lower well-being. In addition, we suggest that the racism directed toward subordinate groups by more dominant groups will also be experienced as stressful and will contribute independently to lowering well-being even further. Thus, community-level stressors contribute to individual-level stress among both dominant and subordinate group members. This stress contributes to dominant groups acting in racist ways toward subordinate groups, which in turn contributes even more stress to the lives of subordinate group members.

We hypothesize that several social-psychological mechanisms may contribute individually or collectively to the hypothesized stress-racism relationship: (a) Stress may influence increased economic competition (e.g., a greater drive to remove potential competitors under stressful conditions); (b) cognitive ability to individuate under stressful conditions may be lowered, leading to greater cognitive categorization and thus increased stereotyping and negative sentiments toward out-groups; (c) stress may help lower psychological barriers against expressing racism; (d) stress may heighten in-group positive biases; and (e) stress may accentuate negative out-group biases and feelings.

In summary, as shown in Figure 2.2, we hypothesize that (a) community-level stressors influence individuals in all dominant and subordinate groups; (b) stress contributes directly to increased racism among both dominant and subordinate groups; (c) racism is stressful to both dominant and subordinate groups; and (d) the lower the subordinate group, the higher the stress and associated experienced group conflict, and group and individual mental health disorders.

Figure 2.3 displays a set of derived, hypothesized empirical relationships among stressors, racism, and well-being within dominant groups and among stressors/stress, perceived/experienced racism, and well-being within subordinate groups. For dominant groups (shown at the bottom

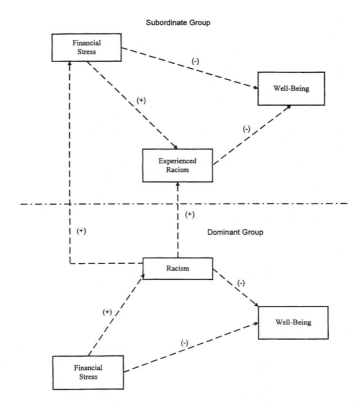

Figure 2.3. Hypothesized Relationships Among Financial Stress, Racism (Experienced Racism), and Well-Being

of Figure 2.3), we predict that economic stress will lead to increased racism and simultaneously to lower well-being. In addition, we predict that expressions of racism will lead to the lowering of a dominant group member's own well-being. Although it is not as directly testable, we also predict that the racism of the dominant group will be reflected in increased perceptions and experiences of racism among members of the subordinate groups. This is reflected in the dashed arrow from Racism of the dominant group members to Experienced Racism for the subordinate group. Similarly, we predict that racism will also contribute, over and above the community stressors, to economic stress as perceived by the subordinate group.

We propose that, among the subordinate groups (shown at the top of Figure 2.3), economic stress and perceived and experienced racism will lower well-being. We also suggest that perceived and experienced racism will raise economic stress but that, simultaneously, economic stress may lead to an increase in perceived and experienced racism. For this chapter, we test these relationships among a dominant (White) group and a subordinate (African American) group in the United States and among dominant groups (Europeans) in Western Europe. (We lack the data to test these predictions among subordinate groups in Western Europe.) Data are from the National Panel Survey of Black Americans (1979-80 and 1987-88), the 1984 General Social Survey (GSS), a recent 1995 Detroit Area Survey (DAS), and the 1988 Eurobarometer Survey in the countries of France, Great Britain, Germany, and the Netherlands (combined data from the four nations).

Data and Analytic Approach

Data Sets

Eurobarometer. The European Omnibus Surveys of the European Union (EU) are a long-running set of opinion polls conducted in the spring and fall on nationally representative samples of countries in the EU. These surveys, in varied forms, have been conducted since 1970. Although the themes of the surveys have changed on each occasion, central concerns have been the attitudes of the EU publics toward the common market, attitudes toward other European countries, and the priority of goals and values within each country. Since 1973, the surveys have added a major continuing series of items related to subjective satisfaction and perceived quality of life.

In 1974, the Commission of the European Communities initiated the Eurobarometer series. This is a supplemental survey within the European Omnibus Survey that is designed to provide a regular monitoring of social and political attitudes of the publics within the EU. The actual sampling and fieldwork were conducted by the Gallup affiliates in each EU country. Representative samples were drawn of the adult populations 15 years of age and older. The sampling designs were a mixture of multistage national probability procedures and national stratified quota procedures, similar to the Gallup polls conducted within the

United States. Appropriate weights are available for the samples in each country and for a combined European sample.

Because of our interest in having salient populations of immigrants and ethnic out-groups as targets for the study and because of cost considerations, we limited our intensive research in the 1988 survey to only 4 of the 12 EEC countries: France ($N = 1,001$), Great Britain ($N = 1,017$), the Netherlands ($N = 1,006$), and West Germany ($N = 1,051$). Data from these countries permit cross-national comparisons for groups at both the same and different status levels. In keeping with the view that multiple comparisons among different groups and cultural contexts are needed to study the nature of out-group rejection, we used a split-ballot questionnaire technique within each country (except Germany). This procedure had the advantage of providing two randomly drawn samples within each nation, each of which reacted to questions about one of two preselected groups. For many purposes, such as this chapter, the data for each target group within and across countries may be combined to provide larger sample sizes.

General Social Surveys (GSS). The General Social Surveys are yearly interviews on a representative sample of the American public, conducted by the National Opinion Research Center (NORC) at the University of Chicago. The initial survey was conducted in 1972. Items that appear on the surveys are of three types: (a) permanent questions that appear each year, (b) questions that appear on two out of every three surveys, and (c) occasional questions that appear mainly as the result of particular investigator interests. Approximately 1,500 interviews are taken yearly, with the numbers fluctuating slightly over the years (1,372 to 1,613). Each survey is an independently drawn sample of English-speaking persons 18 years of age or older living in noninstitutionalized housing arrangements within the continental United States. Both block quota and full probability sampling methods have been used in the 21 years that the GSS has been conducted. The median length of the interview has been approximately 90 minutes. Analyses for this chapter used a total of 1,251 respondents with European backgrounds from the 1984 GSS.

National Survey of Black Americans (NSBA). NSBA panel data were collected in four waves beginning in 1979-80. The original 1979-80 survey used face-to-face interviewing methods in a national multistage household probability sample of 2,107 self-identified Black Americans aged 18 or older living in the continental United States. The overall response rate was approximately 67%. This rate was quite good because 79% of the sample resided in urban areas, one of the most difficult locations for face-to-face interviewing. The 1979-80 NSBA was followed by three more waves of data collection on the original respondents with smaller, but still comprehensive, telephone surveys in 1987-88, 1988-89, and 1992. The 1987-88 NSBA Wave 2 data were used in the analyses for this chapter.

Detroit Area Study, 1995 (DAS). The DAS is a training program in survey research supported by the Department of Sociology and the Survey Research Center at the University of Michigan. It has been in existence for 45 years and currently provides a multistage area probability sample representative of the population, 18 years and older, residing in the tricounty area of Michigan (Wayne, Oakland, and Macomb counties, including the city of Detroit). Our project, Racism and Health, was selected for the 1995 investigation, and supplemental funds were secured to increase the sample size to 1,140. Face-to-face interviews averaging 65 minutes in length were completed with adult respondents, with a response rate of 70%. African Americans were oversampled so that the final sample was about 50% Black. All fieldwork was completed by October 1995.

Table 2.1 displays the items and scales used to measure racism, perceived economic stress, and psychological well-being in the four data sets listed above.

Eurobarometer Measures

Traditional Racism. As shown in Table 2.1, in the Eurobarometer traditional racism was operationalized as a 3-item index—the average of the following three items, each scored on a 4-point scale: (a) extent of unwillingness to have sexual relations with a member of the targeted out-group, (b) extent of agreement with the statement that the "majority can never really be comfortable with members of the out-group," and (c) extent of agreement with the statement that "out-groups take jobs that majority group members should have." This index had an alpha coefficient of .68.

Financial Stress. A 3-item index included the respondent's unemployment status, an item about financial changes that asked, "In the past year, has the financial situation of you and your family gotten worse?" and a sample-standardized measure of family income in quartiles. The items were averaged on a 5-point scale, and this index had a relatively low alpha coefficient of .32.

Subjective Well-Being. This index averaged scores on two items that asked, "In general, how satisfied are you with your life these days?" and "How satisfied will you be with your life in 5 years?" Individuals responded to each item on a 10-point scale of *very satisfied* to *very dissatisfied.* The alpha coefficient of this index was .79.

General Social Survey Measures

Traditional Racism. No really comparable measure of traditional racism was available in the GSS, so an approximation was used, as summarized in Table 2.1. A 4-item index was constructed from the following questions: "Do you think that there should be laws against marriages between Blacks and Whites?"; "How strongly would you object if a member of your family wanted to bring a Black friend home to dinner?"; "Do you think White students and Black students should go to the same schools or to separate schools?"; and "White people have a right to keep Blacks out of their neighborhoods if they want, and Blacks should respect that right." Items were scored on a 5-point scale and averaged, and this index had an alpha coefficient of .71. Although this was a somewhat different operationalization of the racism construct, as shown later the same relationships with traditional racism that were observed among dominant groups in the Eurobarometer Survey also held in the GSS for this measure.

Financial Stress. A 4-item index was developed that included unemployment status, perceptions of financial changes during the last few years, sample-standardized income in quartiles, and opinions that the family's income was not enough. Items were averaged using a 5-point scale, and the index had an alpha coefficient of .52.

Subjective Well-Being. This index included four satisfaction items and one happiness measure. The satisfaction items asked, "For each area of life I am going to name, tell me the number that shows how much satisfaction you get from that area." The areas were (a) city or place of residence, (b) family life, (c) friendships, and (d) health and physical

Table 2.1
Racism, Financial Stress, and Well-Being Measures in the Eurobarometer, General Social Survey, National Survey of Black Americans, and Detroit Area Study

	Eurobarometer 1988	GSS 1984	NSBA Wave 2	DAS 1995
Racism				
Items:	No out-group sexual relations Never comfortable with out-group Take jobs from dominant group	No interracial marriages No Black friends to dinner Segregated schools Segregated neighborhood	Past month had racial problem	Ever treated badly because of race (for Blacks) Out-group should work way up (for Whites) Discrimination no longer a problem (for Whites) Out-groups blame Whites for own problems (for Whites) Out-groups have more than they deserve (for Whites)
alpha	.68	.71		0.68 (for four items)
value range	(1-4)	(1-5)	(0-1)	(0-1) for first item; (1-9) for last four items

Financial Stress

Items:	Unemployed	Unemployed	Unemployed	Unemployed last year more than 3 months
	Financial change last year	Negative financial change last few years	Financial change from 8 years ago	Had financial problems last year
	Income in quartiles	Income in quartiles	Worry about bills	Income in quartiles
		Family income not enough	Income in quartiles	Level of financial difficulty
alpha	.32	.52	.51	.61
value range	(1-5)	(1-5)	(1-5)	(1-5)

Well-Being

Items:	Life satisfaction now	City satisfaction	General life satisfaction	General life satisfaction
	Life satisfaction in 5 years	Family life satisfaction	Family life satisfaction	
		Friendship satisfaction	Friends' relationships satisfaction	
		Health satisfaction	Health satisfaction	
		Happiness	Happiness	
			Family relationships satisfaction	
alpha	.79	.66	.66	
value range	(1-10)	(1-7)	(1-5)	(1-5)

conditions. Individuals responded on a 7-point scale of *a very great deal* to *none.* The happiness measure asked respondents on a 3-point scale, "Taking all things together, how would you say things are these days? Would you say that you are very happy, pretty happy, or not too happy?" Items were averaged using a 7-point scale, and the index had an alpha coefficient of .66.

NSBA Measures

Experienced Racism. As shown in Table 2.1, we used a dichotomous measure of experienced racism that asked respondents to indicate whether they or their families had been treated badly or not treated badly in the past month because of their race.

Financial Stress. This 4-item index included unemployment status, financial changes over 8 years ("In the past 8 years, has the financial situation of you and your family gotten worse?"), extent to which respondents worried about paying bills, and a sample-standardized measure of family income in quartiles. With the items being averaged on a 5-point scale, this index had an alpha coefficient of .51.

Subjective Well-Being. This 6-item index included items asking respondents how satisfied they were with their life these days, and how satisfied they were with their friends, health, family life, and family relationships. The items were scored on a 4-point scale of *very satisfied* to *very dissatisfied.* The final item in the index asked respondents, on a 3-point scale, "Taking all things together, how would you say things are these days? Would you say you are very happy, pretty happy, or not too happy these days?" The items were placed on a 5-point scale and averaged, and the index had an alpha coefficient of .66.

Detroit Area Study Measures

Experienced and Traditional Racism. As shown in Table 2.1, for Blacks, we used a dichotomous measure of experienced racism that asked respondents to indicate whether they had ever been treated badly because of their race. For Whites, a 4-item index was used. The items asked Whites to indicate on a 9-point scale whether Blacks should work their way up as had other groups, whether discrimination was no longer a problem, whether Blacks blame Whites for their own problems, and whether Blacks get more than they deserve. Averaging these items yielded an index with an alpha coefficient of .68.

Financial Stress. A 4-item index included unemployment status, financial problems in the last year on a 4-point response scale, sample-standardized family income in quartiles, and the respondents' perceptions of the extent of their current financial difficulties. The items were placed on a 5-point scale and averaged, and the index had an alpha coefficient of .61.

Subjective Well-Being. A single item was used—"In general, how satisfied are you with your life these days?"—measured on a 5-point scale of *very dissatisfied* to *very satisfied.*

Analysis Strategy

The analyses presented in this chapter provide a preliminary assessment of how racist feelings on the part of dominant group members, and experiences of racism on the part of subordinate group members, may be related to economic stress and psychological well-being in each group. Correlations, ordinary least squares regression, and logistic regression were the major analytic techniques employed. These analyses are summarized in a series of three path analytic models in Figures 2.4, 2.5, and 2.6. In each regression model used to estimate the path coefficients for economic stress, racism (or experienced racism), and well-being, age and gender were included as control variables.

Findings and Discussion

The path model in Figure 2.4 is a summary of the standardized path coefficients connecting perceived financial stress, racism, and well-being for the dominant group in the four West European countries combined. As predicted, financial stress was significantly related (.062, $p < .01$) to increased feelings of racism toward subordinate groups. Independently, financial stress was also related to lowered levels of well-being ($- .259, p < .01$). Also as predicted, increased personal

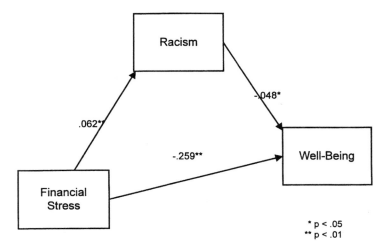

Figure 2.4. Path Models for Dominant Groups in Four West European
Countries

feelings of racism were related to lowered levels of well-being among
dominant group members (− .048, *p* < .05). These significant paths
support the view that financial stress is simultaneously related to increased racist feelings and lowered well-being among dominant group
members and that increased feelings of racism are also related to lower
personal well-being. This suggests that perceived stress has both external effects (on racism) and internal effects (on lowered well-being)
among dominant group members in the four European countries.

Figure 2.5 is a summary of the path analyses for both the dominant
group and the subordinate group (African Americans) in the United
States. Among Americans of European background, as in Western
Europe, increased perceptions of financial stress were related to higher
levels of racism (.101, *p* < .01) and to lower levels of well-being (− .308,
p < .01). Racism, as in the European sample, was associated with lower
levels of well-being, but this was not a significant effect.

The upper half of Figure 2.5 presents the path coefficients among
financial stress, experienced racism, and well-being for African
Americans in the United States. As in the dominant group, increased
stress was strongly associated with lower well-being (− .286, *p* < .01).
It was also significantly and independently associated with experienced

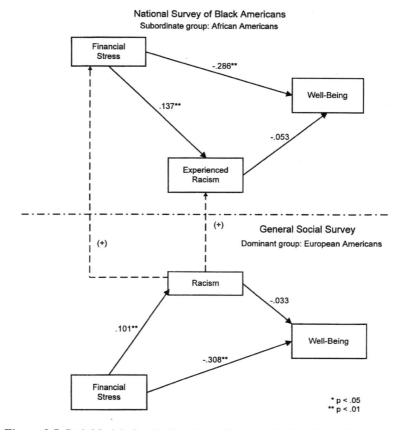

Figure 2.5. Path Models for the Dominant Group and Subordinate Group in the National Survey of Black Americans and General Social Survey

racism (.137, $p < .01$). Experienced racism, however, was only weakly independently associated with lower levels of well-being (− .053, ns).

Finally, Figure 2.6 is a summary of the results of the Detroit Area Study. Among European Americans, financial stress was significantly related to lowered well-being (− .305, $p < .01$) and to heightened levels of racism toward Blacks (.108, $p < .05$). Personal racism, however, was unrelated to lowered levels of well-being (− .008, ns). In the top of Figure 2.6, data for African Americans show that feelings of financial stress were modestly related to experienced racism (.068, $p < .10$) and

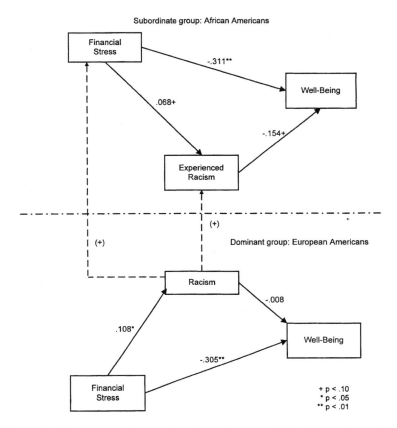

Figure 2.6. Path Models for the Dominant Group and Subordinate Group in the Detroit Area Study

more strongly related to lowered well-being (− .311, p < .01). Finally, experienced racism was modestly linked with lowered well-being (− .154, p < .10).

Overall, these results provide preliminary evidence for the reverberation model of stress and racism that we have hypothesized. In the dominant group, increased stress, represented in this chapter by perceived financial strain, is associated with increased antipathy toward the outgroup(s). These relationships were found in national and regional samples of Whites from the United States and also in combined national samples of Europeans in four major Western countries. It is also clear that perceived economic stress is directly linked with reduced well-being. Simultaneously, racism can have direct effects on lowered well-being, as seen in the data for Western Europe. Thus, costs may be associated with holding racist beliefs. The alternative view that lower levels of well-being might lead to increased racism seems less likely in the light of the pattern of relationships and the direction of stress effects (Jackson et al., 1996).

Finally, a hypothesis that was not easily testable in these data suggests that racism among the dominant group is related to the levels of perceived racism, experienced stress, and well-being among subordinate groups. A test of a related hypothesis among African Americans (in both 1979-80 and 1987-88) showed that reports of experiencing racism and stress were both directly related to reduced well-being and that, over time in the NSBA panel study, economic stress was more strongly related to experiences of racism than experiences of racism were related to economic stress (Jackson et al., 1996).

These findings provide partial support for our reverberation thesis regarding stress and racism in hierarchically organized, mixed-ethnic communities. Results of our path models suggest that stressors, such as unemployment and poor economic conditions, are related to experienced stress and out-group antipathies among the major dominant groups and to experienced racism among subordinate groups. Our results support recent theorizing that stress may increase the propensity of dominant groups to behave in prejudicial and discriminatory ways toward subordinate groups and also that stress may contribute to reduced psychological well-being (Jackson & Inglehart, 1995).

Models of Antiracism in Reducing Intergroup Conflict

As indicated earlier, research on the topics of prejudice and racism has captured the interest and guided the efforts of many social psychologists (Jones, 1997). Remedies to alleviate these social ills, however, have not been as forthcoming (Katz & Taylor, 1988). The paucity of research on antiracism approaches can be attributed, in part, to differences in the overarching philosophies that have directed this field of research during various historical periods (Duckitt, 1992). These guiding paradigms have suggested different causal underpinnings for intergroup conflict, pointing to different types of interventions. Since Allport's (1954) early attempts to develop a remedial program to reduce intergroup conflict, social psychology has made substantive advances both methodologically and theoretically in its understanding of the problem. Still, surprisingly little attention has been directed toward testing the efficacy of his proposals or evolving new intervention strategies that are informed by the progress made in the field. One exception is the research that has been conducted on the contact hypothesis. Research on the efficacy of intergroup contact for ameliorating intergroup conflict dates back at least to 1947, when Williams (1947) noted that White soldiers who fought in integrated units during World War II subsequently held more favorable attitudes toward Black soldiers. Allport (1954) later outlined the specific conditions of contact required to foster such an improvement in intergroup relations. Enthusiasm for the possibilities suggested by this remedy generated numerous studies. The promise of the contact approach was dimmed, however, when this research exposed the difficulty in meeting the contingent conditions that Allport (1954) had outlined—the necessity for "equal status contact between the majority and the minority groups in the pursuit of common goals" (p. 262; see Amir, 1969; Cook, 1985).

Recent work by Elliot Aronson and his colleagues employing the contact hypothesis has been more successful in meeting the conditions proposed by Allport; they used a technique they call the *jigsaw classroom* (Aronson, Blaney, Stephan, Sikes, & Snapp, 1978). In this research, the traditional classroom structure is altered to create an interdependent atmosphere that makes each child in the classroom a primary source of information. Children are placed in six-person, desegregated learning groups. Each child is assigned one unique critical portion of an assignment that she or he must learn and then teach to the other children in that group. The success of each child is dependent on the contributions of the other children in the group, so it is each child's responsibility to encourage and support other students in doing their best work. In this way, the children learn to value and respect each other. The evidence from these studies shows that students in the jigsaw groups exhibit a decrease in prejudice and stereotyping, in comparison with children in traditional classroom settings. In addition, they increase their liking for their group mates both within and across ethnic groups.

Another promising line of research using the framework of the contact hypothesis has been launched in a long-term study that will follow both male and female NCAA athletes before, during, and after their college careers (Brown, Brown, Jackson, Manual, & Coates, 1997). This research is designed to ascertain whether intercollegiate athletic competition meets the conditions for contact as specified by Allport. In a related line of work, Gaertner, Dovidio, and their colleagues (Gaertner, Dovidio, Anastasio, Bachman, & Rust, 1993) have proposed the *common in-group identity model* as an approach to reducing intergroup bias. Similar to the work of Sherif and Sherif (1969), they suggest that lessening group boundaries (decategorization) should reduce in-group bias through changes in several mediating processes involving the redefinition of group membership (recategorization) and the creation of a common group identity. In both experimental and field studies, Gaertner et al. (1993) have demonstrated that cooperative interactions lead to increased positive evaluations of out-group members, primarily through the transformation of an "us and them" representation to an all-encompassing "we" recategorization.

Building on the work of activists, educators, and racial-identity development researchers such as Janet Helms (1990) and William Cross (1991), clinical psychologist Beverly Daniel Tatum (1992, 1994) has been engaged in a program of racial identity development in the classroom since 1980. This program of teaching White college students about racism is designed to nurture and assist White students through a series of six stages of White identity development, culminating in the student becoming what is called a "White ally" (Tatum, 1994). A *White ally* is a person who has constructed a positive, proactive White identity and thus is prepared to confront racism and oppression in his or her daily life. Tatum (1992, 1994) has been conducting antiracism training as part of a psychology of racism course at several undergraduate institutions. Currently, she is leading a community-wide implementation of this program in Northhampton, Massachusetts, as part of the Eastern Massachusetts Initiative, a project that involves training K-12 teachers to be racial-identity development facilitators for their own classrooms. The grant for this project includes funds to conduct a long-term follow-up of the success of this kind of intervention.

These examples of antiracism work and research being conducted by psychologists highlight the possibilities for extending our accumulated knowledge of the problem of intergroup conflict (Essed, 1996). Antiracism research remains a much neglected area of investigation, however. It is difficult to deny that psychologists remain more interested in understanding intergroup conflict than in trying to assuage the problem. Whatever reasons may have stymied research into efficacious, psychologically based, antiracism interventions, it is clear that the urgency created by the current escalation of deadly intergroup strife throughout the world necessitates our commitment to generating more effective approaches.

It has become increasingly clear that prejudice and racism are multiply determined problems involving universal psychological processes, social experiences, and individual-difference dimensions. It seems equally certain that interventions designed to eliminate or diminish the effects of prejudice and racism must also be multifaceted. With this in mind, Duckitt (1992) proposed a multilevel approach that would, at a minimum, address the degree to which prejudice and racism are expressed. According to Duckitt (1992), intervention is required at three levels: social structural, social influence, and individual susceptibility. Like others before him (see Apfelbaum, 1979; Horkheimer & Flowerman, 1950; Sherif & Sherif, 1969), Duckitt warns against using single, individual-level interventions that attempt to change attitudes without addressing social influences or structural issues. He argues that the higher the level of the intervention, the greater the potential for creating enduring change.

Macrolevel changes may seem beyond the purview or expertise of social psychologists, yet successful examples do exist. Tatum's (1992, 1994) work in Massachusetts is one example, and the role played by social psychologists in the U.S. Supreme Court decision to desegregate public schools is another. Thomas (1996) recently proposed a community-level approach applying the "cycle of racial unity" to community race relations. Using Detroit as an example, he suggested a macroapproach. In Step 1, business, education, and community leaders generally should adopt the racial unity model; in Step 2, key people across racial lines commit to a long-term process of community building; and in Step 3, race relation concerns and interests are articulated and policies are formulated regarding race within a racial unity framework.

Given the increasing knowledge about the etiology of intergroup discord, psychologists could turn that knowledge toward investigating more and better ways at least to diminish its expression. Results of our research, however, suggest that group conflict may have analyzable macro and institutional causes (cf. Duckitt, 1992; Jones, 1997). Our work suggests that economic stressors may contribute to a cycle of increased racism and lowered well-being among all groups in the community. Thus, approaches to reduce intergroup conflict will have to use more extensive and greater community-level interventions. It may be that indirect interventions, perhaps like those pioneered by Price and his colleagues (e.g., Price, van Ryn, & Vinokur, 1992; Vinokur, Price, & Schul, 1995), designed to reduce the stressful nature of unemployment experiences, may have more salubrious effects on reducing community racial tensions than do individual change efforts.

Conclusions

In this chapter, we addressed the influence of macrolevel stressors on accumulated stress in dominant and subordinate groups in society. We proposed a framework to account for the interrelationships among community-level stressors, social stress, dominant and subordinate group well-being, and racism. Conceptually, we suggested that stressors such as unemployment and financial difficulties directly influence the extent of discriminatory responses and experienced social stress among both dominant and subordinate groups. This model assumes that dominant and subordinate groups are arranged in social, economic, political, and related status hierarchies, such that a group's status is relative to the group or groups positioned above and below it in the status ordering. Recent theorizing suggests that stress increases the propensity of dominant groups to behave in prejudicial and discriminatory ways toward subordinate groups—in attempts to simplify cognitive perceptions of their environment and for a host of other reasons to which we have alluded. We suggest that these stress effects are not limited to the major dominant group but also appear among all hierarchically arranged subordinate social, economic, or political groups.

Thus, we hypothesized that (a) community-level stressors influence the stress experienced by individuals in all dominant and subordinate groups, (b) stress contributes directly to increased racism in a hierarchical manner among both dominant and subordinate groups, (c) racism is stressful to both dominant and subordinate groups, and (d) the lower the subordinate group's status, the higher the stress and associated experienced group conflict and group and individual psychological and physical health-related disorders. Empirical support for some of these hypothesized relationships was found in analyses of data from a national panel study of African Americans, the 1988 Eurobarometer Survey, the 1984 General Social Survey in the United States, and the 1995 Detroit Area Study.

We believe that it is crucial to consider racism as a community stressor having chronic and pervasive characteristics. Its predicted effects may be modest in comparison to natural disasters, for example. Given the millions of people worldwide who are involved in ethnically and racially stratified hierarchical communities, however, its impact can be enormous—socially, psychologically, and financially. Racism creates a chronic health risk for both its holders and its victims. In most theoretical models of intergroup competition and conflict, the poor social, economic, and psychological outcomes of those lower in the hierarchy are acknowledged—that is, the cost of being Black, Mexican American, and so on. Our work suggests not only a cost to the subordinate group members but also a cost to all members of the larger community. Some causes of racist behaviors may reside in macrolevel events and in community responses to these events. Therefore, we should spend more time and effort focusing on structural and social interventions that address the problem at these more structural and community levels (Duckitt, 1992).

References

Adorno, T., Frenkel-Brunswik, E., Levinson, D., & Sanford, R. N. (1950). *The authoritarian personality.* New York: Harper.

Allport, G. (1954). *The nature of prejudice.* Reading, MA: Addison-Wesley.

Altemeyer, B. (1988). *Enemies of freedom: Understanding right-wing authoritarianism.* San Francisco: Jossey-Bass.

Amir, Y. (1969). Contact hypothesis in ethnic relations. *Psychological Bulletin, 71,* 319-342.

Apfelbaum, E. (1979). Relations of domination and movements for liberation: An analysis of power between groups. In W. G. Austin & S. Worchel (Eds.), *The social psychology of intergroup relations* (pp. 188-204). Pacific Grove, CA: Brooks/Cole.

Aronson, E., Blaney, N., Stephan, C., Sikes, J., & Snapp, M. (1978). *The jigsaw classroom.* Beverly Hills, CA: Sage.

Blumer, H. (1958). Race prejudice as a sense of group position. *Pacific Sociological Review, 1*(1), 3-7.

Bobo, L. (1983). Whites' opposition to busing: Symbolic racism or realistic group conflict? *Journal of Personality and Social Psychology, 45,* 1196-1210.

Bobo, L. (1988a). Attitudes toward the Black political movement: Trends, meaning, and effects on racial policy preferences. *Social Psychology Quarterly, 51,* 287-302.

Bobo, L. (1988b). Group conflict, prejudice, and the paradox of contemporary racial attitudes. In P. A. Katz & D. A. Taylor (Eds.), *Eliminating racism: Profiles in controversy* (pp. 85-116). New York: Plenum.

Bobo, L., Johnson, J. H., Oliver, M. L., Sidanius, J., & Zubrinsky, C. (1992). *Public opinion before and after a spring of discontent: A preliminary report on the 1992 Los Angeles County Survey.* Los Angeles: University of California, Center for the Study of Urban Poverty.

Bowser, B. P. (Ed.). (1995). *Racism and antiracism in world perspective.* Thousand Oaks, CA: Sage.

Brown, K. T., Brown, T. N., Jackson, J. S., Manual, W. J., & Coates, D. (1997). *Testing the Jack Kemp effect: The role of interracial contact on racialized attitudes among intercollegiate student-athletes.* Paper presented at the American Psychological Association meeting, Chicago.

Cohen, S., Kessler, R. C., & Underwood-Gordon, L. (1995). *Measuring stress: A guide on health and social scientists.* New York: Oxford University Press.

Cook, S. W. (1985). Experimenting on social issues: The case of school desegregation. *American Psychologist, 40,* 452-460.

Crocker, J., Thompson, L. L., McGraw, K. M., & Ingerman, C. (1987). Downward comparison, prejudice, and evaluations of others: Effects of self-esteem and threat. *Journal of Personality and Social Psychology, 52,* 907-916.

Cross, W. E., Jr. (1991). *Shades of Black: Diversity in African American identity.* Philadelphia: Temple University Press.

Dollard, J., Doob, L., Miller, N., Mowrer, O. H., & Sears, R. R. (1939). *Frustration and aggression.* New Haven, CT: Yale University Press.

Duckitt, J. (1992). *The social psychology of prejudice.* New York: Praeger.

Essed, P. (1991). *Understanding everyday racism.* Newbury Park, CA: Sage.

Essed, P. (1996). *Diversity: Gender, color, and culture.* Amherst: University of Massachusetts Press.

Gaertner, S. I., Dovidio, J. F., Anastasio, P. A., Bachman, B. A., & Rust, M. C. (1993). The common in-group identity model: Recategorization and the reduction of in-group bias. *European Review of Social Psychology, 4,* 1-26.

Giles, M. W., & Evans, A. S. (1985). External threat, perceived threat, and group identity. *Social Science Quarterly, 66,* 51-66.

Greenberg, J., Simon, L., Pyszczynski, T., Solomon, S., & Chatel, D. (1992). Terror management and tolerance: Does mortality salience always intensify negative reactions to others who threaten one's worldview? *Journal of Personality and Social Psychology, 63,* 212-220.

Hamilton, W. D. (1971). Selection of selfish and altruistic behavior in some extreme models. In J. F. Eisenberg & W. S. Dillon (Eds.), *Man and beast: Comparative social behavior.* Washington, DC: Smithsonian Institution Press.

Helms, J. (Ed.). (1990). *Black and White racial identity: Theory, research, and practice.* Westport, CT: Greenwood.

Horkheimer, M., & Flowerman, S. H. (1950). Studies in prejudice (Foreword). In T. W. Adorno, E. Frenkel-Brunswik, D. J. Levinson, & R. N. Sanford (Eds.), *The authoritarian personality* (pp. v-viii). New York: Harper.

Insko, C. A., Nacoste, R. P., & Moe, J. L. (1983). Belief congruence and racial discrimination: Review of the evidence and critical evaluation. *European Journal of Social Psychology, 13,* 153-174.

Jackman, M. R., & Muha, M. J. (1984). Education and intergroup attitudes: Moral enlightenment, superficial democratic commitment, or ideological refinements. *American Sociological Review, 49,* 751-769.

Jackson, J. S. (Ed.). (1991). *Life in Black America.* Newbury Park, CA: Sage.

Jackson, J. S., Brown, T. B., Williams, D. R., Torres, M., Sellers, S. L., & Brown, K. B. (1996). Racism and the physical and mental health status of African Americans: A 13-year national panel study. *Ethnicity & Disease, 6,* 132-147.

Jackson, J. S., & Inglehart, M. R. (1995). Reverberation theory: Stress and racism in hierarchically structured communities. In S. E. Hobfoll & M. deVries (Eds.), *Stress and communities: Moving beyond the individual* (pp. 353-374). Norwell, MA: Kluwer.

Jackson, J. S., Kirby, D., Barnes, L., & Shepard, L. (1993). Racisme institutionnel et ignorance pluraliste: Une comparaison transnationale. In M. Wievorka (Ed.), *Racisme et modernité* (pp. 246-264). Paris: Éditions La Découverte.

Jones, J. M. (1997). *Prejudice and racism* (2nd ed.). New York: McGraw-Hill.

Katz, D. (1960). The functional approach to the study of attitudes. *Public Opinion Quarterly, 24,* 163-204.

Katz, P. A., & Taylor, D. A. (Eds.). (1988). *Eliminating racism: Profiles in controversy.* New York: Plenum.

Kinder, D. R. (1986). The continuing American dilemma: White resistance to racial change 40 years after Myrdal. *Journal of Social Issues, 42*(2), 151-172.

Krause, N. (1994). Stressors in salient social roles and well-being in later life. *Journal of Gerontology, 49,* 137-148.

McNeilly, M. D., Anderson, N. B., Armstead, C. A., Clark, R., Corbett, M., Robinson, E. L., Pieper, C. F., & Lepisto, E. M. (1996). A Perceived Racism Scale: A multidimensional assessment of the experience of White racism among African Americans. *Ethnicity and Disease, 6,* 154-166.

Milner, D. (1981). Racial prejudice. In J. C. Turner & H. Giles (Eds.), *Intergroup behavior.* Cambridge, MA: Blackwell.

Nielsen, F. (1985). Toward a theory of ethnic solidarity in modern societies. *American Sociological Review, 50,* 133-149.

Olzak, S. (1992). *The dynamics of ethnic competition and conflict.* Stanford, CA: Stanford University Press.

Pettigrew, T. F. (1985). New Black-White patterns: How best to conceptualize them? *Annual Review of Sociology, 11,* 329-346.

Pettigrew, T. F., Jackson, J. S., Ben Brika, J., Lemaine, G., Meertens, R. W., Wagner, U., & Zick, A. (1997). Out-group prejudice in Western Europe. *European Review of Social Psychology.*

Pincus, F. L., & Ehrlich, H. J. (Eds.). (1994). *Race and ethnic conflict: Contending views on prejudice, discrimination, and ethnoviolence.* Boulder, CO: Westview.

Plous, S. (1996). Ten myths about affirmative action. *Journal of Social Issues, 52*(4), 25-31.

Price, R. H., van Ryn, M., & Vinokur, A. D. (1992). Impact of preventive job-search intervention on the likelihood of depression among the unemployed. *Journal of Health and Social Behavior, 33,* 158-167.

Rokeach, M. (1979). Some unresolved issues in theories of beliefs, attitudes, and values. In M. M. Page (Ed.), *Nebraska Symposium on Motivation* (Vol. 27). Lincoln: University of Nebraska Press.

Schuman, H., Steeh, C., & Bobo, L. (1985). *Racial attitudes in America: Trends and interpretations.* Cambridge, MA: Harvard University Press.

Sears, D. O. (1987). Symbolic racism. In P. A. Katz & D. A. Taylor (Eds.), *Eliminating racism: Profiles in controversy* (pp. 53-84). New York: Plenum.

Sears, D. O., & Kinder, D. R. (1985). Whites' opposition to busing: On conceptualizing and operationalizing "group conflict." *Journal of Personality and Social Psychology, 48,* 1141-1147.

Sherif, M., & Sherif, C. W. (1969). *Social psychology.* New York: Harper & Row.

Sidanius, J., Pratto, F., & Bobo, L. (1996). Social dominance orientation and the political psychology of gender: A case of invariance? *Journal of Personality and Social Psychology, 67,* 998-1011.

Smith, C. A., & Ellsworth, P. (1985). Patterns of cognitive appraisal in emotion. *Journal of Personality and Social Psychology, 48,* 813-838.

Sniderman, P. M., & Piazza, T. (1993). *The scar of race.* Cambridge, MA: Harvard University Press.

Sniderman, P. M., & Tetlock, P. E. (1986). Symbolic racism: Problems of motive attribution in political debate. *Journal of Social Issues, 42,* 173-188.

Stephan, W. G., & Stephan, C. W. (1985). Intergroup anxiety. *Journal of Social Issues, 41,* 157-175.

Stephan, W. G., Ybarra, O., & Bachman, G. (1997). *A threat model of prejudice: The case of immigrants.* Unpublished manuscript, New Mexico State University.

Tajfel, H., & Turner, J. C. (1979). An integrative theory of intergroup conflict. In W. C. Austin & S. Worchel (Eds.), *The social psychology of intergroup relations* (pp. 33-47). Pacific Grove, CA: Brooks/Cole.

Tatum, B. D. (1992). Talking about race, learning about racism: The application of racial identity development theory in the classroom. *Harvard Educational Review, 62*(1), 1-24.

Tatum, B. D. (1994). Teaching White students about racism: The search for White allies and the restoration of hope. *Teachers College Record, 95*(4), 462-475.

Thoits, P. A. (1991). On merging identity theory and stress research. *Social Psychology Quarterly, 54,* 101-112.

Thomas, R. W. (1996). *Understanding interracial unity: A study of U.S. race relations.* Thousand Oaks, CA: Sage.

United Nations Economic and Social Council. (1993). *The 1993 report on the world social situaiton.* New York: Author.

Vinokur, A. D., Price, R. H., & Schul, Y. (1995). Impact of the JOBS intervention on unemployed workers varying in risk for depression. *American Journal of Community Psychology, 23,* 39-74.

Weigel, R. H., & Howes, P. W. (1985). Conceptions of racial prejudice: Symbolic racism reconsidered. *Journal of Social Issues, 41,* 117-138.

Williams, R. M., Jr. (1947). *The reduction of intergroup tensions: A survey of research on problems of ethnic, racial, and religious group relations.* New York: Social Science Research Council.

Wilson, E. O. (1978). The genetic evolution of altruism. In L. Wispe (Ed.), *Altruism, sympathy, and helping* (pp. 11-38). San Diego: Academic Press.

Ybarra, O., & Stephan, W. G. (1994). Perceived threat as a predictor of prejudice and stereotypes: Americans' reactions to Mexican immigrants. *Boletín de Psicología, 42,* 39-54.

Yinger, J. M. (1985). Ethnicity. *Annual Review of Sociology, 11,* 151-180.

3

Is Housing the Cure
for Homelessness?

MARYBETH SHINN
SAM TSEMBERIS

omelessness is a continuing scourge on U.S. society. Throughout the 1980s, a debate raged about the number of people who were homeless at any given time, with estimates varying wildly. Perhaps the most credible figure is 350,000—representing the number of people who were literally homeless, living in shelters and public places throughout the United States in a 1-week period in 1987 (Burt, 1992; Jencks, 1994).

More recently, several studies that have attempted to determine how many people have experienced homelessness over a longer period have yielded enormously higher figures. A 1990 telephone survey found that 7.4% of adults in conventional dwellings with telephones—representing a total of 13.5 million people—reported having been literally homeless at some time in their lives. That is, they considered themselves to be homeless and slept in a park, in an abandoned building, on the street, in a train or bus station, in a shelter for homeless people, or in another temporary residence because they did not have another place to stay. In

AUTHORS' NOTE: Preparation of this chapter was funded in part by National Institute of Mental Health Grant #R01MH46116 and by contract #1UD9SM51970 from the Substance Abuse and Mental Health Services Administration.

the same survey, 3.1%—representing 5.7 million people—had been homeless during the past 5 years. This study found only slightly higher 5-year rates (3.4%) among residents of the 20 largest Standard Metropolitan Statistical Areas than among residents of all other areas (3.1%) (Link et al., 1994). Unduplicated counts of people using shelters in two cities yielded remarkably similar numbers: Over a 5-year period, 3.3% of New York City's population used shelters, as did 2.8% of Philadelphia's population over 3 years (Culhane, Dejowski, Ibanez, Needham, & Macchia, 1994); an unknown additional proportion were homeless on the streets.

Thus, converging evidence from telephone surveys and shelter counts indicates that slightly over 3% of the nation's population has been literally homeless over a 5-year period. From these numbers, we draw two critical conclusions: First, temporary homelessness is far more common than even the most exaggerated claims of the advocates in the 1980s suggested; and second, most homelessness is temporary. Homelessness is a state through which many people pass, and not a permanent trait.

The realization that, for most people, homelessness is temporary raises a new set of important questions for research. Rather than conduct endless surveys of homeless people to examine the characteristics that differentiate them from other poor people who are housed, and rather than infer (with faulty logic) that the differences are causes of homelessness, we can ask what it takes to end homelessness. Can people find their own ways out of homelessness without assistance? Is provision of subsidized housing sufficient to enable people who have been homeless to attain residential stability and avoid returns to homelessness? To what extent are additional supportive services necessary, and how should those services be organized? Or, to what extent are neither housing nor services sufficient to extricate people from a permanent state of homelessness or a vicious cycle of intermittent episodes? This chapter attempts to address these questions.

We must say at the outset that we shall not address them very well. Although the body of research on the characteristics of homeless people is substantial, few studies have been conducted on *exits* from homelessness. One reason for the paucity of such research is that it requires longitudinal methods: A sample of homeless people must be identified and followed over time to obtain dependent measures of housing and residential stability. Longitudinal studies are far more difficult to conduct and more expensive than cross-sectional surveys.

A second problem is conceptual. The assumption that individual disability is central to homelessness is so ubiquitous that efforts to house people without elaborate services have rarely been put to an empirical test. Researchers and service providers tied to the mental health system have assumed that housing must be linked to services and treatment. Running counter to this assumption is a small but growing body of evidence that not all homeless people require specialized services, and even in the case of homeless individuals with mental illness and substance abuse problems, housing programs and mental health or social services can be offered separately, with housing being offered first as the most critical factor in ending homelessness.

In suggesting that housing is the cure for homelessness, we do not mean to deny that many homeless people have characteristics that make them vulnerable to loss of housing, particularly when the stock of affordable housing is inadequate. We agree with the growing consensus that homelessness has multiple correlates, including poverty, disability, demographic characteristics, childhood histories, and lack of access to families or friends with resources, often in combination (Koegel, Burnam, & Baumohl, 1996). Explanations for homelessness that are confined to any one factor falter in the face of the evidence. For example, researchers who emphasize structural explanations based on our nation's growing poverty rates and loss of affordable housing must contend with the fact that, among poor people, those who experience homelessness have higher levels of disability than those who do not experience homelessness. Researchers who emphasize disability must acknowledge that mental illness and substance abuse are far more broadly distributed over the socioeconomic spectrum than is homelessness; in fact, few differences in demographic characteristics are found between single homeless adults with and without mental illness (Tessler & Dennis, 1989). The fact that there are many correlates of homelessness, however, does not require that all receive equal emphasis in programs to help homeless people obtain permanent housing. Some characteristics, such as age, race, and disruptive childhood experiences, cannot be changed. Among factors that can be manipulated, some may be more potent than others; those most potent in causing homelessness may not be those that are most potent in alleviating it.

In the remainder of this chapter, we briefly describe the associations between homelessness and mental illness and substance abuse, and findings concerning the resulting assumption that housing programs for

homeless people with such problems—or even for those without them—
should be linked with services. First in the case of families, and then in
the case of single individuals with mental illness and substance abuse
problems, we examine the conventional wisdom about the organization
of services. In each case, we offer modest evidence that housing without
specialized services, or with services driven by consumer requests
rather than by requirements of the service system, is often sufficient to
end homelessness.

Mental Illness and
Substance Abuse

The link between homelessness and mental illness or substance
abuse is frequently exaggerated. Methodologically rigorous studies
report that, of the single adult homeless population, 25% to 37% either
have a history of or exhibit serious mental disorders (Plapinger, Gounis,
& Dennis, 1988; Struening, 1987; Susser, Struening, & Conover, 1988;
Tessler & Dennis, 1989). When the mental illness is required to be
current, and both severe and persisting, estimates shrink to 13% to 26%
(Lehman & Cordray, 1994). Estimates for lifetime substance use disorders of single, adult homeless individuals are less stable, ranging, in
rigorous studies, from 30% to 70%, with an average of about 50% (Lehman
& Cordray, 1994; Tessler & Dennis, 1989). Fewer studies examine current
substance use disorders, with levels averaging 28% for alcohol use
disorder and 11% for substance use disorder. Dual diagnoses (lifetime)
of concurrent mental health and substance abuse problems characterize
a relatively large subset of the mentally ill, ranging from 12% to 26%
of the single adult homeless population (Lehman & Cordray, 1994).

Interestingly, Koegel, Burnam, and Farr (1990) reported, on the basis
of ethnographic studies, that mental illness and substance abuse played
only a small role in the day-to-day subsistence strategies of inner-city
homeless adults in Los Angeles. Across groups with mental illness,
substance abuse, both, or neither, about one third ate as often as three
times a day, three fifths reported difficulty finding shelter, one half had
difficulty finding clothing, and two fifths had difficulty finding a setting
for personal hygiene. (The situation may be worse outside the inner city,

which is comparatively rich in services.) Differences among groups were surprisingly small, leading Koegel et al. (1990, p. 104) to remark on the "leveling" quality of homelessness. The condition is sufficiently handicapping "by itself that each homeless person's adaptation suffers radically." Within this context, disability makes relatively little difference.

Although people with mental illness are a minority of those who are homeless, they are the most visible segment of the homeless population; these are the individuals who walk the streets, carrying their bundled belongings, or who sit disheveled in parks, subway stations, and other public places, talking to others only they can see. They also have a special claim on society's resources by virtue of their disabilities.

Families make up about 40% of those who become homeless, although a much smaller portion of those who are homeless on any given night (Shinn & Weitzman, 1996). Rates of both mental illness and substance abuse among parents in homeless families are far lower than in homeless single adults (Bassuk et al., 1997; Rossi, 1994; Shinn & Weitzman, 1996). Indeed, in recent studies using diagnoses rather than symptom scales, homeless and housed poor mothers have not differed in rates of mental illness, although they have differed in use of substances (Bassuk et al., 1997; Shinn et al., in press). One reason why the prevalence of mental illness is relatively low in homeless families is that parents with serious mental illnesses or substance abuse problems, especially those who become visible by virtue of homelessness, are likely to lose access to their children and to become part of the single adult population. In the words of a service provider, "You have to be pretty together to hold on to your kids through an episode of homelessness" (Shinn, 1992, p. 14). Families have a special claim on society's resources because of the needs of their children.

Although we would argue that housing is a human right, not reserved for those with special vulnerabilities, our society makes relatively few supports available to single individuals without mental illnesses who become homeless, and consequently scant research has been conducted on exits from homelessness for such groups. An exception is a study by Sosin, Piliavin, and Westerfelt (1990), which followed new entrants to homelessness in Minneapolis, as well as a cross-sectional sample in the same city. The authors found that relatively few people were able to exit from homelessness during a 6-month period without some assistance from either government or private sources. The remainder of this chapter focuses first on homeless families and then on homeless single individuals with serious mental illnesses.

Families

Assumptions About Services

Although homeless families have fewer mental health needs than single individuals, research has found elevated levels of other problems, including disruptive experiences in childhood and, in many but not all studies, higher rates of domestic violence in adulthood and poorer social networks than among housed poor families. Other common characteristics, such as limited education, lack of employment, and single parenthood, are shared by many very poor families irrespective of homelessness (Shinn & Weitzman, 1996).

Perhaps because of these problems, the conventional wisdom is that housing for homeless families should be linked with services. For example, a program design manual prepared by the Better Homes Foundation advocates tying "essential services," such as case management, to permanent housing to prevent returns to homelessness. "Service-enriched" housing might range "from a collective housing arrangement entered into by a group of single mothers, to housing staffed with house managers trained in social services." With these options available for permanent housing, "only the most troubled families with severe or multiple special needs . . . would require lengthy stays in specially designed transitional facilities" (Bassuk & Harvey, 1990, pp. 14-15). The foundation report notes that transitional housing can promote dependency among those who do not need it and that it is unfortunate that "some self-sufficient families" enter costly transitional facilities because affordable housing is not available; it is not clear whether the authors believe that any homeless families should avoid case management (Bassuk & Harvey, 1990, p. 15).

A report of the New York City Commission on the Homeless (1992), commonly dubbed the "Cuomo report" because it was chaired by Andrew Cuomo, who later became secretary of the Department of Housing and Urban Development, suggested similarly that most homeless families require "some form of social service assistance before moving to permanent housing," although "the few" homeless families "whose only need is affordable housing" should be eligible for housing directly (pp. 76-77). The commission recommended a three-phase system in which families would move from assessment centers, where eligibility would be determined and needs assessed, to transitional

housing, where "social and related services" including training in independent living would be provided, and only then, on to permanent
housing. (The linear continuum model for adults with mental illness, to
be described later, is a more elaborate version of this system.)

Evidence

A major problem with these analyses is that, of the 5.7 million people
estimated to have been homeless at some time in the late 1980s, very
few passed through the sorts of service programs envisioned in these
reports, but most are currently housed. The longest-term longitudinal
study of homelessness of which we are aware took place in New York
City in the system that the Cuomo report deemed inadequate (Shinn
et al., in press). Most families stayed in congregate shelters or welfare
hotels, which were often abysmal places to which no one should be
subjected (e.g., Kozol, 1988). But 5 years after the initial entry into
homelessness, 80% of 244 previously sheltered families were housed
in their own places, typically apartments, and 61% had met the additional criterion for stability of having been in those places for at least
1 year. (Note that the percentage of readers of this book who are in their
own place may approach 100%, but the proportion who have not moved
in the past year would be lower.) On average, the families who met the
criterion of stability had been in a single place of their own for 35
months.

The primary predictor of long-term stability was the family's receipt
of one of five forms of subsidized housing at any time after entering
shelter. The most common types of subsidized housing were apartments
in New York City Housing Authority "projects" or in buildings that had
been taken over from landlords who had abandoned them or failed to
pay taxes and that typically were rehabilitated and managed by the City
Department of Housing Preservation and Development. In either case,
rents were capped at 30% of income. Other options were federal Section
8 certificates, which pay the difference between the market rent on an
apartment and 30% of the recipient's income, a private-landlord program in which landlords were given bonuses for renting cheaply to
formerly homeless families, and court-ordered rent supplements to
prevent eviction. Very few families (18%) who did not receive one of
these forms of subsidy were stable, whereas 97% of those who received

subsidies were in their own apartment and 80% were stable at Time 2, figures as good or better than those in the comparison group that was randomly sampled from the welfare caseload (92% in own apartment, 80% stable). Controlling for age, the odds of attaining stability were increased 20-fold for families who received subsidized housing. In the context of subsidized housing, no additional factor other than age contributed to stability. Neither indexes of disability (mental illness, substance use disorders, physical health problems), social relationships, childhood histories, nor other demographic characteristics made any contribution to stability, although several of these factors predicted which families became homeless in the first place. We conclude that subsidized housing is very close to a necessary and sufficient condition for housing stability among formerly homeless families in New York.

In this study, receipt of subsidized housing was not confounded with individual characteristics. The primary predictors of who received subsidized housing were the type of shelter to which the family was assigned (by a computer algorithm based on family size and composition, availability of shelter space that matched those characteristics, and current system priorities for using particular shelters or hotels) and length of time in shelter. The latter variable indexed whether the family waited in shelter long enough to come to the head of the queue for housing and was unrelated to stability, once receipt of subsidized housing was controlled. Domestic violence was the only individual or family characteristic associated with a lower probability of receiving housing, probably because batterers pursued some women into the shelter or because some women who experienced violence returned to live with the men who had abused them.

Further analyses (Stojanovic, Weitzman, Shinn, Labay, & Williams, 1997) of the paths followed by individual families showed that those who received subsidized housing but nevertheless returned to shelter did so primarily because of building problems or problems with safety in the neighborhood. They were less likely than those who stayed housed to have been given apartments in New York City's Housing Authority projects, which in New York are well run and provide some of the best housing available to poor people.

Services did little to promote stability. Only 22% of families spent the longest time in shelters that provided enriched and coordinated services. These families had a greater probability of receiving subsidized housing, but this seems more likely to be a result of efforts by these shelter operators to secure housing for their residents than to services focused on families' psychological well-being. Families from the services-enriched shelters were no more likely to stay stably housed than other families, once receipt of subsidized housing was controlled. One fifth (19%) of the families received a one-time grant of money for furniture and utensils, but very few (6%) received other services to help them stay housed, although they were free to access the usual mix of services available in their communities. Families who had been in a shelter were somewhat more likely than those in the comparison group to report that "someone at a welfare, school, health, housing, legal or other service organization" told them about service for which they were eligible (16% vs. 10%) but were no more likely to get help in filling out paperwork or forms to get services (9% vs. 6%). Having a caseworker was actually negatively associated with long-term stability, perhaps because caseworkers were most often from the agency responsible for child welfare, and mothers who were separated from their children lost eligibility for family housing.

Two other studies designed to examine the effects of case management services in the context of housing for families leaving shelter also support the conclusion that most homeless families who are given subsidized housing attain residential stability (see the following paragraphs). Because all families in these studies received subsidized housing, no test of the relationship of subsidized housing to stability is possible.

The first of these studies, also conducted in New York City (Weitzman & Berry, 1994), focused on families deemed to be at especially high risk for returning to shelter, on the basis of a set of individual and family characteristics. The primary question addressed was whether intensive case management services would enhance the stability of families who were given subsidized housing. This question could not really be answered, however, because at the end of the 1-year follow-up period, the vast majority of families were housed whether or not they had received the intensive case management services. Only 8 of 169 high-risk families—just under 5%—had returned to shelter. Receipt of case management services was partially confounded with the type of housing into which families were placed, and also with some individual characteristics, but type of housing was the strongest single predictor of who would return. As in the study by Shinn et al. (in press), New York City Housing Authority projects fostered the most stability. Families who received case management services (and, on average, better housing) were slightly more likely to be primary tenants in their own apartments at the end of a year than families who did not (87% vs. 80%).

Other interesting findings concerned services. Families who received intensive case management and comparison families were equally likely to use long-term services or support groups in the community; comparison families were somewhat more likely to use one-shot services (e.g., a furniture program, food pantry). No differences were found between the groups in family reunification or prevention of out-of-home placement, school enrollment or attendance, or health care use; that is, it is not clear that intensive case management provided much added value, even for these high-risk families, beyond the mix of services already available in communities—which families could and did access on their own.

Similar findings are emerging from a nine-city study of homeless families chosen for long-term patterns of recurrent homelessness and needs for services and given both Section 8 housing certificates and case management services. Among 601 families on whom 18 months of follow-up data were available, 88% remained in permanent housing (Rog, Holupka, & McCombs-Thornton, 1995). This study suggests that services-enriched housing works, but it does not speak to the issue of housing without services. Interestingly, the case management services differed in intensity across the nine cities. Analyses of relationships between service receipt and housing stability at the individual level are not yet available, but at the level of cities, no relationship appears to exist between the intensity of the programs and the levels of housing stability (Rog et al., 1994)—contrary to what might be expected if the services were the critical factor.[1]

Tentative Conclusions

On the basis of these data, we claim that in many cases receipt of subsidized housing is sufficient to end homelessness for families. The additional value of specialized services in promoting stability is less clear. Our claim is a limited one. The formerly homeless families in all these studies did not lead idyllic lives. Many grappled with health problems, domestic violence, or substance abuse. Mortality rates were high. Some mothers became separated from their children, who went to live with relatives or in foster care. Receipt of housing did not solve all the problems in these families' lives, but in most cases it did solve the problem of homelessness. Services might well help with some of the families' other problems and should be offered, but it is not clear that such services need to be linked with housing.

There is at least a hint that specialized services may be counterproductive. Some of the best services available to homeless families in New York shelters are health services, offered on-site at shelters or by mobile medical vans staffed by dedicated health care professionals. Yet, 5 years after initial entry into shelter, formerly homeless families in the longitudinal study described previously (Shinn et al., in press) were less likely to have a usual source of medical care than other poor families in the comparison group and were more likely to rely on emergency rooms. Shelter use contributed to this pattern above and beyond family mobility (Duchon, Weitzman, & Shinn, 1997). Differences may have been attributable to unmeasured family characteristics or to screening out of formerly homeless families by health care providers. But it is possible that specialized services in shelter interrupted families' ties to the medical care system and failed to link families with ordinary services after the families ceased to be eligible for the transitional ones.

Two additional caveats need to be raised. First, all three studies were completed before the recent limitations on eligibility for welfare went into effect. Most families in all three studies received public assistance, which although insufficient for them to procure housing on the open market, provided a base on which the subsidies could build. Very few formerly homeless families left the public assistance caseload even during the longest follow-up period (5 years). If families who exhaust their eligibility for welfare payments cannot maintain their income by other means, housing subsidies would need to be much larger to prevent a return to homelessness. It seems unlikely, in the current political climate, that such large subsidies would be provided.

Second, although families held the leases to their apartments in the programs just described, subsidy arrangements were not equivalent to provision of unrestricted income. Subsidies were tied directly to housing, reducing families' rent. Further, at least in New York, the nonsubsidized portion of families' rent was typically taken out of welfare checks and paid directly from the welfare authority to the housing authority, guaranteeing that, whatever other needs of families went unmet, rent would be paid. Liberals might argue that such arrangements are paternalistic; conservatives might find them more palatable than providing (additional) direct subsidies to income via welfare or other mechanisms. The studies suggest only that housing subsidies work to end homelessness and produce residential stability;

they allow no conclusion about whether additional income supports would work as well.

Homeless Single Individuals With Mental Illness and Substance Abuse

Needs for Services

The success of subsidized housing in ending homelessness for most families without major mental health problems cannot be generalized to the situation of adults with serious and persistent mental illnesses. Nevertheless, the fact that homelessness did not arise during the first great waves of deinstitutionalization from mental hospitals, but only much later in the context of a general housing shortage, suggests that housing is also an essential part of any effort to reduce homelessness for this group. The central question here is how best to organize housing and services.

It must be recognized that individuals who are homeless and who have mental illnesses and co-occurring disorders, such as substance abuse or alcohol addictions, are a fragile, extremely vulnerable population. They are more likely than other subpopulations of homeless people to need help securing housing. Many studies have noted the difficulty of engaging this population in traditional services (Asmussen, Romano, Beatty, Gasarch, & Shaughnessey, 1994; Cohen, Putnam, & Sullivan, 1984; Shern et al., 1994; Tsemberis, Cohen, & Jones, 1993). Some authors hypothesize that rejection of services is based on individuals' distrust and frustration born of experience with a mental health system unable to meet their needs. Among the principal causes of this systemic failure is the fragmentation of the current mental health system and the bifurcation between mental health and addiction services (Bachrach, 1984; Barrow, Hellman, Lovell, Plapinger, & Struening, 1989; Goldfinger & Chavetz, 1984; Osher & Drake, 1996).

Not all researchers view homeless individuals with mental illnesses and substance use disorders who reject services as being uncooperative (Baxter & Hopper, 1982). Studies have shown that many otherwise uncooperative people are willing to accept help if they can determine the service plan or if they view the help as relevant to their needs (Asmussen et al., 1994; Dattalo, 1990; Lovell, 1992; Martin & Nayowith, 1988; Shern et al., 1994; Tessler & Dennis, 1989). Homeless consumers often perceive their need for services differently from providers, placing higher value on meeting basic needs than on addressing mental health problems (Barrow et al., 1989; Cohen & Tsemberis, 1991; Dattalo, 1990; Martin, 1990; Plapinger et al., 1988; Struening, 1987).

Nontraditional mental health services specifically designed for these individuals, such as outreach, drop-in centers, and case management, have been shown to be successful in engaging this group (Barrow et al., 1989; Lovell, 1992; Martin, 1990; Tsemberis, 1995). Successful as these models are, programs characterized by consumer preferences and low-demand approaches have not been used by traditional housing providers.

The Linear Continuum Model

The dominant model for community-based treatment of clients with mental illness and previously homeless clients is currently characterized by a linear continuum of care in which treatment options that vary simultaneously in the intensity of services and the restrictiveness of living arrangements are organized into a continuum along which clients are expected to progress. In this model, the client is matched by the service provider to an appropriate setting on the basis of the provider's assessment of the client's level of functioning and need for restriction. Clients served in a particular setting are supposed to represent a homogeneous grouping of individuals, all of whom function at the same level and require the same intensity of services. The entry point is typically a congregate setting with 24-hour staff supervision. After mastering such skills as cleaning, shopping, budgeting, and bathing (often referred to as "activities of daily living") and becoming an active participant in psychiatric treatment, including taking medications, the individual "graduates" to a higher level of housing with more independence and less staff involvement. Eventually, the person graduates to independent living with little or no staff support (New York City Commission on the Homeless, 1992; Randolph, Ridgway, & Carling, 1991; Ridgway & Zipple, 1990).

Despite its widespread acceptance among service providers, serious questions regarding the linear continuum model have been raised by consumers, advocates, and some program planners. First, the model fails to distinguish between residential treatment and housing; clients must become clinically stable and treatment-compliant to gain more independent housing. Second, the continuum model does not represent the kind of housing most consumers want. Studies have documented that, given the option, most consumers prefer to live alone or with a chosen partner (Owen et al., 1996; Schutt & Goldfinger, 1996; Tanzman, 1993). They want jobs and social integration in the community. Although consumers generally understand that they may need special support to attain their goals, they think that this support should be focused on practical matters, such as acquiring and maintaining apartments, jobs, and a social network, and that they should decide its extent themselves (Howie the Harp, 1990). Third, the entry point to the model, in particular, is often more restrictive than clients will accept—that is, shared living spaces, continuous staff supervision, and forced treatment. Some individuals prefer the relative independence of the streets to loss of privacy and control in residential facilities (Howie the Harp, 1990). This kind of highly structured environment can lead to social disability (Grunberg & Eagle, 1990).

Fourth, moving an individual through a series of time-limited stays in various specialized housing arrangements is stressful; paradoxically, support is reduced just as transitions cause stress. Fifth, in many cases it has proved unrealistic to expect people with psychiatric disabilities to fit into this highly structured linear progression with standardized levels of care. Clients who experience an exacerbation of psychiatric symptoms or who relapse into drug and alcohol use are returned to a more restrictive service setting with more intensive services (Carling, 1993; Ridgway & Zipple, 1990). Sixth, individuals with co-occurring disorders who are currently not complying with psychiatric or substance abuse treatment are excluded by the continuum model. And seventh, the continuum model teaches skills for independent living in structured settings, whereas rehabilitation studies suggest that the most effective way to learn such skills is in the environment in which they will be applied (Anthony & Blanch, 1989; Carling, 1993).

Choice is an extremely important factor when helping homeless individuals regain or obtain housing. Newer research has shown that providing consumers with choices has a very positive effect on both staff and tenants. One study found that when a shift in housing policy occurred from congregate care facilities to independent living, the attitudes of the case managers changed. The case managers began to see the tenants as more competent and capable when they were living independently even though the tenants themselves had not changed (Pandiani, Edgar, & Pierce, 1994). The studies involving tenants are even more impressive. It has been found that choice in housing options is correlated with housing satisfaction, housing stability, and psychological well-being (Srebnik, Livingston, Gordon, & King, 1995). Another study showed that when tenants were allowed to choose where and how they lived and to have their choice of support services, hospitalizations decreased and positive roles such as work, school, and social activities increased (Chipperfield & Aubry, 1990).

A Consumer-Preference Independent Living Model

Although much has been written about consumer-driven independent models, few have actually been implemented. One of the most radical examples is the Consumer Preference Independent Living program of Pathways to Housing, Inc., in New York City (Tsemberis, 1997). This program targets individuals who are homeless—literally living on the streets or in other public places—and have a psychiatric disability and/or a substance abuse disorder; it offers them their own apartments with their own leases, not as a final step in a continuum model, but directly from the streets. It views housing as a human right that is not contingent on housing readiness or treatment success, and it provides housing in scattered sites, not in congregate living arrangements. The program accepts active substance abusers who decline treatment, as well as people with histories of violence or criminal records that are often barriers to many treatment programs. The Pathways model is based on the belief, and research findings that support this belief, that housing problems relate less closely to psychiatric disability than to economic and social factors (Carling, 1995; Cohen & Thompson, 1992); thus, given suitable housing and supports, individuals with mental illnesses or co-occurring disorders can function in independent apartments of their own. This view mirrors that of consumers, who see lack of income, not mental disability, as their main barrier to stable housing (Tanzman, 1993).

Further, the model assumes that services will be more successful once tenants are housed and when tenants have selected the services they want. This belief, too, is based on research showing that individuals do better in substance abuse treatment once they are housed (Lapham, Hall, & Skipper, 1995; Smith, North, & Fox, 1995) and that a program combining housing and treatment results in stronger housing stability (Stahler, Shipley, Bartelt, DuCette, & Shandler, 1995). Another study found that willingness to be in treatment predicted success in treatment and that the living condition of the individual greatly influenced the motivation or willingness to be in treatment. Those in stable housing were more apt to participate in and complete treatment (Erickson, Stevens, McKnight, & Figueredo, 1995). Thus, Pathways offers extensive services, but with two exceptions they are driven by consumer choices rather than by staff decisions. The exceptions are that tenants must agree to participate in money management to ensure that the rent gets paid and must meet with a case manager to set goals and select whatever additional services they want. Table 3.1 compares the Pathways model with the more traditional continuum-of-care model.

A randomized trial comparing housing and psychological outcomes for homeless individuals with mental illness assigned to the Pathways model versus alternative linear-continuum models is about to be conducted. But it is already clear that the program is more successful than typical alternatives in stabilizing clients. According to a psychiatrist with New York City's Human Resources Administration, 62% of individuals who enter linear-continuum models in the city leave within the first month (Lipton, personal communication, 1997). By contrast, 139 of the first 162 consumers to enter Pathways to Housing's program (86%) were still housed at the end of the program's first 4 years (Tsemberis, 1995). Further, a descriptive study of 52 Pathways tenants found significant negative correlations between the number of months spent in an apartment and both depressive symptoms and alcohol consumption. Depressive symptoms were also negatively correlated with being able to obtain services when needed and with an increase in the number of visits with friends (Tsemberis, 1995). These are only correlational results on a small sample, but barring any systematic change in the tenants entering Pathways over time, they suggest that stable housing, with voluntarily selected services and control over one's own social life, is associated with better psychological outcomes. Such results need to be confirmed with a more rigorous design.

Table 3.1
Comparison of the Pathways to Housing Program
With the Linear-Continuum Model

Pathways Scatter-Site Supported Housing	*Linear Continuum-of-Care Model*
Housing is a basic right; every person who is homeless and has a psychiatric disability and/or substance abuse problem is given immediate access to permanent housing.	Individuals must prove they are "housing ready" after first completing a series of treatments or successfully living in a series of transitional congregate living settings or residences.
Consumers select housing (apartments) that is owned and operated by community landlords or real estate agencies.	Clients are placed into housing owned and operated by the social services provider; housing is selected by providers and includes the provider's determination of the level of supervision based on client disability.
The agency providing case management, treatment, and other supports is different from the agency providing housing.	Treatment and housing are related; treatment must be successfully engaged before housing placement occurs, and it continues to be required thereafter.
Continued tenancy is not contingent upon the consumer's acceptance or participation in services or treatment.	Clients must participate in treatment, meet curfews, attend groups, etc.; high level of clinical staff supervision/control.
Services and supports are mostly provided in vivo, in the community.	Services are provided on-site or in an office setting.
Staff practices radical acceptance of the consumer's point of view regarding all aspects of supports and services needed by consumers; consumer preferences are honored; consumers set goals, pace, and outcomes.	Housing and treatment services are planned by the provider and include a series of specified goals that require completion before the client can graduate to the next level.
Sobriety and treatment are not required to maintain housing; staff practice harm-reduction to intervene quickly and prevent emergencies for consumers with drug or alcohol addictions.	The sobriety and abstinence model is used to treat drug and alcohol addictions; use of alcohol or drugs may lead to loss of housing.
There are no live-in support staff, but services are available 24 hours a day; there is a long-term commitment to the consumer.	Clients' graduation to increasingly independent levels of living results in a reduction of supports.

Source: Tsemberis (1997)

The Pathways program is in some ways more easily implemented than programs involving congregate care. Engaging homeless people with mental illness on the streets takes time and skill, but the offer of immediate access to an apartment of one's own is a greater draw for program participation than the offer of a supervised, congregate treatment facility. The housing is with private landlords in scattered sites, with no more than 5% of tenants in a given building being in the program. Landlords are surprisingly welcoming of program tenants because they are assured of regular rent payments. No zoning or community-board approval is required. The cost of the Pathways model, including rent and all services, is about $1,500 a month per client, comparable to the cost of congregate shelters in New York City and substantially less expensive than the cost of linear-continuum models. The cost of the latter programs is inflated by the need to have 24-hour staffing. Although Pathways' staff are on call 24 hours a day, this availability requires many fewer staff members than regular round-the-clock shifts.

Additional Evidence

A growing literature on effective models for housing people with psychiatric disabilities supports the idea that homeless individuals with mental illness can be stably housed in the community (rather than in dedicated treatment settings) with appropriate supports. In a recent review of clinical research demonstration projects undertaken with Stewart B. McKinney Homeless Assistance Act Funds in five cities, the authors concluded that programs offering a range of housing alternatives, when coupled with case management services, could effectively engage and stably house homeless individuals with severe mental illness (Shern et al., 1997). The experimental manipulation in these studies was the intensity level of case management services. Follow-up data, available for four of the five studies, indicated that 78% of the experimental group were stably housed after more than 18 months. Just as informative was the fact that approximately 60% of the control group, who received no special case management services, were housed and that the difference between experimental and control was diminishing at each time interval. Across cities, housing provided an important base for establishing stability, and intensive case management enhanced success. One major clinical variable that was negatively related to stable housing across these studies was alcohol or substance abuse.

More detailed within-city studies of the same data showed more mixed results. In the San Diego project, homeless people (ones who had no stable home of their own) with severe and chronic mental illness (schizophrenia, bipolar disorder, or major depression) were randomly assigned, in a 2 × 2 design, to access versus no access to Section 8 certificates and to traditional versus comprehensive case management (Hurlburt, Wood, & Hough, 1996). Excluded from the study were clients who had a history of violence or drug dealing or a substance abuse addiction for which they refused treatment. Not surprisingly, a significant number of clients underreported these problems. Results of the project indicated that an enormous effect was produced by access to Section 8 certificates. Almost 60% of participants with access to the certificates achieved stability in independent housing, compared with 31% of participants who did not have that access. No effect on housing outcomes was found for the type of case management.

In New York City, two substudies focused on a "critical time" intervention and a street sample of homeless individuals. Results of the "critical time" intervention showed that intensive services offered in the first 9 months after men entered a variety of unspecified forms of community housing from a shelter institution were associated with a substantial reduction in homeless nights (from 91 to 30) over the 18-month follow-up period (Susser et al., 1997). A second street-homeless sample was less successful overall (Shern et al., 1997); however, the 13 individuals from both the experimental and control groups who ended up at Pathways to Housing were far less likely to remain on the streets (0%) than the remainder of the experimental group (25%) or control group (50%). The Pathways subgroup was also more likely to be in their own apartments (69%) than the remainder of the experimental group (3%) or control group (1%).

Additional research on the effectiveness of case management services has shown that, with adequate supports, even persons with severe mental illness and those with dual diagnoses of mental illness and substance abuse can maintain stable housing in the community (Brown, Ridgway, & Anthony, 1991; Goldfinger, 1994; Livingston, Srebnik, King, & Gordon, 1992). Other studies that have looked at this question have found effects of housing type over and above personality characteristics and psychiatric diagnosis in a sample of veterans (Rosenheck,

1995) and in a sample of people who presented themselves in a psychiatric emergency room (Lipton, Nutt, & Sabatini, 1988).

Conclusion

We have provided partial answers to the questions we raised at the start of this chapter. The number of individuals who have experienced homelessness compared with the number of people who are homeless at any given point in time indicates that some people can find their own way out of homelessness without assistance. But the studies of particular populations suggest that, at least in housing markets such as New York's, housing assistance is very important. Indeed, in studies with homeless families in New York City, receipt of subsidized housing was very close to both a necessary and a sufficient condition for families to attain stability; with it, very high rates of stability were obtained without specialized services. Subsidized housing did not cure other problems that families had, any more than day care or psychotherapy would be likely to cure homelessness, but it at least provided a stable base from which families could begin to access other services available in their communities.

Adults with mental illnesses and substance abuse can also be stabilized in community settings, but supportive services are probably necessary for them. Certainly, we found no studies that offered housing without services. Housing subsidies were more important than the intensity of case management in stabilizing homeless adults with mental illness in a San Diego study, but intensive services mattered (and housing options were not examined) in a study in New York City. These results suggest that the availability of housing, as well as of services, should be systematically studied in future research. Just as Koegel et al. (1990) found that mental illness contributed little variance to the daily subsistence strategies of homeless adults in the Los Angeles inner city, it may be that mental illness plays a surprisingly small role in the ability of formerly homeless tenants to maintain apartments with appropriate supports. Finally, it is possible to organize services so that they are under client control. Although we do not have data, it seems reasonable to assume that tenants would find such programs more empowering than programs that tie housing to compliance to, and success in, treatment. The Pathways to Housing example shows that it is often possible to move homeless individuals with mental illness and concurrent substance abuse directly from the streets to their own apartments and to provide them with services of their choosing.

If subsidized housing, with or without services, is the cure for homelessness, it is an expensive cure, although subsidized housing is less expensive than such housing with services attached, and supported housing with services is, in turn, less expensive than linear-continuum models of care. Society is faced with a moral choice of whether to continue to allow people to live on sidewalks, heating grates, and benches, and in subways and cars. People in those circumstances challenge the humanity of the rest of us who walk by, and change relationships among citizens who have learned to avert their eyes rather than to intervene. Ironically, the problem of homelessness may be more readily solved for individuals with serious disabilities, because their numbers are more limited, than for people who are simply poor. Also, society seems less likely to withdraw the social safety net from individuals having disabilities than from poor adults and families without disabling conditions.

Large numbers in the latter group are poorly housed and receive no federal subsidies. For example, of 6.05 million households with incomes below 25% of the area median in 1989, fewer than half (2.27 million) received any housing assistance. Of the 3.78 million unsubsidized units, only 8% had housing judged adequate in the American Housing Survey (conducted by the Bureau of the Census) and that cost less than half of their total income (Joint Center for Housing Studies of Harvard University, 1993, p. 32).

The public costs of subsidized housing may seem more reasonable if we realize that government housing subsidies to wealthy households in the top fifth of the income distribution are more than three times as great as subsidies to those in the bottom fifth. These subsidies are in different forms, with those for households at the top primarily made up of tax expenditures, such as income tax deductions for mortgage interest and property taxes, whereas subsidies for those at the bottom are primarily direct outlays for assisted housing, including voucher programs. In fiscal year 1992, the bottom fifth of households, by income, received about 17% of the combined forms of subsidy, whereas the top fifth received 56% (Dolbeare, 1992, p. 20). Equating or reversing those proportions would go a long way toward curing homelessness.

Note

1. This is our conclusion, rather than one presented by the study authors. The three cities with the least intensive services (Table V-17) ranked second, third, and seventh out of nine in the percentage of families who were presumed to be in stable housing at the time of the interim report (Table V-20); the city with the most intensive services ranked fourth. This conclusion is, at best, tentative; many other characteristics besides intensity of services varied across cities.

References

Anthony, W. A., & Blanch, A. (1989). Research on community support services: What have we learned? *Psychosocial Rehabilitation Journal, 12*, 55-81.

Asmussen, S. M., Romano, J., Beatty, P., Gasarch, L., & Shaughnessey, S. (1994). Old answers for today's problems: Helping integrate individuals who are homeless with mental illnesses into existing community-based programs. *Psychosocial Rehabilitation Journal, 17*, 17-34.

Bachrach, L. L. (1984). Interpreting research on the homeless mentally ill: Some caveats. *Hospital and Community Psychiatry, 35*, 914-917.

Barrow, S. M., Hellman, F., Lovell, A. M., Plapinger, J. D., & Struening, E. L. (1989). *Effectiveness of programs for the mentally ill homeless: Final report.* New York: New York State Psychiatric Institute, Community Support Systems Evaluation Program.

Bassuk, E. L., Buckner, J. C., Weinreb, L. F., Browne, A., Bassuk, S. S., Dawson, R., & Perloff, J. N. (1997). Homelessness in female-headed families: Childhood and adult risk and protective factors. *American Journal of Public Health, 87*, 241-248.

Bassuk, E. L., & Harvey, M. R. (1990). Family homelessness: Recommendations for a comprehensive policy response. In E. L. Bassuk, R. W. Carmen, L. F. Weinreb, & M. M. Herzig (Eds.), *Community care for homeless families: A program design manual* (pp. 13-16). Washington, DC: Interagency Council on Homelessness.

Baxter, E., & Hopper, K. (1982). The new mendicancy: Homeless in New York City. *American Journal of Orthopsychiatry, 52*, 393-408.

Brown, M. A., Ridgway, P., & Anthony, W. A. (1991). Comparison of outcomes for clients seeking and assigned to supported housing services. *Hospital and Community Psychiatry, 42*, 1150-1153.

Burt, M. (1992). *Over the edge.* New York: Russell Sage.

Carling, P. J. (1993). Housing and supports for persons with mental illness: Emerging approaches to research and practice. *Hospital and Community Psychiatry, 44*, 439-449.

Carling, P. J. (1995). *Return to community: Building support systems for people with psychiatric disabilities.* New York: Guilford.

Chipperfield, S., & Aubry, T. (1990). The supportive housing program in Winnipeg. *Psychosocial Rehabilitation Journal, 13*, 91-94.

Cohen, C. I., & Thompson, K. S. (1992). Homeless mentally ill or mentally ill homeless? *American Journal of Psychiatry, 6*, 505-509.

Cohen, N. L., Putnam, J. F., & Sullivan, A. M. (1984). The mentally ill homeless: Isolation and adaptation. *Hospital and Community Psychiatry, 35,* 922-924.

Cohen, N. L., & Tsemberis, S. (1991). Emergency psychiatric interventions on the street. *New Directions for Mental Health Services, 52,* 3-16.

Culhane, D. P., Dejowski, E. F., Ibanez, J., Needham, E., & Macchia, I. (1994). Public shelter admission rates in Philadelphia and New York City: The implications of turnover for sheltered population counts. *Housing Policy Debate, 5,* 107-128.

Dattalo, P. (1990). Widening the range of services for the homeless mentally ill. *Administration and Policy in Mental Health, 17,* 247-256.

Dolbeare, C. N. (1992). *The widening gap: Housing needs of low income families.* Washington, DC: Low Income Housing Information Service.

Duchon, L. M., Weitzman, B. C., & Shinn, M. (1997). *Health care use after homelessness among poor families in New York City.* Manuscript submitted for publication.

Erickson, J. R., Stevens, S., McKnight, P., & Figueredo, A. J. (1995). Willingness for treatment as a predictor of retention and outcomes. *Journal of Addictive Diseases, 14,* 135-150.

Goldfinger, S. M. (1994). The Boston project: Promoting housing stability and consumer empowerment. In *Making a difference: Interim status report of the McKinney Research Demonstration Program for Mentally Ill Adults* (pp. 43-61; DHHS Publication No. [SMA] 94-3014 SAMHSA). Washington, DC: U.S. Department of Health and Human Services, Substance Abuse and Mental Health Services Administration, Center for Mental Health Services.

Goldfinger, S. M., & Chavetz, L. (1984). Developing a better service system for the homeless mentally ill. In H. R. Lamb (Ed.), *The homeless mentally ill: A task force report of the American Psychiatric Association.* Washington, DC: American Psychiatric Association.

Grunberg, J., & Eagle, P. (1990). Shelterization: How the homeless adapt to shelter living. *Hospital and Community Psychiatry, 41,* 521-525.

Howie the Harp. (1990). Independent living with support services: The goals and future for mental health consumers. *Psychosocial Rehabilitation Journal, 13,* 85-89.

Hurlburt, M. S., Wood, P. A., & Hough, R. L. (1996). Providing independent housing for the mentally ill homeless: A novel approach to evaluating long-term housing patterns. *Journal of Community Psychology, 24,* 291-310.

Jencks, C. (1994). *The homeless.* Cambridge, MA: Harvard University Press.

Joint Center for Housing Studies of Harvard University. (1993). *The state of the nation's housing, 1993.* Cambridge, MA: Author.

Koegel, P., Burnam, M. A., & Baumohl, J. (1996). The causes of homelessness. In J. Baumohl (Ed.), *Homelessness in America* (pp. 24-33). Phoenix, AZ: Oryx.

Koegel, P., Burnam, M. A., & Farr, R. K. (1990). Subsistence adaptation among homeless adults in the inner city of Los Angeles. *Journal of Social Issues, 46*(4), 83-107.

Kozol, J. (1988). *Rachel and her children: Homeless families in America.* New York: Crown.

Lapham, S. C., Hall, M., & Skipper, B. J. (1995). Homelessness and substance use among alcohol abusers following participation in Project HART. *Journal of Addictive Disease, 14,* 41-55.

Lehman, A. F., & Cordray, D. S. (1994). Prevalence of alcohol, drug, and mental disorders among the homeless: One more time. *Contemporary Drug Problems, 20*(3), 355-381.

Link, B. G., Susser, E., Stueve, A., Phelan, J., Moore, R. E., & Struening, E. (1994). Lifetime and 5-year prevalence of homelessness in the United States. *American Journal of Public Health, 84,* 1907-1912.

Lipton, F. R., Nutt, S., & Sabatini, A. (1988). Housing the homeless mentally ill: A longitudinal study of a treatment approach. *Hospital and Community Psychiatry, 39,* 40-45.

Livingston, J. A., Srebnik, D., King, D. A., & Gordon, L. (1992). Approaches to providing housing and flexible supports for people with psychiatric disabilities. *Psychosocial Rehabilitation Journal, 16,* 27-43.

Lovell, A. (1992). Classification and its risks: How psychiatric status contributes to homeless policy. *New England Journal of Public Policy, 8,* 247-263.

Martin, M. A. (1990). The homeless mentally ill and community-based care: Changing a mind-set. *Community Mental Health Journal, 26,* 435-447.

Martin, M. A., & Nayowith, S. A. (1988). Creating community: Groupwork to develop social support networks with homeless mentally ill. *Social Work With Groups, 11,* 79-93.

New York City Commission on the Homeless. (1992). *The way home: A new direction in social policy.* New York: Author.

Osher, F. C., & Drake, R. R. (1996). Reversing a history of unmet needs: Approaches to care for persons with co-occurring addictive and mental disorders. *American Journal of Orthopsychiatry, 66,* 4-11.

Owen, C., Rutherford, V., Jones, M., Wright, C., Tennant, C., & Smallmann, A. (1996). Housing accommodation preferences of people with psychiatric disabilities. *Psychiatric Services, 47,* 628-632.

Pandiani, J. A., Edgar, E. R., & Pierce, J. E. (1994). A longitudinal study of the impact of changing public policy on community mental health client residential patterns and staff attitudes. *Journal of Mental Health Administration, 21,* 71-79.

Plapinger, J., Gounis, K., & Dennis, D. L. (1988). *The development of the residential placement management program: Issues and implications for housing mentally ill homeless persons* (Final report submitted to Office of Mental Health, contract #C001917). Philadelphia: Research Institute.

Randolph, F. L., Ridgway, P., & Carling, P. J. (1991). Residential programs for persons with severe mental illness: A nationwide survey of state-affiliated agencies. *Hospital and Community Psychiatry, 42,* 1111-1115.

Ridgway, P., & Zipple, A. M. (1990). The paradigm shift in residential services: From the linear continuum to supported housing approaches. *Psychosocial Rehabilitation Journal, 13,* 20-31.

Rog, D. J., Hambrick, R. S., Jr., Holupka, C. S., McCombs, K. L., Gilbert, A. M., & Brito, M. C. (1994). *The homeless families program: Interim benchmarks* (Interim evaluation report to Robert Wood Johnson Foundation). Washington, DC: Vanderbilt Institute for Public Policy Studies.

Rog, D. J., Holupka, C. S., & McCombs-Thornton, K. L. (1995). Implementation of the Homeless Families Program: 1. Service models and preliminary outcomes. *American Journal of Orthopsychiatry, 65,* 502-513.

Rosenheck, R. (1995, October). *Review of research on homeless veterans and on the development of VA-community programs for homeless veterans during the past decade.* Paper presented at the American Public Health Association meeting, San Diego.

Rossi, P. H. (1994). Troubling families: Family homelessness in America. *American Behavioral Scientist, 37,* 342-395.

Schutt, R. K., & Goldfinger, S. M. (1996). Housing preferences and perceptions among homeless mentally ill persons. *Psychiatric Services, 47,* 381-386.

Shern, D. L., Felton, C. J., Hough, R. L., Lehman, A. F., Goldfinger, S., Valencia, E., Dennis, D., Straw, R., & Wood, P. A. (1997). Housing outcomes for homeless adults with mental illness: Results from the second-round McKinney program. *Psychiatric Services, 48,* 239-241.

Shern, D. L., Lovell, A. M., Tsemberis, S., Anthony, W., LaComb, C. A., Richmond, L., Winarski, J., & Cohen, M. (1994). The New York City Street Outreach Project. In *Making a difference: Interim status report of the McKinney Research Demonstration Program for Mentally Ill Adults* (pp. 62-78; DHHS Publication No. [SMA] 94-3014 SAMHSA). Washington, DC: U.S. Department of Health and Human Services, Substance Abuse and Mental Health Services Administration, Center for Mental Health Services.

Shinn, M. (1992). Homelessness: What is a psychologist to do? *American Journal of Community Psychology, 20,* 1-24.

Shinn, M., & Weitzman, B. C. (1996). Homeless families are different. In J. Baumohl (Ed.), *Homelessness in America* (pp. 109-122). Phoenix, AZ: Oryx.

Shinn, M., Weitzman, B. C., Stojanovic, D., Knickman, J. R., Jimenez, L., Duchon, L., James, S., & Krantz, D. H. (in press). Predictors of homelessness from shelter request to housing stability among families in New York City. *American Journal of Public Health.*

Smith, E. M., North, C. S., & Fox, L. W. (1995). Eighteen-month follow-up data on a treatment program for homeless substance abusing mothers. *Journal of Addictive Diseases, 14,* 57-72.

Sosin, M., Piliavin, I., & Westerfelt, H. (1990). Toward a longitudinal analysis of homelessness. *Journal of Social Issues, 46*(4), 157-174.

Srebnik, D., Livingston, J., Gordon, L., & King, D. (1995). Housing choice and community success for individuals with serious and persistent mental illness. *Community Mental Health Journal, 31,* 139-152.

Stahler, G. J., Shipley, T. F., Bartelt, D., DuCette, J. P., & Shandler, I. W. (1995). Evaluating alternative treatments for homeless substance-abusing men: Outcomes and predictors of success. *Journal of Addictive Diseases, 14,* 151-167.

Stojanovic, D., Weitzman, B. C., Shinn, M., Labay, L., & Williams, N. P. (1997). *Tracing the path out of homelessness: The housing patterns of families after exiting shelter.* Manuscript submitted for publication.

Struening, E. L. (1987). *A study of residents of the New York City shelter system* (Report supported by contracts #85206/86206 with the New York City DMHMRAS). New York: New York State Psychiatric Institute.

Susser, E., Struening, E. L., & Conover, S. (1988). *Psychiatric problems of homeless men in NYC shelters.* New York: New York State Psychiatric Institute, Epidemiology of Mental Disorders Research Department, CSS Evaluation Program.

Susser, E., Valencia, E., Conover, S., Felix, A., Tsai, W.-Y., & Wyatt, R. J. (1997). Preventing recurrent homelessness among mentally ill men: A "critical time" intervention after discharge from a shelter. *American Journal of Public Health, 87,* 256-262.

Tanzman, B. (1993). An overview of surveys on mental health consumers' preferences for housing and support services. *Hospital and Community Psychiatry, 44,* 450-455.

Tessler, R. C., & Dennis, D. L. (1989). *A synthesis of NIMH-funded research concerning persons who are homeless and mentally ill.* Rockville, MD: National Institute of Mental Health.

Tsemberis, S. J. (1995, October). *Housing homeless people with psychiatric disabilities directly from the streets.* Paper presented at the American Public Health Association meeting, San Diego.

Tsemberis, S. J. (1997). *Pathways to Housing: An innovative model of supported housing for the homeless mentally ill in New York City.* Manuscript submitted for publication.

Tsemberis, S. J., Cohen, N. L., & Jones, R. M. (1993). Conducting emergency psychiatric evaluations on the street. In S. E. Katz, D. Nardacci, & A. Sabatini (Eds.), *Intensive treatment of the homeless mentally ill.* Washington, DC: American Psychiatric Association.

Weitzman, B. C., & Berry, C. (1994) *Formerly homeless families and the transition to permanent housing: High-risk families and the role of intensive case management services* (Final report to the Edna McConnell Clark Foundation). New York: Wagner Graduate School, Health Research Program.

4

Violence Among Urban
African American Adolescents
The Protective Effects of Parental Support

MARC A. ZIMMERMAN
KENNETH J. STEINMAN
KAREN J. ROWE

> Saturday, my big brother got killed. He was going to pick up somebody
> because it was his birthday. He was found in an alley near a police station
> . . . then a few minutes later the police found him and got in touch with our
> mother . . . she was crying and mad . . . I did not eat the rest of my food.
> . . . They did not tell his son yet . . . whoever killed him killed the wrong
> person. He was nice and going to get married. He is 23 years old and
> treated people nice. I loved him very much. Now I don't have a brother.
>
> *Urban fifth grader (e-mail communication)*

Τhis chapter is about assaultive youth violence. We define *assaultive youth violence* as interpersonal behavior that

AUTHORS' NOTE: This research was funded by the National Institute of Drug Abuse, Grant No. DA07484. The research reported here does not necessarily represent the views or policies of the National Institute of Drug Abuse. The authors thank Alice Hart and the Project for Urban and Regional Affairs at the University of Michigan, Flint Campus, for their assistance in collecting the data reported in this paper, and the Flint public schools and students for their cooperation and time.

is intended to coerce or to cause harm, injury, or death. Examples of such behavior are carrying a knife or gun, using a weapon to force someone to do something (e.g., hand over one's wallet), and hurting someone badly enough to need medical attention. This definition distinguishes between the more common types of aggressive behavior such as fighting, and more dangerous weapon-related violent behavior. Our definition of assaultive youth violence parallels the definition proposed by Rosenberg and Mercy (1991) but emphasizes weapon-related behaviors. They defined assaultive violence as both nonfatal and fatal interpersonal violence, where physical force by one person is used with the intent of causing harm, injury, or death to another.

A growing body of evidence suggests that weapon carrying is related to antisocial and violent behavior (Centers for Disease Control and Prevention [CDC], 1991). Researchers have reported rates of knife carrying among urban adolescents ranging from 29% in the last 3 months to 47% in their lifetime (Schubiner, Scott, & Tzelepis, 1993; Vanderschmidt, Lang, Knight-Williams, & Vanderschmidt, 1993; Webster, Gainer, & Champion, 1993). The number of students who reported carrying a firearm during the last 30 days has almost doubled from 1990 to 1995; 1 in 12 students reported carrying a gun in 1995 (CDC, 1991, 1996b). In addition, the National Institute of Justice (NIJ, 1995) reported that 22% of urban high school students owned a firearm and that 12% carried it to school. Similarly, the 1995 Youth Risk Behavior Survey, a national study of high school students, found that almost 11% of the youths carried a gun in the last 30 days (CDC, 1996b).

African American youths reported higher rates of weapon carrying than those found in national surveys (see Hammond & Yung, 1994). Schubiner et al. (1993), for example, found that 18% of inner-city, African American youths carried a gun. Researchers reported that the most common reason given for youths carrying a gun was to protect themselves (NIJ, 1995; Price, Desmond, & Smith, 1991). Webster et al. (1993), however, found that carrying a gun was more commonly associated with aggressive action. Callahan and Rivara (1992) found that one third of 11th graders in Seattle high schools who reported owning a gun admitted shooting at another person. Not surprisingly, weapon carrying among youths has been accompanied by an increase in homicide rates.

Homicide rates among adolescents, especially males, have increased during the last 30 years, and they began to climb dramatically in the last decade (Fingerhut, Kleinman, Godfrey, & Rosenberg, 1991). Since

1988, more than 80% of homicide victims 15 to 19 years old were killed with a firearm (CDC, 1996a). Nonfirearm homicides have actually decreased 29% during the same 10-year period (Fingerhut, Ingram, & Feldman, 1992). The firearm homicide rate for teenagers in the United States in 1989 was the highest in the world (Fingerhut & Kleinman, 1990). The risk of dying from a firearm injury has more than doubled for 15- to 19-year-olds from 1985 to 1994 (CDC, 1996b). The annual homicide rate for 15- to 19-year-olds increased from 6.9 to 11.1 per 100,000 during the last 10 years. Arrest rates for homicide from 1985 to 1994 have increased by 41% for youths aged 14 to 17 years (CDC, 1996b). Half of the arrests for murder in 1991 were of youths under 25 years old (C. S. Mott Foundation, 1994).

Urban African American youths had the highest rates for homicide and nonlethal assaultive violence (Hammond & Yung, 1994). African American males between the ages of 15 and 24 were homicide victims at an annual rate of 154.4 per 100,000 versus 17.5 per 100,000 for their White male counterparts (National Center for Education Statistics [NCES], 1996). Homicide was the leading cause of death among African American youths aged 15 to 24 (CDC, 1996a). Most homicides among African American males involved firearms (CDC, 1990). Ninety percent of African American homicide victims were murdered by other African Americans (Federal Bureau of Investigation, 1989). Several theories begin to explain the high incidence of weapon carrying and violence.

Theories of Violent Behavior

Social learning and social cognitive theories of violent behavior provide an explanatory framework that involves person-environment interactions. Social learning theory posits that youths learn to be aggressive from modeling behavior (observational learning), direct experience from achieving desirable outcomes through aggressive behavior, or self-regulation (e.g., they rationalize means as justification for desired ends). Social-cognitive theory includes many explanations of violent behavior. One social-cognitive explanation is *script theory:* Aggressive behavior is considered to be a product of learned cognitive schemata or scripts, which are activated from memory when one is faced with environmental cues similar to those present when the script was learned (Huesmann, 1988). Dodge (1993) suggested that dysfunctional information processing by children may result in aggressive behavior. Youths may have difficulty with any one of five steps involved with processing information: (a) encoding, (b) mental representation, (c) response access, (d) response evaluation, and (e) enactment. During the mental representation phase of information processing, for example, an aggressive youth may have difficulty considering others' perspectives. Youths may develop aggressive scripts and processing capabilities from observations of friends, family members, and nonfamily adults.

Pepler and Slaby (1994) presented several other theoretical explanations of violent behavior as diverse as individual biological explanations and contextual factors. Original theories of violent behavior focused on biological theories, which suggest that aggression is a basic human instinct that can be expressed with no antecedent learning. Another individual-level theory suggested that frustration leads to aggressive behavior. Pepler and Slaby (1994) pointed out, however, that these theories have limited empirical support.

Contextual factors provide explanations at the opposite end of the continuum. Several researchers have suggested that poverty, urban residence, and living in physically run-down neighborhoods account for adolescent violence (Greenberg & Schneider, 1994; Guerra, Huesmann, Tolan, & Van Acker, 1995; McLloyd, 1990; Wilson, 1987). Urban areas in the United States have violent crime rates 3 to 30 times the national average (Guerra et al., 1995). Insofar as these conditions disproportionately affect African Americans, they are often presented as an explanation for why African American youths are more violent than White youths.

Another contextual perspective suggests that cultural norms and values provide the conditions for sanctioning violent behavior. The cultural perspective includes the notion that, in general, U.S. society is desensitized to violence because violent behavior is ubiquitous. Huston et al. (1992) reported that, by the time children leave adolescence, they will have witnessed more than 200,000 violent acts in the media. More than 3.3 million youths witnessed or experienced violence in the home (C. S. Mott Foundation, 1994). One in six youths aged 10 to 17 years has seen or knows someone who has been injured by a firearm. Another viewpoint is that a subculture of violence, particularly in low-income settings, teaches youths that violence is an appropriate and acceptable means for solving problems (Berkowitz, 1995; Wolfgang, 1981). This subculture may be more closely associated with drug dealing and use, gang membership, and the easy availability of guns, than with ethnicity. Although theories provide explanations of violent behavior, researchers also have identified several risk factors that predict violent behavior.

Risk Factors for
Violent Behavior

Several researchers have found that early aggressive behavior is a risk factor for predicting later violent behaviors (see Guerra et al., 1995). Similarly, researchers have pointed out that antisocial behavior in childhood was a strong predictor of adolescent violence (Capaldi & Patterson, 1993; Loeber et al., 1993). Individual factors that may lead to antisocial and aggressive behaviors include temperament and limited cognitive, social, and negotiation skills (Pepler & Slaby, 1994).

Peer influences on antisocial behavior, including aggressive behavior, have been well documented (Cairns & Cairns, 1991; Hill, Soriano, Chen, & LaFromboise, 1994). Cairns and Cairns (1991) suggested that aggressive children are frequently rejected by their socially competent peers and that, as a result, they establish relationships in marginalized cliques of individuals who resemble themselves in terms of their rejected status and antisocial behavior. Youths who belong to such groups may reinforce each other's aggressive behavior and limit their exposure to prosocial methods of problem solving (Parker & Asher, 1987). Their low social status may also encourage their peers, teachers, and other significant figures to expect them to be violent. Among adolescents, violent behavior may be influenced by peers through increased access to weapons and by the availability of willing comrades to participate in group fights and carry weapons.

Few researchers have studied the influence of nonfamilial adults on youths' aggressive behavior. Nonfamilial adults who appear in youths' lives may be significant figures and serve as role models. Although most research on role models and mentoring has focused on positive influences (Hamilton & Darling, 1996; Rhodes, Contreras, & Mangelsdorf, 1994; Rhodes & Davis, 1996; Rhodes, Ebert, & Fischer, 1992), adults outside the home may also present youths with role models for aggressive and violent behavior. These role models may provide examples for developing aggressive scripts. Although patterns of aggressive behavior emerge during childhood, it is useful to consider how the social influences of friends, family, and adults can maintain such behavioral patterns during adolescence (Eron & Huesmann, 1990).

Adolescent Resiliency and Violence

Most research on adolescent violence and other problem behaviors has emphasized identification of risk factors associated with their effects on violent behavior. Yet, several longitudinal studies have indicated that most individuals who are aggressive as youths will not become adult violent offenders (Huesmann, Eron, Lefkowitz, & Walder, 1984; Wolfgang, Figlio, & Selin, 1972). In addition, most violent offenses are perpetrated by a small number of people (Kolvin, Miller, Fleeting, & Kolvin, 1988; Weiner, 1989; Wolfgang et al., 1972). Others have also pointed out that more than half of the children possessing a risk factor do not exhibit the negative outcome predicted by risk models (Garmezy, 1991; Rutter, 1987). *Resiliency theory* provides a useful framework for understanding the youths who do not fit the risk models. It provides an alternative approach that helps us understand why some youths avoid the negative consequences of the risks they face.

Resiliency refers to those factors and processes that interrupt the trajectory from risk to problem behaviors or psychopathology (Garmezy, 1991; Masten, 1994; Rutter, 1987; Werner, 1993). Garmezy and Masten (1991) defined *resilience* as "a process of, or capacity for, or the outcome of, successful adaptation despite challenging and threatening circumstances" (p. 459). Werner (1993) used the concept of *resiliency* to refer to those children who successfully coped with biological and social risk factors. Researchers have described several mechanisms by which environmental and individual factors helped reduce or offset the adverse effects of risk factors (Zimmerman & Arunkumar, 1994). Garmezy, Masten, and Tellegen (1984) have proposed three models that describe resiliency: (a) the compensatory model, (b) the challenge model, and (c) the protective factor model.

Models of Resiliency

Compensatory Model

Compensatory factors are variables that neutralize exposure to risk or that operate in a counteractive fashion against the potential negative consequences introduced by a risk (Garmezy et al., 1984; Masten et al., 1988). Compensatory factors have a direct and independent effect on outcomes. Both the risk and the compensatory factors contribute additively to the prediction of the outcome (Masten et al., 1988). The compensatory model examines how different variables may directly reduce negative outcomes associated with risk factors. Analysis of this model would examine the direct main effects of the compensatory and risk factors in a linear regression analysis. An example of compensation may be seen in aggressive children (risk factor) whose parents help them modify their aggressive behavior (compensatory factor) so that they do not become violent adolescents (outcome). These children may receive vital help to channel their aggressive tendencies into less aggressive or possibly productive behavior.

Challenge Model

In the challenge model of resiliency, stressors (risk factors) are treated as potential enhancers of successful adaptation, provided they are not excessive. In this model, too little stress is not challenging enough, and very high levels render the individual helpless. Moderate levels of stress, however, provide the individual with challenges that, when overcome, strengthen competence over time. The individual develops effective patterns of adaptation and is better prepared to handle future challenges as each ensuing challenge is successfully met. Rutter (1987) has called this process *steeling* or *inoculation.* In contrast, if effective patterns are not developed, an individual may become increasingly more vulnerable to risk. The Yerkes-Dodson law of arousal and performance is an analogous model. The challenge model could be represented analytically by introducing quadratic trends in a regression equation (testing for a curvilinear relationship), but longitudinal data are necessary. Panel analysis or structural equation models may also be used to explore inoculation effects. An example of steeling is that of a youth who, having successfully avoided a fistfight with a peer with his social status intact, is now better prepared to avoid subsequent pressure to join a gang.

Protective Factor Model

The protective factor model has received the most attention in the research literature. *Protective factors,* unlike compensatory factors, modify the effects of risks in an interactive fashion (Rutter, 1985). A protective factor may also have direct effects on outcomes (compensatory effect), but the effect is heightened in the presence of the risk. These effects may vary in degree, depending on the mechanism by which the protective factor functions. Brook, Brook, Gordon, and Whiteman (1990) proposed that effects may be associated with a risk-protective mechanism or a protective-protective mechanism. A *risk-protective variable* functions to lessen the negative effect of a risk factor, whereas a *protective-protective variable* enhances the positive effects of factors found to decrease negative outcomes. This model is evaluated by examining the interaction effects of the risk and protective factors (or one protective factor with another). An example of a risk-protective factor is the effect parental support may have on risks associated with assaultive violence. Youths with high levels of parental support would be less susceptible to the influence of violent friends than youths with low levels of support, because parents help protect youths from friends' negative effects.

Our approach for examining the protective effects of parental support was based on social learning and cognitive theories. We used a social learning perspective to examine the risk of violent friends and adults on assaultive youth violence. Violent friends and adults provide role models (social learning) for violent behavior. We also examined the risk associated with less serious aggressive behavior—fighting—by using a social cognitive perspective because fighting was considered to help youths learn more aggressive (violent) scripts as new social contexts present themselves. A risk-protective effect was supported if evidence of a statistical interaction was found between parental support and the risk factor in predicting violent behavior. We studied these two theories in a cross-sectional sample of urban high school students.

Methods

Sample

The sample came from Year 1 of a 4-year longitudinal study of 850 ninth-grade adolescents. They were selected from the four public high schools in the second largest school district in Michigan. The students selected were enrolled in the school system at the start of fall 1994 and had grade point averages of 3.0 and below on a 4-point scale. This grade cutoff was used because one goal of the larger project was to study youths at risk for leaving school before graduation. Students who were diagnosed as having either emotional impairment or developmental disability were not recruited for the study. The sample included 679 African American youths (80%), 145 White youths (17%), and 26 mixed African American and White youths (3%) and was equally divided by sex. Only the African American youths were included in this study. The sample included 333 males (49%) and 346 females (51%). Their mean age was 16.6 years ($SD = .66$), and the average eighth-grade GPA was 2.02 ($SD = .70$). Data missing because of incomplete responses reduced the total number of youths in any one analysis.

Procedure

Face-to-face interviews were conducted by trained African American and White male and female interviewers. Interviewers and students were not matched for ethnicity. Students were called from their regular classrooms and taken to selected areas within the school to be interviewed. Each interview lasted 50 to 60 minutes. Youths who could not be found in school were interviewed in a community setting (e.g., home, community organization).

Measures

Table 4.1 reports the means, standard deviations, degree of skewness, and Cronbach's alphas for all study variables (described below).

Table 4.1
Descriptive Statistics for All Study Variables
for the Total Sample

Variable	Number of Items	N	Mean	SD	Skew	Range	Cronbach's Alpha
Number of assaultive violent acts	4	647	.80	2.61	1.84	1-6	.72
Number of fights	3	645	1.65	.89	1.59	1-5	.72
Number of violent friends	3	638	2.14	.95	.97	1-5	.73
Number of violent adults	4	642	1.81	.85	1.21	1-5	.82
Mother's support	5	637	4.01	.96	-1.21	1-5	.88
Father's support*	5	578	3.10	1.36	-.21	1-5	.94

NOTE: *Includes those youths who had living fathers whom they knew.

Violent Behavior. Violent behavior was measured with four items using a 5-point frequency scale (1 = *never;* 5 = *4 or more times*). The four items included the frequency during the last year of carrying a gun, carrying a knife or razor, using a weapon coercively, and hurting someone badly enough to need medical attention. The four items were summed into a single scale that could range from 4 to 20. The scores for this 4-item scale were collapsed into six categories because the original scale was skewed (skewness = 2.5; kurtosis = 6.98). The six new categories were 0, 1-2, 3-4, 5-6, 7-8 and 9 or more times. This six-category variable was used as the dependent variable in all the regression analyses described below.

Fighting Behavior. Fighting behavior was measured with three items using the same frequency scale as violent behavior. Scores could range from 1 to 5 (mean of the three items). The three items included the number of times in the last year youths got into group fights, fights in school, and fights outside school.

Friends' Violent Behavior. Friends' violent behavior was measured with three items indicating how many friends respondents knew who (a) got into fights, (b) carried a knife or razor, and (c) carried a gun. The items used a 5-point scale (1 = *none;* 5 = *all*). The variable was the mean of the 3-item index.

Adult Violent Behavior. Youths reported the number of adults they knew (not including their parents or adults with whom they lived) who carried a gun, carried a knife or razor, threatened to hurt people, or got into fights with others. The same 5-point scale as for friends' violent behavior was used. The mean of the 4-item measure was used.

Parental Support. Parental support was measured with a shortened version of the Parental Support Scale developed by Procidano and Heller (1983). The items asked youths about emotional, moral, and problem-solving support. Father's and mother's levels of support were measured separately, using the same 5-point, 5-item scale (1 = *not true,* 5 = *very true*); 101 youths (13%) were missing father's support data. If youths did not know their fathers and did not have another father figure in their lives, they were not asked the father's support questions. The mean for each variable was used.

Other Variables. In addition to demographic characteristics, youths reported the occupations of both parents. Occupations were allotted a prestige score assigned to 20 major occupational classifications (Nakao & Treas, 1990a, 1990b). The average prestige score for each occupational group was used. The highest occupational group received a score of 64.38 (professional), and the lowest group received a score of 27.84 (private household work). If scores were provided for both parents, the highest prestige score was used for analysis. Parents of youths in this sample were mostly blue-collar workers from the local factories. The mean prestige score was 39.78 (*SD* = 10.44; skewness = 1.41).

Data Analytic Strategy

First, we conducted a factor analysis that included all the students' fighting and violent behavior items. We did this to test empirically our hypothesis that fighting and assaultive violent behavior are distinct measures. Second, we examined descriptive statistics and gender differences for fighting and violent behavior, as well as the association of socioeconomic status (SES) with violent behavior. Third, we tested the risk-protective mechanism of friends' and parental influences by using hierarchical multiple regression to predict assaultive youth violence. Each equation included, in order, a risk factor, parental support, and the interaction term for both of these variables. Sample size for each analysis changed slightly because of missing data, but no analysis had more than 10% of the sample missing.

Results

Descriptive Analysis
of Violent Behaviors

A principal components analysis of the seven items measuring self-reported frequency of fighting and violent assaultive behavior was conducted. This was done to validate a distinction between fighting and more violent behavior. A particular number of factors was not specified in advance. Results indicated two separate factors that explained 60% of the variance. The loadings for each item after a Varimax rotation provided simple structure. All items loaded .50 or greater on their respective factor and .28 or lower on the other factors. Our measures of fighting and violent behavior described above coincided with the factor results. The two measures correlated .57.

We recoded the fighting and violent behavior into three categories (none, 1 or 2, and 3 or more events) and crossed the two variables to examine further the relationship and distinction between them. We found further evidence that whereas fighting is associated with a greater likelihood of violent behavior, a sizable proportion of youths who fight do not engage in violent behavior. Table 4.2 reports the cell-by-cell frequencies for the three-category recoded variables, $\chi^2(4) = 155.30$, $p < .01$. We found that 232 youths (36%) did not engage in any fighting or violent behavior but that 255 youths (40%) reported at least one violent behavior in the last year. Almost 400 youths ($n = 390$; 60%) did not engage in any violent behavior, but 158 (41%) of these youths did participate in at least one fight. Conversely, almost 300 youths ($n = 286$; 44%) did not get into any fights, but 54 of these youths (19%) reported at least one violent behavior. Among youths who reported fighting ($n =$

Table 4.2
Number of Fights Crossed With Number
of Assaultive Violent Acts

Number of assaultive violent acts	Number of fights			Total
	0	1-2	3+	
0	232	107	51	390
1-2	41	38	48	127
3+	13	32	83	128
Total	286	177	182	645

359), 56% ($n = 201$) also reported at least one violent behavior. Eighty-three (13%) youths reported getting into three or more fights and engaging in three or more violent behaviors. Almost one third of the youths ($n = 201$; 31%) got into fights and engaged in violent behavior at least once in the last year. Thirty-two youths (8%) reported carrying a gun in the last year. A similar pattern of relationships was found for males and females separately. The remaining analyses used the six-category violent behavior measure and the mean of the three-item fighting behavior measure.

Analysis of Gender Differences and SES

Males ($\overline{X} = 1.78$; $SD = .97$) were more likely than females ($\overline{X} = 1.53$; $SD = .80$) to report fighting behavior, $t(604.8) = 3.54, p < .01$. Males ($\overline{X} = 1.46$; $SD = 1.40$) were also more likely than females ($\overline{X} = .03$; $SD = 1.20$) to report violent behavior $t(615.6) = 4.19, p < .01$. Parents' occupational status was not correlated with fighting behavior ($r = -.04$) or violent behavior ($r = -.03$). Table 4.3 includes zero-order correlations for all other study variables for males (above the diagonal) and females (below the diagonal). The highest correlations for both males and females were among friends' and adults' violent behavior. The correlations among the parental support variables and the other study variables

Table 4.3
Zero-Order Correlation Matrix of
All Study Variables by Gender
(Males Are Above and Females Are Below the Diagonal)

	1	*2*	*3*	*4*	*5*	*6*
1. Assaultive violence	—	.65	−.20	−.21	.62	.53
2. Fighting	.48	—	−.20	−.11	.51	.48
3. Father's support	−.14	−.08	—	.31	−.19	−.17
4. Mother's support	−.28	−.14	.24	—	−.24	−.28
5. Number of violent friends	.54	.44	−.09	−.14	—	.54
6. Number of violent adults	.54	.47	−.04	−.25	.54	—

NOTE: All correlations .14 and above are significant at the .05 level.

were in the negative direction (most, but not all, were significant at the .05 or .01 level).

Prediction of Violent Behavior

We used hierarchical multiple regression to determine whether mother's or father's support compensated for (main effect) or protected against (interaction effect) three risk factors: (a) friends' violent behavior, (b) adults' violent behavior, and (c) fighting behavior. We conducted separate analyses for males and females because they differed on reported levels of violent behavior. We did three sets of analyses that paired the risk factor with mother's support and father's support separately. The equations that included father's support did not include the 58 youths with missing data on this variable. When the father's support scores for these youths were recoded (from missing) to the lowest father's support scores in the sample, the bivariate correlations with other variables were nearly identical to those computed without these 58 youths. In each equation, the risk factor was entered first, the protective factor was entered second (testing the compensatory model), and the interaction of the risk and protective factor (multiplicative term) was entered last (testing the protective factor model). As suggested by Aiken and West (1991), all variables were centered (each individual score was sub-

Table 4.4
Final β, Adjusted R^2, and Change in R^2
for Compensating and Protective Effects

Variable	Final β	Adjusted R^2	Change in R^2
Males			
Violent friends	.61	.39	.39**
Mother's support	−.00	.39	.00
Interaction	−.12	.41	.02**
Females			
Violent friends	.48	.30	.30**
Mother's support	−.14	.33	.03**
Interaction	−.10	.34	.01**
Males			
Violent friends	.61	.38	.38**
Father's support	−.01	.39	.01
Interaction	.00	.39	.00
Females			
Violent friends	.50	.29	.29**
Father's support	−.01	.30	.01*
Interaction	−.01	.30	.00
Males			
Violent adults	.57	.30	.30**
Mother's support	−.01	.30	.01
Interaction	−.00	.30	.00
Females			
Violent adults	.40	.28	.28**
Mother's support	−.01	.29	.02**
Interaction	−.17	.35	.05**
Males			
Violent adults	.54	.28	.28**
Father's support	−.13	.29	.01*
Interaction	.01	.29	.01
Females			
Violent adults	.42	.28	.28**
Father's support	−.12	.29	.02**
Interaction	−.19	.34	.05**
Males			
Fighting	.60	.37	.37**
Mother's support	−.17	.39	.02**
Interaction	−.00	.39	.00

Table 4.4
Continued

Variable	Final β	Adjusted R^2	Change in R^2
Females			
Fighting	.42	.23	.23**
Mother's support	−.17	.27	.04**
Interaction	−.12	.29	.02**
Males			
Fighting	.65	.42	.42**
Father's support	−.01	.42	.00
Interaction	−.00	.42	.00
Females			
Fighting	.43	.23	.23**
Father's support	−.13	.24	.01*
Interaction	−.17	.27	.03**

$*p < .05$; $**p < .01$.

tracted from the group mean) before they were entered in the regression equation to reduce multicollinearity.

The final equation betas, adjusted R^2, and change in R^2 are reported in Table 4.4. The variance explained by the equations ranged from 27% (females fighting and father's support) to 42% (males fighting and father's support). Mother's support was a protective factor for the influence of violent friends for both males and females. Father's support helped compensate for the effects of violent friends for females but had no effect for males. Although R^2 change was the same for both groups, it only reached statistical significance for females, probably because of greater error variance for males. Mother's support helped protect females from the effects of violent adults but had no effect for males. Father's support was found to be a compensating factor for the effects of violent adults for males and a protective factor for females. A similar pattern was found for risk-protective effects of fighting and mother's support. Results showed protective effects of father's support for fighting among females but no father's support effects for males.

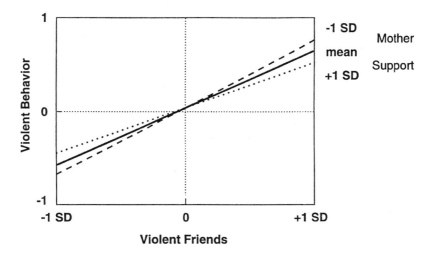

Figure 4.1. Interaction Effect of Mother's Support and Violent Friends for Predicting Violent Behavior Among Males

Decomposition of Interaction Effects

We examined the interaction terms by following the procedure described by Aiken and West (1991). We computed separate equations to examine the association between the risk factor and violent behavior at the mean, and one standard deviation above and below the mean, for mother's or father's support. The lines in Figures 4.1 and 4.2 represent the linear relationship between the risk factor and violent behavior at these three values of mother's or father's support. Figure 4.1 represents the interaction effect for mother's support and violent friends among males. Figure 4.2 represents the interaction effect for father's support and fighting among females. The x-axis represents the value of the standardized risk factor; the y-axis displays the standardized value of the dependent variable (violent behavior). Only two interaction effects are illustrated, but all the interaction effects indicated the same pattern of results. The slopes for each line in all the interaction analyses were greater than zero. In addition, within each analysis, the slopes differed from each other. In other words, the slope of the lines graphed for a specific protective factor was different at each value of the protective factor.

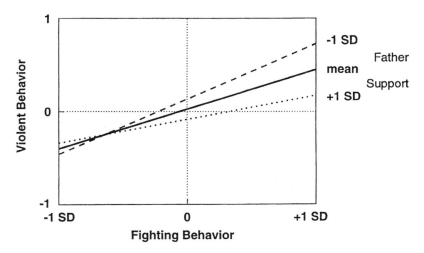

Figure 4.2. Interaction Effect of Father's Support and Number of Fights for Predicting Violent Behavior Among Females

The steepest lines represent the relationship between the risk factor (violent friends or fighting) and violent behavior when mother's or father's support was one standard deviation below the mean. The middle regression line shows the relationship between the risk and outcome for youths who reported average support from their mothers or fathers. The flattest line in each figure represents those youths whose parental support was one standard deviation above the mean. This decomposition of interaction effects suggests that parental support has a moderating influence on the relationship between risks and outcomes. Figure 4.1, for example, indicates that mother's support helps reduce the effects of violent friends for predicting violent behavior among males. Males with a relatively high number of violent friends were at greatest risk for violent behavior, but this risk diminished if they reported relatively high levels of mother's support. Similarly, Figure 4.2 suggests that females who engaged in relatively more fights than their counterparts were at greatest risk for violent behavior, but father's support helped reduce that risk. In each case where we found interaction effects, youths who had relatively low levels of the risk factor engaged in similarly low levels of violent behavior regardless of the amount of support they received from parents. As the risk factor increased, however, parental support helped reduce the effects of the risk on assaultive violent behavior.

Discussion

We found that fighting and violent behavior were distinct. Fighting is a relatively common behavior among adolescents and may not lead to more violent behavior. Our results supported this and further suggested that assaultive youth violence is a uniquely aggressive act. A relatively small number of youths engaged in high levels of both fighting and violent behavior, but over half of the youths who fought also engaged in at least one assaultive violent behavior. Fighting appeared to be a precursor to more violent behavior, but a significant portion of youths who fought did not report violent behavior. Second, we found that males were more likely to be aggressive and violent than females. This was expected because of the disproportionate victimization of African American males (NCES, 1996).

We did not find an association between SES and fighting or violent behavior. Others, however, have found low SES to be a risk factor for violent behavior (Greenberg & Schneider, 1994; Guerra et al., 1995; McLloyd, 1990; Wilson, 1987). Several possibilities may explain this discrepancy. It is possible, for example, that our SES measure was problematic. It may not be adequate to detect vital differences among youths, or youths may not have reported their parents' occupations accurately. In addition, occupational status may not be the best measure of SES for this sample. Most youths' parents worked in the local factories, which may have inflated occupational prestige scores even though the neighborhood context might have indicated lower SES conditions. A more precise test of the poverty context theory would be to use neighborhood indicators from census information. Also, it is possible that SES was relatively constant in the sample and we had limited variance to explain. This seems unlikely, however, because the variable was only slightly skewed and the standard deviation suggested ample variation.

Perhaps the most significant findings in this study were those supporting resiliency theory. Results indicating interaction effects for parental support provided evidence for a risk-protective resiliency model

(Garmezy et al., 1984; Zimmerman & Arunkumar, 1994). Mother's support moderated the influence (interaction effect) of violent friends, violent adults, and fighting for predicting violent behavior among females. Mother's support also moderated the effects of violent friends on violent behavior among males. Father's support, however, was only protective for females for the risk factors of violent adults and fighting. Results indicated that mothers may be particularly protective, for example, for youths who report many violent friends but have less effect among youths with few violent friends. These findings suggest that parents may not be able to prevent their children from having violent friends or from knowing violent adults, but they can help protect against friends' and adults' effects on their children's violent behavior. Similarly, although parental support may not prevent youths from getting into fights, it seemed to help reduce the likelihood that these youths would become more violent.

The disparate findings for males and females seemed to be counterintuitive. We expected father's support to have greater effects on males and mother's support to have greater effects on females. Yet, we found support from either parent to be most predictive of resiliency for females' violent behavior as compared with males' (11 significant effects for females vs. 3 for males). One explanation for this contrasting finding may be that parental support may have a greater influence on female versus male adolescents regardless of the outcome. Windle (1992) found, for example, that females were more adversely affected by low parental support than boys for predicting problem behaviors. Block (1983) also suggested that females may be socialized toward interpersonal domains, whereas boys are socialized toward independence. This different socialization pattern may be especially relevant because the period of middle adolescence is one of sex role and self-identity formation. Conversely, Zimmerman, Salem, and Maton (1995) found that African American male adolescents who reported emotional support from their fathers had higher self-esteem and less depression than youths who did not receive emotional support. These findings suggest that future research may benefit from a more detailed look at the gender differences found for effects of parental support.

Results also supported a compensatory resiliency model for some risks. We found that father's support had a main effect on violent behavior for females when we examined violent friends as the risk factor. Father's support had a similar effect for the risk factor of violent adults among males. Similarly, mother's support compensated for fighting behavior risks among males. Thus, parental support seemed to operate in a counteractive fashion to reduce some risks associated with violent behavior. Yet, father's support had no effects for males when violent friends or fighting were analyzed, and it had fewer effects overall as compared with mother's support. It is possible that support from fathers may not be as vital a resource as support from mothers for adolescent violence. Some researchers have found that fathers and mothers play different roles in the family and vary in the way they influence their adolescent children (Lamb, 1986; Youniss & Smollar, 1985). Youniss and Smollar (1985) found that adolescents rely on their fathers for approval and advice about concerns for the future and for problems in which the father may have specialized experience. In that study, adolescents indicated that their fathers adopted a more indirect, authoritative role, without keeping up with their children's activities, whereas mothers were more active with day-to-day monitoring and support. The measure of support we used may have emphasized emotional support and an intimate relationship. Thus, our support measure may have been more consistent with the roles that youths expected from their mothers than their fathers. This may also help explain why we found that females benefited the most from parental support.

The percentage of variance explained by either main (compensatory) or interaction (protective) effects in some analyses was small. This finding raises some questions as to the value of minimal effects. Abelson (1985), however, pointed out that the percentage of variance accounted for may be a misleading index of influence because it does not consider the notion that cumulative influence may produce meaningful outcomes. He also suggested that an effect, however small, may be theoretically relevant. Our results may be meaningful because of both aspects. First, this study adds to the cumulative evidence that parental support is vital for healthy adolescent development (Dubow & Luster, 1990; Emery & Forehand, 1994; Grossman et al., 1992; Maccoby & Martin, 1983; Werner & Smith, 1992). Second, parental support is relevant for resiliency theory because parents play a central role in youths' lives. Adolescents generally spend more time with their parents than with any other adults during the day (Csikszentmihalyi & Larson, 1984), and parents are generally the most significant adults in the lives of adolescents (Galbo, 1986).

Another issue is that our results may have capitalized on chance. We computed three statistics in 12 equations. Thus, two significant results might be a chance finding using a 95% confidence interval ($p < .05$).

However, 23 of the 36 tests we conducted reached statistical significance at the .01 level. Consequently, it is unlikely that the findings can be explained by chance alone. In fact, it is noteworthy that many results were replicated across different risk and protective factor pairings. This further supports the notion that cumulative effects may be present. It is also notable that our results may not generalize to White or other non-White adolescents.

The fact that our measure of violent behavior was based on self-report data in a face-to-face interview may reduce confidence in our results. One possible implication is that our rates of violent behavior are underestimated, and this would reduce the variance in our dependent variable. Thus, it would be more difficult to reach statistical significance. Consequently, one could argue that our analyses may have actually underestimated the effects of parents. Greater variance in the dependent variable might also increase the amount of variance explained by the protective factors. Our data collection procedure may also explain why our rates of gun carrying were somewhat lower than national averages, but in addition, our sample was younger than national studies and included only one age-group. It would be useful to examine the validity of self-reported violent behavior by comparing results from different data collection procedures.

Conclusion

Assaultive youth violence is a growing public health concern. Most research on youth violence has focused on cataloging risk factors and documenting their adverse effects on adolescents' behavior. In this study, we consistently found that mother's support, and to some extent father's support, helped mitigate negative effects of fighting and of modeled behavior from friends and adults. Results suggest that efforts to prevent violence may benefit from enhancing parent-child relationships and from nurturing the positive influences in youths' lives. This study provides an alternative approach for understanding assaultive youth violence in particular, and other problem behaviors more generally. Resiliency theory presents a useful framework for understanding why some youths avoid negative consequences of the risks they face.

Resiliency theory directs the study of youth violence toward a strengths model, rather than a deficit and problem-oriented approach.

References

Abelson, R. (1985). A variance paradox: When a little is a lot. *Psychological Bulletin, 97,* 129-133.

Aiken, L. S., & West, S. G. (1991). *Multiple regression: Testing and interpreting interactions.* Newbury Park, CA: Sage.

Berkowitz, L. (1995). Guns and youth. In L. D. Eron, J. H. Gentry, & P. Schlegel (Eds.), *Reason to hope: A psychosocial perspective on violence and youth* (pp. 251-279). Washington, DC: American Psychological Association.

Block, J. H. (1983). Differential premises arising from differential socialization of the sexes: Some conjectures. *Child Development, 54,* 1335-1354.

Brook, J. S., Brook, D. W., Gordon, A. S., & Whiteman, M. (1990). The psychosocial etiology of adolescent drug use: A family interactional approach. *Genetic, Social, and General Psychology Monographs, 116,* 111-267.

Cairns, R. B., & Cairns, B. D. (1991). The sociogenesis of aggressive and antisocial behaviors. In J. McCord (Ed.), *Facts, frameworks, and forecasts.* New Brunswick, NJ: Transaction Publishing.

Callahan, C. M., & Rivara, F. P. (1992). Urban high school youth and handguns: A school-based survey. *Journal of the American Medical Association, 267,* 3038-3042.

Capaldi, D. M., & Patterson, G. R. (1993). *The violent adolescent male: Specialist or generalist?* Paper presented at the biennial meeting of the Society for Research in Child Development, New Orleans, LA.

Centers for Disease Control and Prevention (CDC). (1990). Homicide among young black males—United States, 1978-1987. *Morbidity and Mortality Weekly Report, 39,* 869-873.

Centers for Disease Control and Prevention (CDC). (1991). Weapon-carrying among high school students—U.S. 1990. *Morbidity and Mortality Weekly Report, 40,* 681-684.

Centers for Disease Control and Prevention, National Center for Injury Prevention and Control (CDC). (1996a). *National summary of injury mortality data, 1987-1994.* Atlanta, GA: Author.

Centers for Disease Control and Prevention (CDC). (1996b). Youth risk behavioral surveillance—United States, 1995. *Morbidity and Mortality Weekly Report, 45,* 1-84.

Csikszentmihalyi, M., & Larson, R. (1984). *Being adolescent.* New York: Basic Books.

Dodge, K. A. (1993). Social-cognitive mechanisms in the development of conduct disorder and depression. *Annual Review of Psychology, 44,* 559-584.

Dubow, D. L., & Luster, T. (1990). Adjustment of children born to teenage mothers: The contribution of risk and protective factors. *Journal of Marriage and the Family, 52,* 393-404.

Emery, R. E., & Forehand, R. (1994). Parental divorce and children's well-being: A focus on resilience. In R. J. Haggerty, L. R. Sherrod, N. Garmezy, & M. Rutter (Eds.), *Stress, risk, and resilience in children and adolescents* (pp. 64-99). Cambridge, UK: Cambridge University Press.

Eron, L. D., & Huesmann, L. R. (1990). The stability of aggressive behavior—even unto the third generation. In M. Lewis & S. M. Miller (Eds.), *Handbook of developmental psychology* (pp. 147-156). New York: Plenum.

Federal Bureau of Investigation. (1989). *Uniform crime reports for the United States, 1988.* Washington, DC: Author.

Fingerhut, L., Ingram D., & Feldman J. (1992). Firearm and non-firearm homicide among persons 15 through 19 years of age: Differences by level of urbanization, United States, 1979-1989. *Journal of the American Medical Association, 267,* 3048-3053.

Fingerhut, L., & Kleinman, J. (1990). International and interstate comparisons of homicide among young males. *Journal of the American Medical Association, 263,* 3292-3295.

Fingerhut, L., Kleinman, J. C., Godfrey, M. S., & Rosenberg, H. (1991). Firearm mortality among children, youth, and young adults 1-34 years of age, trends, and current status: United States 1979-1988. *Monthly Vital Statistics Report, 39,* 1-15.

Galbo, J. (1986). Adolescents' perceptions of significant adults. *Children and Youth Services Review, 8,* 37-51.

Garmezy, N. (1991). Resilience and vulnerability to adverse developmental outcomes associated with poverty. *American Behavioral Scientist, 34,* 416-430.

Garmezy, N., & Masten, A. S. (1991). The protective role of competence indicators in children at risk. In E. M. Cummings, A. L. Green, & K. H. Karraker (Eds.), *Life-span developmental psychology: Perspectives on stress and coping* (pp. 151-174). Mahwah, NJ: Lawrence Erlbaum.

Garmezy, N., Masten, A. S., & Tellegen, A. (1984). The study of stress and competence in children: A building block of developmental psychopathology. *Child Development, 55,* 97-111.

Greenberg, M., & Schneider, D. (1994). Violence in American cities: Young Black males is the answer, but what was the question? *Social Science & Medicine, 39,* 179-187.

Grossman, F. K., Beinashowitz, J., Anderson, L., Sakurai, M., Finnin, L., & Flaherty, M. (1992). Risk and resilience in young adolescents. *Journal of Youth and Adolescence, 21,* 529-549.

Guerra, N. G., Huesmann, L. R., Tolan, P. H., & Van Acker, R. (1995). Stressful events and individual beliefs as correlates of economic disadvantage and aggression: Implications for preventive interventions among inner-city children. *Journal of Consulting and Clinical Psychology, 63,* 518-528.

Hamilton, S. F., & Darling, N. (1996). Mentors in adolescents' lives. In K. Hurrelmann & S. F. Hamilton (Eds.), *Social problems and social contexts in adolescence.* Hawthorne, NY: Aldine.

Hammond, W. R., & Yung, B. (1994). African Americans. In L. D. Eron, J. H. Gentry, & P. Schlegel (Eds.), *Reason to hope: A psychosocial perspective on violence and youth* (pp. 105-118). Washington, DC: American Psychological Association.

Hill, H. M., Soriano, F. I., Chen, S. A., & LaFromboise, T. D. (1994). Sociocultural factors in the etiology and prevention of violence among ethnic minority youth. In L. D. Eron, J. H. Gentry, & P. Schlegel (Eds.), *Reason to hope: A psychosocial perspective on violence and youth* (pp. 59-97). Washington, DC: American Psychological Association.

Huesmann, L. R. (1988). An information-processing model for the development of aggression. *Aggressive Behavior, 14,* 13-24.

Huesmann, L., Eron, L., Lefkowitz, M., & Walder, L. (1984). Stability of aggression over time and generations. *Developmental Psychology, 20,* 1120-1134.

Huston, A. C., Donnerstein, E., Fairchild, H., Feshbach, N. D., Katz, P. A., Murray, J. P., Rubinstein, E. A., Wilcox, B. L., & Zuckerman, D. (1992). *Big world, small screen: The role of television in American society.* Lincoln: University of Nebraska Press.

Kolvin, I., Miller, F. J. W., Fleeting, M., & Kolvin, P. A. (1988). Social and parenting factors affecting criminal offence rates. *British Journal of Psychiatry, 152,* 80-90.

Lamb, M. E. (1986). *The father's role: Applied perspectives.* New York: John Wiley.

Loeber, R., Wung, P., Keenan, K., Giroux, B., Stouthamer-Loeber, M., Van Kammen, W. B., & Maughan, B. (1993). Developmental pathways in disruptive childhood behavior. *Development and Psychopathology, 5,* 103-133.

Maccoby, E. E., & Martin, J. A. (1983). Socialization in the context of the family: Parent-child interaction. In E. M. Hetherington & P. H. Mussen (Eds.), *Handbook of child psychology: Vol. 4. Socialization, personality, and social development* (pp. 1-101). New York: John Wiley.

Masten, A. S. (1994). Resilience in individual development: Successful adaptation despite risk and adversity. In M. Wang & E. W. Gordon (Eds.), *Educational resilience in inner-city America* (pp. 3-25). Mahwah, NJ: Lawrence Erlbaum.

Masten, A. S., Garmezy, N., Tellegen, A., Pelligrini, D. S., Larkin, K., & Larsen, A. (1988). Competence and stress in schoolchildren: The moderating effects of individual and family qualities. *Journal of Child Psychology and Psychiatry, 29,* 745-764.

McLloyd, V. C. (1990). The impact of economic hardship on Black families and children: Psychological distress, parenting, and socioemotional development. *Child Development, 61,* 311-346.

C. S. Mott Foundation. (1994). *A fine line: Losing American youth to violence.* Flint, MI: Author.

Nakao, K., & Treas, J. (1990a). *Computing 1989 occupational prestige scores* (GSS Methodological Report No. 70). Chicago: National Opinion Research Center.

Nakao, K., & Treas, J. (1990b). *The 1989 socioeconomic index of occupations: Construction from the 1989 occupational prestige scores* (GSS Methodological Report No. 74). Chicago: National Opinion Research Center.

National Center for Education Statistics (NCES). (1996). *Youth indicators 1996: Trends in the well-being of American youth.* Washington, DC: Author.

National Institute of Justice (NIJ). (1995, May). *Juvenile crime part III.* Washington, DC: Author.

Parker, J. G., & Asher, S. R. (1987). Peer relations and later personal adjustment: Are low-accepted children at risk? *Psychological Bulletin, 102,* 357-389.

Pepler, D. J., & Slaby, R. G. (1994). Theoretical and developmental perspectives on youth and violence. In L. D. Eron, J. H. Gentry, & P. Schlegel (Eds.), *Reason to hope: A psychosocial perspective on violence and youth* (pp. 27-58). Washington, DC: American Psychological Association.

Price, J. H., Desmond, S. M., & Smith, D. (1991). A preliminary investigation of inner city adolescents' perceptions of guns. *Journal of School Health, 61,* 255-259.

Procidano, M. E., & Heller, K. (1983). Measures of perceived social support from friends and from family: Three validation studies. *American Journal of Community Psychology, 11,* 1-24.

Rhodes, J. E., Contreras, J. M., & Mangelsdorf, S. C. (1994). Natural mentors' relationships among Latino adolescent mothers: Psychological adjustment, moderating processes, and the role of early parental acceptance. *American Journal of Community Psychology, 22,* 211-228.

Rhodes, J. E., & Davis, A. B. (1996). Supportive ties between nonparent adults and urban adolescent girls. In B. J. R. Leadbeater & N. Way (Eds.), *Urban girls.* New York: New York University Press.

Rhodes, J. E., Ebert, L., & Fischer, K. (1992). Natural mentors: An overlooked resource in the social networks of African American adolescent mothers. *American Journal of Community Psychology, 20,* 445-462.

Rosenberg, M., & Mercy, J. (1991). Assaultive violence. In M. Rosenberg & J. Mercy (Eds.), *Violence in America: A public health approach.* New York: Oxford University Press.

Rutter, M. (1985). Resilience in the face of adversity: Protective factors and resistance to psychiatric disorder. *British Journal of Psychiatry, 147,* 598-611.

Rutter, M. (1987). Psychosocial resilience and protective mechanisms. *American Journal of Orthopsychiatry, 57,* 316-331.

Schubiner, H., Scott, R., & Tzelepis, A. (1993). Exposure to violence among inner-city youth. *Journal of Adolescent Health, 14,* 214-219.

Vanderschmidt, H. F., Lang, J. M., Knight-Williams, V., & Vanderschmidt, F. G. (1993). Risks among inner-city young teens: The prevalence of sexual activity, violence, drugs, and smoking. *Journal of Adolescent Health, 14,* 282-288.

Webster D. W., Gainer, P. S., & Champion, H. R. (1993). Weapon-carrying among inner-city junior high school students: Defensive behavior vs. aggressive delinquency. *American Journal of Public Health, 83,* 1604-1608.

Weiner, N. A. (1989). Violent criminal careers and violent career criminals: An overview of the research literature. In N. A. Weiner & M. E. Wolfgang (Eds.), *Violent crime, violent criminals.* Newbury Park, CA: Sage.

Werner, E. E. (1993). Risk, resilience, and recovery: Perspectives from the Kauai Longitudinal Study. *Development and Psychopathology, 5,* 503-515.

Werner, E. E., & Smith, R. S. (1992). *Overcoming the odds: High-risk children from birth to adulthood.* Ithaca, NY: Cornell University Press.

Wilson, W. J. (1987). *The truly disadvantaged.* Chicago: University of Chicago Press.

Windle, M. (1992). A longitudinal study of stress buffering for adolescent problem behaviors. *Developmental Psychology, 28,* 522-530.

Wolfgang, M. E. (1981). Sociocultural overview of criminal violence. In J. R. Hays, T. K. Roberts, & K. S. Solway (Eds.), *Violence and the violent individual* (pp. 97-115). New York: S. P. Medical and Scientific Books.

Wolfgang, M. E., Figlio, R., & Selin, T. (1972). *Delinquency in a birth cohort.* Chicago: University of Chicago Press.

Youniss, J., & Smollar, J. (1985). *Adolescent relations with mothers, fathers, and friends.* Chicago: University of Chicago Press.

Zimmerman, M. A., & Arunkumar, R. (1994). Resiliency research: Implications for schools and policy. *Social Policy Report, 8,* 1-18.

Zimmerman, M. A., Salem, D. A., & Maton, K. I. (1995). Family structure and psychosocial correlates among urban African American adolescent males. *Child Development, 66,* 1598-1613.

5

Involving Schools and Communities in Preventing Adolescent Dating Abuse

VANGIE A. FOSHEE

P artner violence is a significant public health problem in the United States (Biden, 1993). It often begins during adolescence, with the first episode typically occurring by age 15 (Henton, Cate, Koval, Lloyd, & Christopher, 1983). The percentage of high-school-aged adolescents reporting ever being involved in dating violence ranges from 12.1% to 26.9% (Henton et al., 1983; O'Keeffe, Brockopp, & Chew, 1986; Roscoe & Callahan, 1985). Studies have found that 16% of high-school-aged adolescents report hitting a partner with an object (Plass & Gessner, 1983); 22% report being kicked, bitten, or punched by a partner (Plass & Gessner, 1983); and 6.5% report having "beaten up" a partner (O'Keeffe et al., 1986). The few published studies measuring *sexual* violence among adolescent dating partners found that 16% of females report experiencing sexual abuse from a partner (Bergman, 1992) and that 6% of high school students (Smith & Williams, 1992) report being a perpetrator of sexual violence to a partner.

AUTHOR'S NOTE: This chapter is primarily based on work that is presented in Foshee et al. (1996) and Foshee et al. (1998). I acknowledge the significant contribution to this chapter of the coauthors of these two publications. This study was funded by the Centers for Disease Control and Prevention, Cooperative Agreement Number U81/ CCU409964-03.

Several developmental factors may increase adolescent susceptibility to partner violence. Dating is a developmental process that serves many functions. It prepares youths for adult relationships, it plays an important role in attaining prestige and status, and it develops and hones skills used in marital relationships (Deal & Wampler, 1986). Although dating serves these desirable functions, the importance placed on dating may put adolescents at increased risk for partner violence. Because of dating pressures, an adolescent may remain in an abusive relationship just to have someone to date. The fear of not being liked may prompt a teenager to do things that an abusive partner requests so that the teenager will be liked. Because adolescents are just beginning to date, they may not know what constitutes abusive behaviors. In addition, adolescents have less-developed communication skills than adults, and gender stereotyping, which has been associated with dating violence (Burt, 1980; Check & Malamuth, 1983; Finn, 1986), is stronger during adolescence than at any other time in the life span (Galambos, Petersen, Richards, & Gitelson, 1985).

Being involved in an abusive dating relationship as an adolescent has many negative developmental consequences. First is the obvious mortality and morbidity. About 70% of female victims of dating violence and 50% of male victims of dating violence report receiving injuries from the violence they experienced (Foshee, 1996). Second, being involved in an abusive dating relationship may lead to abusive adult relationships because dating develops skills and provides models for later marital relationships (O'Keeffe et al., 1986). In one study from a domestic violence shelter, approximately 30% of respondents reported having married their violent adolescent partners (Roscoe & Benaske, 1985). Finally, adolescence is a crucial period for developing identity and for gaining independence, and being in a controlling abusive relationship may affect these developmental stages.

Despite the magnitude of this problem and the serious consequences of dating violence for adolescents, scant research has been conducted on adolescent dating violence. Of the 50 or so studies that have been published on dating violence, about 6 have been with adolescents. The rest have focused almost entirely on college students. Especially lacking is research evaluating the effectiveness of dating violence prevention programs targeted at adolescents, despite the obvious need for early intervention.

This chapter (a) describes the Safe Dates study, which is an evaluation of a school- and community-based adolescent dating abuse prevention program, (b) reports outcome effectiveness results from the Safe

Dates study, and (c) presents strategies for involving schools and communities in the prevention of adolescent dating abuse.

The Safe Dates Study

The Safe Dates project was developed in response to the need for adolescent dating violence research and early intervention. The study, funded by the Centers for Disease Control and Prevention (CDC), began in October 1993. It was one of 12 studies funded by the CDC to determine the effectiveness of various youth violence prevention programs. The Safe Dates study was the only study to focus specifically on the prevention of violence between dating couples.

The study was conducted in Johnston County, North Carolina, a primarily rural county with approximately 82,000 residents. Collaborators included community agencies such as the Health Department; Harbor, Inc. (the county domestic violence and sexual assault organization); the public school system; the hospital; the mental health organization; social services; the Johnston County Sheriff's Department; and the nine police departments in the county.

The purpose of the study was to develop and evaluate an adolescent dating abuse prevention program. The study examined the effect of the program on the primary and secondary prevention of partner violence. *Primary prevention* refers to prevention of the first dating violence event. *Secondary prevention* occurs when victims stop being victimized or perpetrators stop being violent. The Safe Dates program aimed for the primary prevention of dating violence perpetration by both males and females, for studies consistently find that both male and female adolescents are perpetrators of partner violence (Foshee, 1996; Henton et al., 1983; O'Keeffe et al., 1986; Plass & Gessner, 1983). Secondary prevention activities encouraging the prevention of further victimization and perpetration were also aimed at both males and females.

The Safe Dates Program

The program that was developed, the Safe Dates program, included both school and community activities. School activities included (a) a

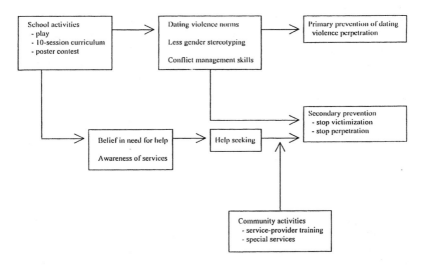

Figure 5.1. Safe Dates Theoretical Model

theater production performed by peers, (b) a 10-session curriculum (the Safe Dates Curriculum), and (c) a poster contest. Community activities included (a) special services for adolescents in violent relationships (e.g., a crisis line, support groups, materials for parents) and (b) community service provider training. The program promoted primary prevention through school activities, and secondary prevention through school and community activities. Figure 5.1 displays the theoretical process through which these activities were expected to influence the primary and secondary prevention of dating violence.

Changes in norms, coupled with improvements in prosocial skills, served as the theoretical base for primary prevention school activities. *Norms* are standards for acceptable behavior, and conformity to norms thus has a significant effect on individuals' behavior. In the dating violence context, norms concerning the use of violent behavior toward dating partners (Bergman, 1992; Deal & Wampler, 1986; O'Keeffe et al., 1986; Stets & Pirog-Good, 1987) and concerning gender role expectations (Burt, 1980; Check & Malamuth, 1983; Finn, 1986) are associated with the use of violence toward partners. Weak conflict management skills are associated with youth aggression in general (Slaby & Guerra, 1988) and with partner violence specifically (Lloyd, 1987; Lloyd, Koval, & Cate, 1989). Thus, school activities were expected to lead to the primary prevention of dating violence perpetration by (a) changing norms associated with partner violence, (b) decreasing gender stereotyping, and (c) improving conflict management skills.

Changes in norms, gender stereotyping, and conflict management skills may also be important for adolescents in abusive relationships if they are to leave those relationships or to stop being violent. In addition to these influences, secondary prevention activities encouraged victims and perpetrators to seek help by addressing cognitive factors associated with help seeking. Cognitive factors influencing help seeking that were emphasized were belief in the need for help and awareness of community services, as suggested by Weinstein's (1988) precaution adoption theory.

School Activities. Each of these mediating variables was addressed in the school activities. The play described how an adolescent victim and a perpetrator of dating violence sought help for their violent relationship, thus providing victims and perpetrators in the audience with a model for help seeking. It addressed cognitive factors associated with help seeking, such as beliefs in the need for help and awareness of community resources. For example, in the play, friends pointed out to the victim the negative consequences of remaining in the abusive relationship, and they described community resources for seeking help with dating violence. These aspects of the play were intended to motivate both victims and perpetrators in the audience to seek help.

The theoretically based teaching objectives for each of the ten 45-minute sessions of the curriculum are presented in Table 5.1. Norms were addressed, for example, when adolescents completed worksheets with peers on the consequences of dating violence for victims and perpetrators, and when they worked with peers to analyze scenarios of dating conflicts to create definitions of abusive dating behaviors. These activities were intended to increase the likelihood that teens would see dating violence as an inappropriate and punishable behavior and thus not do it. Gender stereotyping was addressed when adolescents wrote a story about a time when someone had stereotypic or unfair expectations of them and when they analyzed scenarios and discussed how gender stereotypes affect dating interactions that could lead to dating abuse. To improve conflict management skills, adolescents practiced communication while role-playing dating situations that involved conflict. Two curriculum sessions included activities in which peers practiced helping friends in violent relationships. Most adolescents rely on peers for help with violent dating relationships (Henton et al., 1983; Levy, 1991), but adolescents report receiving unhelpful advice from peers, and they often are supported in being perpetrators of violence or are blamed for the violence when they have been victimized (Koval, 1989). These two sessions were included to enhance the chances that adolescent victims and perpetrators would receive helpful advice and support when seeking help from friends.

The poster contest was described during Day 10 of the curriculum, and interested students developed posters that addressed themes in the Safe Dates Curriculum. Thus, posters also addressed the proposed mediating variables. The themes most commonly addressed by the posters were the controlling aspects of abuse, the negative consequences of remaining in abusive relationships, warning signs of abusive relationships, tips for successful communication, and community resources.

Community Activities. The purpose of the community activities was to improve the resources available to adolescents involved in dating violence. Improving the quantity and quality of resources was a key component to achieving secondary prevention (getting perpetrators to stop being violent or helping victims end victimization) through help seeking. One way to increase community resources for partner violence is to train service providers to be more helpful. Adolescents rarely seek help from professional service providers, however, because they fear being blamed and are concerned that information will not be held in confidence. Many studies have documented that service providers are often not helpful to victims and perpetrators of partner violence (Dobash & Dobash, 1979; Hamilton & Coats, 1993; Kurz, 1987). Thus, in addition to providing direct services to those involved in partner violence (e.g., a crisis line, support groups, materials for parents), the Safe Dates program included community service provider training.

Studies indicate that the way professionals label partner violence influences public attitudes, agency practices, and legal decisions (Borkowski, Murch, & Walker, 1983); that abuse-related stereotypes and attributions for blame influence the type of help that is given to battered women by therapists (Washburn, Frieze, & Knoble, 1979); and that professionals often lack knowledge of the appropriate community resources for battered women (Ball, 1977; Bass & Price, 1979), believe that their actions will not help (Walter, 1981), and believe that they do not have the skills to help (Walter, 1981). The training for service providers involved interactive exercises designed to alter these cognitive factors associated with help giving.

Table 5.1
Teaching Objectives of the "Safe Dates" Dating Violence Prevention Curriculum

DAY 1: DEFINING CARING RELATIONSHIPS

Promote students' consideration of the qualities that are most important to them in dating relationships.

Discuss ways that people act to show they care.

Draw out characteristics that are similar in all caring relationships, romantic and platonic.

Promote students' consideration of how they want to be treated by dating partners and how they want to treat dating partners.

Emphasize that students have a choice in how they are treated in dating relationships and how they treat their girlfriends and boyfriends.

DAY 2: DEFINING DATING ABUSE

Describe dating behaviors that can be harmful.

Differentiate between harmful and abusive behaviors.

Differentiate and define physically and emotionally abusive behaviors.

Discuss facts about dating abuse.

DAY 3: WHY DO PEOPLE ABUSE?

Discuss reasons why people abuse.

Discuss the roles of manipulation, power, and control in dating abuse.

Challenge the attribution that violence from jealousy indicates love.

Demonstrate that a person's feelings, actions, and thinking can be a target for abusive control.

Foster an awareness of consequences of both physical and emotional abuse.

Outline warning signs for abuse.

DAY 4: HOW TO HELP FRIENDS

Demonstrate the reasons that people do not or cannot "just leave" an abusive relationship.

Acknowledge the difficulties in seeking help as a victim of dating violence.

Describe different methods of giving help to friends who are in abusive relationships.

Describe community resources.

Encourage people who are victims of abuse and perpetrators of abuse to seek help.

DAY 5: HELPING FRIENDS

Discuss the red flags for being a perpetrator and a victim of dating abuse.

Have students practice talking with a friend who is violent toward his or her dating partner.

Have students practice talking with a friend who is being abused by his or her dating partner.

Equip students with the skills to confront dating abuse with their peers.

Table 5.1
Continued

DAY 6: IMAGES OF RELATIONSHIPS
  Increase awareness that our images of dating relationships influence how we treat,
    and are treated by, our dating partners.
  Increase students' understanding of how their images of relationships are created.
  Define gender stereotyping.
  Explain how gender stereotyping can influence images and dating interactions.
  Illustrate the link between gender stereotyping and dating abuse.

DAY 7: EQUAL POWER THROUGH COMMUNICATION
  Describe eight communication skills that can be helpful in resolving conflict.
  Give students an opportunity to practice their communication skills.
  Give students an opportunity to think about nonviolent strategies to use when their
    girlfriends or boyfriends do not use communication skills.

DAY 8: HOW WE FEEL—HOW WE DEAL
  Discuss the importance of acknowledging feelings.
  Provide the students with an extended list of words that describe feelings.
  Acknowledge anger as a powerful and valid emotion.
  Facilitate discussion of hot buttons, cues to anger, and nonabusive responses to anger.
  Emphasize that the way one responds to anger is a choice.

DAY 9: SEXUAL ASSAULT
  Define sexual assault.
  Discourage victim blaming for rape.
  Promote opposing rape norms, rather than prescribed rape norms.
  Illustrate verbal and nonverbal cues that indicate someone is unsure or not ready to
    have sex.
  Promote the use of self-defense techniques in potential rape situations.
  Encourage students to be clear with their partners about their sexual boundaries.
  Discuss ways to reduce the risk of rape in a dating situation.

DAY 10: SUMMARY AND POSTER CONTEST
  Obtain student feedback on the curriculum.
  Describe the poster contest.

Research Design

The Safe Dates program was evaluated by using an experimental design. The 14 public schools in Johnston County with students in the eighth or ninth grade were stratified by grade and matched on school size. One school of each matched pair was then randomly assigned to the treatment and the control conditions. Treatment adolescents were exposed to the program's school and community activities; control adolescents were exposed only to the community activities. Thus, the effects of the school activities over and above the effects of the community activities were assessed.

Adolescents were eligible for the study if they were enrolled in the eighth or ninth grade on September 10, 1994. In October 1994, baseline data were collected from adolescents during 50-minute sessions in school through self-administered questionnaires. Questionnaires were completed by 81% (N = 1,965) of the 2,434 eligible adolescents. This overall baseline sample was 50.4% female, 75.9% White, 20.2% African American, and 3.9% other racial/ethnic groups. Student ages ranged from 12 to 17 years, with a mean of 13.9 years. Of the 1,965 adolescents completing baseline questionnaires, 1,405 (72%) reported that they had been on a date. Of the adolescents who were dating at baseline, 36.5% of females and 39.4% of males reported being a victim of partner violence at least once (χ^2 = 1.2, p = .27), and 27.8% of females and 15.0% of males reported being a perpetrator of partner violence at least once (χ^2 = 33.5, p < .001). Most male and female victims in the sample reported being victimized by partners in grades higher than those included in the study sample.

Program activities occurred from October 1994 through March 1995. In October and November, twenty 3-hour workshops were offered to community service providers, including social service, emergency room, health department, mental health, crisis line, and health department staff, school counselors, sheriff's deputies, and officers from the nine police departments in the county. Approximately 63% of eligible service providers received the training. Service providers were eligible for training if they interacted with adolescents as part of their professional activities.

In November, the 45-minute play was performed at each of the seven treatment schools by eight students enrolled in a theater course in one of the high schools; 97% of students in the treatment schools were present for the performance.

In November, the 16 teachers (10 men and 6 women) who taught required health courses in the seven treatment schools received 20 hours of training from Safe Dates staff on teen dating violence and the Safe Dates Curriculum; they then delivered the curriculum to the students in January and February 1995. Because of differences in school practices, some teachers taught it as a 45-minute class for 10 days in a row; some taught it every other day until the 10 sessions were covered; one teacher taught it once a week for 10 weeks; and others taught it in five 1½-hour sessions, covering two topics per day. Approximately 35% of classes were monitored unannounced by Safe Dates staff. Monitors documented, on standardized forms, intended activities that were completed, skipped, or modified by the teachers. On the basis of monitoring data, 90.7% of intended curriculum activities were covered by the teachers. Classroom attendance in Safe Dates sessions ranged from 95.0% to 97.0%.

The poster contest occurred in March. Although not all students created posters, all were exposed to the messages in the posters because each student was required to vote for the best three posters in her or his school, each of which earned a cash prize.

Before the Safe Dates project, Harbor, Inc. staffed a domestic violence and rape crisis line, which was rarely marketed for, or used by, adolescents. As part of the Safe Dates project, adolescents were told about this crisis line in the play, the curriculum, and the poster contest (most posters included the crisis line number). Additionally, crisis line volunteers received training on how to respond to calls from adolescents. Materials for parents of adolescents in abusive relationships were made available throughout the study at Harbor, Inc. A weekly support group was offered to victims of partner violence.

Of the 1,965 adolescents completing baseline questionnaires in October 1994, 1,909 (97%) completed questionnaires again in May 1996, 1 month after program activities ended; and 1,892 (96%) completed questionnaires 1 year after program activities. At each follow-up, data were collected by mail from school dropouts, transfer students, and students who were absent twice during school data collection.

Baseline and 1-month postintervention (7 months postbaseline) data were used to (a) assess the effects of the Safe Dates program on primary and secondary prevention of dating abuse, (b) assess the effects of the Safe Dates program on theoretically based mediating variables, and (c) determine whether the Safe Dates program prevented dating violence through the proposed mediating variables. At this date, the 1-year follow-up data have not yet been examined.

Measures

The questionnaires included about 116 items and were approximately 40 pages long. For these analyses, we used measures of each mediating variable presented in Figure 5.1 and of dating abuse victimization and perpetration.

Early in the questionnaire, adolescents were asked whether they had ever been on a date (either very informal activities like meeting at a mall or a park, or more formal activities). Adolescents who responded "no" skipped all questions on dating abuse.

Four victimization and four perpetration outcome variables were measured. *Psychological abuse victimization* was measured by asking, "How often has anyone that you have ever been on a date with done the following things to you?" Fourteen acts were listed (see Table 5.2). Response options ranged from 0 for *never* to 3 for *very often*. Items were summed, and to normalize the distribution, summed scores were recoded so that 0 indicated no victimization of psychological abuse, 1 (a summed score of 1 to 5) indicated mild victimization, 2 (a summed score of 6 to 10) indicated moderate psychological abuse, and 3 (a summed score of 10 or greater) indicated severe psychological abuse victimization. Cronbach's alpha for psychological abuse victimization was .91. A parallel scale was used to measure *psychological abuse perpetration* (alpha = .88). Adolescents were asked, "How often have you done the following things to someone you have ever had a date with?" The same 14 acts were listed.

Nonsexual violence victimization was measured by asking respondents, "How many times has anyone that you have been on a date with done the following things to you? Only include when they did it to you first. In other words, don't count it if they did it to you in self-defense." Sixteen behaviors were listed (see Table 5.2). Response options ranged from 0 for *never* to 3 for *10 or more times*. The 16 items were summed. To normalize the distribution, the summed scores were recoded so that 0 indicated a summed score of 0, 1 indicated a summed score of 1, and 2 indicated a summed score of greater than 1.

Sexual violence victimization was measured with the same base question and the two behavioral items "forced me to have sex" and "forced me to do other sexual things that I did not want to do." These two items were summed. As with the nonsexual victimization variable, to normalize the distribution, the summed score was recoded so that 0 indicated a summed score of 0, 1 indicated a summed score of 1, and 2 indicated a summed score of greater than 1.

Nonsexual and *sexual violence perpetration* variables were created by using a parallel question. The base question was, "How many times have you ever done the following things to a person that you have been

Table 5.2
Psychological Abuse and
Dating Violence Scales

PSYCHOLOGICAL ABUSE
Damaged something that belonged to me
Threw something at me but missed
Started to hit me but stopped
Threatened to hurt me
Would not let me do things with other people
Told me I could not talk to someone of the opposite sex
Made me describe where I was every minute of the day
Insulted me in front of others
Put down my looks
Blamed me for bad things they did
Said things to hurt my feelings on purpose
Threatened to start dating someone else
Did something just to make me jealous
Brought up something from the past to hurt me

NONSEXUAL VIOLENCE
Scratched me
Slapped me
Physically twisted my arm
Slammed or held me against a wall
Kicked me
Bent my fingers
Bit me
Tried to choke me
Pushed, grabbed, or shoved me
Dumped me out of the car
Threw something at me that hit me
Burned me
Hit me with a fist
Hit me with something hard besides a fist
Beat me up
Assaulted me with a knife or gun

SEXUAL VIOLENCE
Forced me to have sex
Forced me to do other sexual things that I did not want to do

---

on a date with? Only include when you did it to him or her first. In other words, don't count it if you did it in self-defense." The same 18 behaviors were listed, and the recoding procedures were the same as with victimization.

To measure *violence in the current relationship,* adolescents were first asked whether they were currently dating someone (referred to as Partner X). If so, then they were asked the questions "How many times has Partner X ever used any kind of physical force against you that was not used in self-defense?" and "How many times have you used any kind of physical force against Partner X that was not used in self-defense?" Response options ranged from 0 for *never* to 3 for *10 or more times.*

Four variables measuring dating violence norms were created: (a) *acceptance of prescribed norms* (norms accepting dating violence under certain circumstances); (b) *acceptance of opposing norms* (norms considering dating violence unacceptable under all circumstances); (c) *perceived positive consequences of dating violence;* and (d) *perceived negative consequences of dating violence.* The same Likert scale format was used to measure all four constructs. Students were asked how strongly they agreed or disagreed with a series of statements measuring each construct. Response options ranged from 0 for *strongly disagree* to 3 for *strongly agree.* Items measuring each construct were averaged to create composite scores (prescribed norms, eight items, alpha = .71; perceived positive consequences, three items, alpha = .47; perceived negative consequences, three items, alpha = .57). One item was used to measure acceptance of opposing norms: "Hitting a dating partner is never ok."

The same Likert scale format was used to measure *gender stereotyping* (11 items, alpha = .69) and *beliefs in need for help* (two items, alpha = .67). Examples of gender stereotyping items were "Swearing is worse for a girl than for a boy," "On a date, the boy should be expected to pay all the expenses," and "It is more important for boys than girls to do well in school." The two items measuring beliefs in need for help were "Teens who are victims of dating violence need to get help from others," and "Teens who are violent to their dates need to get help from others."

To measure *awareness of services,* subjects were asked whether they knew of county services for victims and perpetrators of dating violence. To measure *help seeking,* victims of dating violence were asked, "Have you ever asked anyone what you should do about the violence in your dating relationships?" and perpetrators were asked, "Have you ever asked anyone for help on how to stop using violence toward dates?"

Four conflict management variables were measured: *constructive communication skills, destructive communication skills, constructive responses to anger,* and *destructive responses to anger.* Communication skills were measured by asking, "During the last 6 months, when you

Table 5.3
Items Assessing Conflict
Management Variables

CONSTRUCTIVE COMMUNICATION SKILLS
Told the person how I felt
Tried to calm down before I talked to them
Asked lots of questions so that I could get the whole story
Asked them what they were feeling
Let them know what was important to me
Tried to find a solution that suited both of us
Listened to their side of the story

DESTRUCTIVE COMMUNICATION SKILLS
Hung up the phone on them
Refused to talk to them about the problem
Gave them the silent treatment
Stomped off during arguments
Acted like nothing was wrong

CONSTRUCTIVE RESPONSES TO ANGER
I asked someone for advice on how to handle it
I told the person why I was angry
I had a discussion with the person about it
I tried to calm myself down before I talked to the person

DESTRUCTIVE RESPONSES TO ANGER
I yelled and screamed insults at the person I was mad at
I made nasty comments about the person to others
I tried to mess up something the person was trying to do
I damaged something that belonged to the person
I fantasized about telling the person off
I fantasized about hurting the person

had a disagreement with someone, how much of the time did you do the following things?" The items are listed in Table 5.3. Response options ranged from 0 for *never* to 3 for *most of the time.* Seven items measuring constructive communication skills (alpha = .88) and five items measuring destructive communication skills (alpha = .69) were averaged to create composite variables for each construct.

To measure responses to anger, adolescents were asked, "During the last 6 months, when you were angry at someone, how often did you do or feel the following things?" The items are listed in Table 5.3. Response options ranged from 0 for *never* to 3 for *very often.* The four items measuring constructive responses to anger (alpha = .78) and the six items measuring destructive responses to anger (alpha = .76) were averaged to create composite variables for each construct.

Analysis Strategy

Although few participants dropped out between baseline and follow-up, concern was expressed that dropping out might be related to some of the variables. To investigate this possibility, correlations were calculated between dropout status and each of the 22 variables measured at baseline. Eleven bivariate correlations were statistically significant. Logistic regression was used to evaluate the multivariate relationship of these 11 variables and dropout status through odds ratios (OR). Only three measures—White racial status, gender stereotyping, and nonsexual violence victimization—were associated with dropout at the .05 level. White students were slightly less likely to drop out (OR = .994) than other students. The odds of dropping out increased with gender stereotyping (OR = 1.8 per unit) and increased with nonsexual violence (OR = 1.5 per unit). All three variables were controlled in later multivariate analyses.

The panel completing both baseline and 1-month follow-up questionnaires was divided into three subsamples based on dating violence experience. The primary prevention subsample included dating adolescents who reported at baseline that they had never been a victim or perpetrator of dating violence (N = 862). The victims secondary prevention subsample included dating adolescents who reported at baseline that they had been a victim of dating violence (N = 438), and the perpetrators secondary prevention subsample included dating adolescents who reported at baseline that they had been a perpetrator of dating violence (N = 247). Consistent with other studies of dating violence (Bergman, 1992; Henton et al., 1983; O'Keeffe et al., 1986; Plass & Gessner, 1983), most adolescents reporting experience with dating violence reported being both a victim and perpetrator. Thus, many of the same adolescents were in the victims and perpetrators subsamples.

In the full sample and each subsample, treatment and control groups were compared at baseline and follow-up on demographic, mediating, and outcome variables. These analyses were conducted with school (N = 14) as the unit of analysis while taking into consideration the matching design. Matching allowed consideration of each matched pair as a primary sampling unit. Schoolwide means for each outcome of interest were compared by using the nonparametric Wilcoxon signed rank test for differences from matched pairs. The small sample size ($N = 7$) dictated a nonparametric procedure, such as the Wilcoxon signed rank test, rather than a parametric procedure, such as the paired t test, because the t test's assumptions about the distribution of the sample could not be ensured with a sample size of 7.

In analyzing variables that mediated program effects, the focus was on assessing patterns of change in individuals, rather than in schools. Thus, the mediation analyses were performed at the individual level. Mediation was indicated when the treatment condition beta was attenuated by 20% or more when controlling for proposed mediators.

Results

None of the study samples displayed significant differences between treatment and control groups in outcome, mediating, or demographic variables at baseline. Also, no significant interactions were found between gender and treatment when predicting outcomes at follow-up. Therefore, Gender × Treatment interactions were dropped, and the main effects of treatment on outcomes at follow-up were assessed.

As indicated in Table 5.4, several perpetration variables differed significantly by treatment condition at follow-up. In the full sample, adolescents in the treatment condition reported significantly less psychological abuse perpetration and significantly less perpetration of violence against a current dating partner than did those in the control condition. In the primary prevention subsample, adolescents in the treatment condition, as compared with those in the control condition, reported initiating significantly less psychological abuse perpetration. Baseline data are not presented for the primary prevention subsample because the baseline prevalence of each type of dating abuse was zero in this subsample. In the perpetrators subsample, treatment and control group differences in psychological abuse perpetration and sexual violence perpetration exhibited suggestive trends in the predicted direction.

At follow-up, no significant differences were found in victimization by psychological abuse, nonsexual violence, sexual violence, or violence in the current relationship between the treatment and control groups in any of the samples.

Table 5.4
Treatment and Control Group Comparisons
of Mean Outcome Variables at Baseline and
Follow-up in the Full Sample, Primary Prevention
Subsample, and Perpetrators Subsample (N = 14)

| | Full Sample | | | | Primary Prevention | | Perpetrators | | | |
| | Baseline | | Follow-up | | Follow-up | | Baseline | | Follow-up | |
Variable	C	T	C	T	C	T	C	T	C	T
Perpetration										
Psychological										
abuse	.58	.58	.67	.50**	.63	.45**	1.75	1.64	1.56	1.14*
Nonsexual										
violence	.22	.26	.26	.22	.18	.12	1.58	1.66	.91	.77
Sexual										
violence	.03	.04	.05	.02*	.04	.01	.21	.25	.18	.07*
Violence in										
current										
relationship	.03	.04	.05	.02**	.03	.01	.20	.31	.16	.17

NOTES: C = Control group; T = Treatment group.
Asterisks indicate significance level using Wilcoxon signed rank test: $*p < .10$; $**p < .05$.

As indicated in Tables 5.5 and 5.6, many of the proposed mediating variables varied by treatment condition at follow-up. In the full sample (Table 5.5), adolescents in the treatment group, as compared with those in the control group, were less supportive of prescribed dating violence norms, were more supportive of opposing dating violence norms, perceived fewer positive consequences from using dating violence, used more constructive communication skills and responses to anger, were less likely to gender-stereotype, and were more aware of victim and perpetrator services. In the primary prevention subsample (Table 5.5), treatment adolescents were more supportive than controls of opposing dating violence norms, perceived more negative consequences from using dating violence, and gender-stereotyped less. Treatment group adolescents in the victims subsample (Table 5.6), compared with the control group adolescents, were less accepting of prescribed dating violence norms, less accepting of traditional gender stereotypes, and more aware of victim services. Treatment group adolescents in the perpetrators subsample (Table 5.6), compared with the control group

Table 5.5
Treatment and Control Group Comparisons of Mediating Variables at Baseline and Follow-up in the Full Sample and Primary Prevention Subsample (*N* = 14)

| | Full Sample | | | | Primary Prevention | | | |
| | Baseline | | Follow-up | | Baseline | | Follow-up | |
Variable	C	T	C	T	C	T	C	T
Norms								
Prescribed norms	.54	.52	.56	.42**	.46	.43	.49	.38*
Opposing norms	2.52	2.51	2.51	2.69**	2.60	2.57	2.58	2.75**
Positive consequences	.29	.28	.29	.24**	.22	.22	.24	.21
Negative consequences	1.83	1.85	1.85	1.94*	1.90	1.92	1.93	2.00**
Conflict management skills								
Constructive communication	1.85	1.89	1.75	1.83**	1.90	1.99	1.78	1.88
Destructive communication	1.03	.99	1.12	1.07	.94	.96	1.08	1.01*
Constructive anger response	1.54	1.58	1.49	1.58**	1.54	1.63	1.49	1.62
Destructive anger response	.89	.88	.95	.86	.76	.81	.84	.78
Gender stereotyping	.72	.73	.73	.61**	.66	.66	.67	.56**
Belief in need for help	2.63	2.68	2.54	2.68*	—	—	—	—
% aware of victim services	18.94	20.87	28.24	80.18**	—	—	—	—
% aware of perp. services	20.75	21.71	24.71	70.88**	—	—	—	—
% victims sought help	21.07	23.18	27.33	31.62	—	—	—	—
% perpetrators sought help	32.44	20.05	22.80	17.42	—	—	—	—

NOTES: C = Control group; T = Treatment group.
Asterisks indicate significance level using Wilcoxon signed rank test: *$p < .10$; **$p < .05$.

adolescents, perceived more negative consequences for using dating violence and were more aware of services for perpetrators.

Analyses for assessing mediation were conducted next. In the full sample, controlling for gender, variables associated with attrition, and

Table 5.6
Treatment and Control Group Comparisons of Mediating Variables at Baseline and Follow-up in the Secondary Prevention Subsamples (*N* = 14)

| | Victims | | | | Perpetrators | | | |
| | Baseline | | Follow-up | | Baseline | | Follow-up | |
Variable	C	T	C	T	C	T	C	T
Norms								
Prescribed norms	.78	.72	.80	.51**	.83	.87	.79	.62
Opposing norms	2.22	2.35	2.31	2.56*	2.13	2.18	2.29	2.54
Positive consequences	.44	.39	.47	.32	.47	.51	.50	.36
Negative consequences	1.64	1.67	1.64	1.81	1.42	1.62	1.37	1.73**
Conflict management skills								
Constructive communication	1.85	1.90	1.66	1.87	1.99	1.98	1.79	1.80
Destructive communication	1.25	1.14	1.26	1.25	1.37	1.18	1.32	1.32
Constructive anger response	1.55	1.66	1.55	1.61	1.66	1.68	1.66	1.61
Destructive anger response	1.14	1.08	1.23	1.02	1.34	1.22	1.34	1.11
Gender stereotyping	.85	.78	.87	.65**	.75	.84	.80	.70
Belief in need for help	2.37	2.59	2.21	2.54	2.45	2.55	2.26	2.50
% aware of victim services	21.65	20.58	30.38	76.82**	—	—	—	—
% aware of perp. services	—	—	—	—	29.81	18.54	30.41	67.90**
% victims sought help	21.08	23.18	30.36	40.20	—	—	—	—
% perpetrators sought help	—	—	—	—	32.44	20.05	36.12	32.49

NOTES: C = Control group; T = Treatment group.
Asterisks indicate significance level using Wilcoxon signed rank test: *$p < .10$; **$p < .05$.

baseline values of the dependent variables, the treatment condition was significantly associated with changes in psychological abuse perpetration ($b = -.08$, $p < .001$), sexual violence perpetration ($b = -.06$, $p < .009$), and violence perpetrated in the current relationship ($b = -.06$,

$p < .014$). The association between treatment condition and psychological abuse perpetration was mediated by changes in prescribed norms, gender stereotyping, and awareness of victim services. The association between treatment condition and sexual violence perpetration was mediated by changes in prescribed norms, gender stereotyping, awareness of victim services, and awareness of perpetrator services. The relationship between treatment condition and violence perpetrated in the current relationship was mediated only by changes in prescribed norms.

In the primary prevention subsample, the controlled analyses indicated that the treatment condition was significantly associated with the initiation of psychological abuse perpetration ($b = -.11, p < .001$). This relationship remained statistically significant when controlling for proposed mediators, indicating that this program effect occurred through mechanisms other than the mediation effects proposed.

In the perpetrators subsample, the treatment condition was associated with psychological abuse perpetration ($b = -.12, p < .048$) and with sexual violence perpetration ($b = -.14, p < .026$). The association between treatment condition and psychological abuse perpetration was mediated by changes in awareness of perpetrator services, whereas the association between treatment condition and sexual violence perpetration was mediated by changes in perceived negative consequences for using dating violence and awareness of perpetrator services.

Discussion

On the basis of 1-month follow-up data, the Safe Dates program shows promise for preventing adolescent partner violence. At follow-up, in the full sample, 25% less psychological abuse perpetration, 60% less sexual violence perpetration, and 60% less violence perpetration against the current dating partner was reported in treatment schools than in control schools. In the primary prevention subsample, 28% less psychological abuse was initiated in treatment schools than in control schools. At follow-up, dating violence perpetrators reported 27% less psychological abuse perpetration and 61% less sexual violence perpetration in treatment schools than in control schools. In addition, school activities had effects on several proposed mediating variables, with the largest effects being on dating violence norms, gender stereotyping, and awareness of services, the variables targeted most heavily by school activities. Mediation analyses suggested that the effects of the school activities on perpetration of violence toward partners occurred primarily through changes in these three variables.

One goal of secondary prevention was to encourage victims and perpetrators to seek help. Although victims and perpetrators in the treatment group became significantly more aware of services than those in the control condition, no between-group differences were found in help seeking. Help seeking increased substantially from baseline to follow-up in both conditions (see Table 5.6). Still, only a minority of victims (35%) and perpetrators (34%) reported seeking help from any-one. When they did seek help, they generally sought it from friends and parents, rather than from community service providers.

Exposure to Safe Dates school activities did not increase the likeli-hood that victims would stop being victimized. One explanation is that many study adolescents were dating people who were not in the sample. For example, 75% of females were dating partners in older grades than the study sample, and 75% of males were dating partners in younger grades than the study sample (Foshee, 1996). Therefore, it is likely that a significant portion of the victims were being victimized by partners who were not in the study and therefore not exposed to the intervention.

This study had several limitations. One, because of the timing of follow-up data collection and the way dating violence was measured, program effects were likely to be underestimated. Follow-up data were collected 1 month after the program activities, and therefore there was not much time for behavior change. Two, when adolescents answered follow-up questions about "ever" involvement in dating violence, they would be including new violence that happened between baseline (October) and follow-up (May). Much of what was reported may have occurred before the program was completed. Therefore, the follow-up measure is not as pure as might be desired. This limitation was ad-dressed in the 1-year follow-up data by asking respondents to report violent and abusive behaviors experienced during the prior year.

Another limitation of the study was that it relied on self-reports of dating violence victimization and perpetration. Unfortunately, there are no other options for measuring dating violence among adolescents because these behaviors are rarely reported to or observed by others. The prevalence of dating violence victimization and perpetration found in the Safe Dates study was comparable with that found in other prevalence studies of adolescents using self-reports. Approximately 38% of dating adolescents reported victimization, and 21% reported perpetration of dating violence. This represents 27% and 15% of the total sample (dating and nondating) for victimization and perpetration, respectively. Previous estimates of adolescent dating violence victimization and perpetration have ranged from 17% to 20% of total samples (Bergman, 1992; O'Keeffe et al., 1986).

Another limitation was that the sample was limited to adolescents living primarily in rural areas, thus limiting the generalizability of study findings. Although approximately 77% of U.S. counties are classified as rural (Gesler & Ricketts, 1992), geographic, ethnic, and cultural variations make it difficult to generalize these findings to all rural counties. Study findings, however, can be generalized to similar rural counties. Compared with the nation, the study county had an overrepresentation of minority residents (20%), lower-income households (40% with less than $10,000 annual income), and individuals with limited education (53% of people over age 25 had less than a high school education). Follow-up studies should determine the effects of the Safe Dates programs in other areas.

The primarily rural sample, however, was probably responsible for several of the study's strengths. Because of the stability of the community, study attrition was low, and therefore potential for bias was low because of loss of respondents at follow-up. This stability also contributed to maintaining the integrity of study conditions. Between the administration of baseline measures and the follow-up questionnaire, only 15 students changed schools within the county: 5 changed from treatment to treatment schools or control to control schools; 2 changed from treatment to control schools; and 8 changed from control to treatment schools. Also, on the basis of school attendance records, almost all treatment group adolescents were exposed to the intended activities: 97% of treatment adolescents were present when the play was performed, and classroom attendance at each curriculum session ranged from 95% to 97%.

Strategies for Involving Schools and Communities in Dating Violence Prevention

The Safe Dates project has had substantial community support. The cooperation of 33 organizations was required for the successful conduct of this study, and all 33 organizations actively participated. Each of these organizations provided a letter of support in the initial grant proposal to the Centers for Disease Control and Prevention, and therefore extensive community work occurred even before the study was funded.

While the grant proposal was being written, each organization was visited several times. A researcher, Dr. Harold Cook, who lived in the study community and who knew community members well, provided entrée into the community. He arranged the initial contact with each school and community agency representative. At the initial meetings, we found that the problem of dating violence was unfamiliar to many school and community people, although it was very familiar to others and considered to be a serious problem. Many expressed the opinion that dating violence was "no big deal" or that it was something that teens grow out of. Educating school and community members about the prevalence and negative consequences of dating violence was very important to gaining support for the project. When obtaining support from community members for participation in the study, we also described very specifically the expected activities of each organization and the amount of time that would be required to accomplish those activities.

The schools expressed specific concerns about the project. Youth violence prevention programs in general were of more interest to the schools than were programs specifically for dating violence prevention. We pointed out that many topics covered in the Safe Dates program (e.g., anger management, communication skills) were appropriate for prevention of both youth violence in general and dating violence. A second concern was over the additional topics that health and physical education teachers would have to cover in their classes to follow the Safe Dates Curriculum. In response to this concern, the curriculum was developed by keeping North Carolina state-mandated topics for health education in mind. When the curriculum was final, we could point out to the teachers the state-mandated topics that were covered by each Safe Dates activity (conflict management skills, relationship skills). This was actually helpful to the teachers because lesson plans for many state-mandated topics were already prepared for them. New topics were introduced by the curriculum, but fewer were introduced because the curriculum was guided by state-mandated topics. The schools were also concerned about parental reactions to the curriculum. Therefore, we formed a teacher-parent advisory committee headed by the school's director of health and physical education to review drafts of the curriculum.

We used several strategies to maintain school and community support. We met frequently and in person with community and school colleagues. We involved known and trusted members of the community (e.g., retired schoolteachers) in answering questions from parents about the project. We encouraged school principals to include on the questionnaire questions of interest to them for making school policy. We worked with schools to help them obtain resources for addressing other health problems of concern to them. The intervention activities were developed to accommodate variations in school practices, and the schools were given many choices in the logistics of delivering the program in individual schools.

Much effort went into the community component of the Safe Dates project. The primary purpose of the community component was to enhance services for preventing and dealing with adolescent dating violence. As indicated above, however, the program was not effective in promoting help seeking by victims or perpetrators. In addition to the self-report questionnaires completed by adolescents, we measured help seeking by adolescents by collecting monthly reports on the number of teens who talked with school counselors about dating violence, who called the crisis line, and who participated in the social support groups. The number of adolescents using these services was so small that, after a year, we stopped collecting these data. Adolescents who seek help for dating violence typically seek it from friends or family members; therefore, interventions targeted at improving help giving by friends and family members hold promise.

Several strategies were used to encourage continuation of program activities after the study was over. The primary strategy was to train community, rather than university, staff to conduct program activities. For example, initially the service provider training was conducted by a Safe Dates staff person. Staff from Harbor, Inc. participated in these workshops. Eventually, the Safe Dates staff person stopped conducting the training, and the training was conducted solely by Harbor, Inc. staff. The play script was given to a high school theater teacher, and she set the play for her students. Schoolteachers were trained to deliver the Safe Dates Curriculum. Training of the schoolteachers was conducted by Safe Dates staff and the director of health education at the Johnston County Health Department. Safe Dates activities have continued after the conclusion of the study.

In conclusion, dating violence among adolescents is prevalent, and consequences of involvement in dating violence are severe. It is encouraging that the Safe Dates program shows promise for the prevention of adolescent dating abuse.

Epilogue

In October 1996, a follow-up study, the Safe Dates Long-Term Effects Study, was funded by the Centers for Disease Control and Prevention. Two-year follow-up data will be collected from the same cohort of adolescents involved in the original study. After the 2-year follow-up data are collected, a random half of the original treatment group adolescents will receive a booster intervention involving a mail-home newsletter and a telephone call from a health educator. Three-year follow-up data and 4-year follow-up data will be collected. The purpose of that study is to determine whether the positive effects of the Safe Dates program last over time.

References

Ball, M. (1977). Issues of violence in family casework. *Social Casework, 58,* 3-12.

Bass, D., & Price, J. (1979). Agency response to abused women. *Social Casework, 10,* 338-342.

Bergman, L. (1992). Dating violence among high school students. *Social Work, 37,* 21-27.

Biden, J. (1993). Violence against women: The congressional response. *American Psychologist, 48,* 1059-1061.

Borkowski, M., Murch, M., & Walker, V. (1983). *Marital violence: The community response.* London: Tavistock.

Burt, M. (1980). Cultural myths and support for rape. *Journal of Personality and Social Psychology, 38,* 217-230.

Check, J., & Malamuth, N. M. (1983). Sex role stereotyping and reactions to depictions of stranger versus acquaintance rape. *Journal of Personality and Social Psychology, 45,* 344-356.

Deal, J. E., & Wampler, K. (1986). Dating violence: The primacy of previous experience. *Journal of Social and Personal Relationships, 3,* 457-471.

Dobash, R. E., & Dobash, R. P. (1979). *Violence against wives: A case against the patriarchy.* New York: Free Press.

Finn, J. (1986). The relationship between sex role attitudes and attitudes supporting marital violence. *Sex Roles, 14,* 235-244.

Foshee, V., Bauman, K., Arriaga, X., Helms, R., Koch, G., & Linder, G. F. (1998). An evaluation of Safe Dates, an adolescent dating violence prevention program. *American Journal of Public Health, 88*(1), 45-50.

Foshee, V., Linder, G. F., Bauman, K., Langwick, S., Arriaga, X., Heath, J., McMahon, P., & Bangdiwala, S. (1996). The Safe Dates project: Theoretical basis, evaluation design, and selected baseline findings. *American Journal of Preventive Medicine, 12,* 39-47.

Foshee, V. A. (1996). Gender differences in adolescent dating abuse prevalence, types, and injuries. *Health Education Research, 11,* 275-286.

Galambos, N. L., Petersen, A. C., Richards, M., & Gitelson, I. B. (1985). The Attitudes Toward Women Scale for Adolescents (AWSA): A study of reliability and validity. *Sex Roles, 13,* 343-354.

Gesler, W. M., & Ricketts, T. C. (1992). *Health in rural North America.* New Brunswick, NJ: Rutgers University Press.

Hamilton, B., & Coats, J. (1993). Perceived helpfulness and use of professional services by abused women. *Journal of Family Violence, 8,* 313-324.

Henton, J., Cate, R., Koval, J., Lloyd, S., & Christopher, S. (1983). Romance and violence in dating relationships. *Journal of Family Issues, 4,* 467-482.

Koval, J. (1989). Violence in dating relationships. *Journal of Pediatric Health Care, 3,* 298-304.

Kurz, D. (1987). Emergency department responses to battered women: Resistance to medicalization. *Social Problems, 34,* 69-80.

Levy, B. (1991). *Dating violence: Young women in danger.* Seattle, WA: Seal.

Lloyd, S. (1987). Conflict in premarital relationships: Differential perceptions of males and females. *Family Relations, 36,* 290-294.

Lloyd, S., Koval, J., & Cate, R. (1989). Conflict and violence in dating relationships. In M. Pirog-Good & J. Stets (Eds.), *Violence in dating relationships: Emerging social issues* (pp. 126-142). New York: Praeger.

O'Keeffe, N. K., Brockopp, K., & Chew, E. (1986). Teen dating violence. *Social Work, 31,* 465-468.

Plass, M. S., & Gessner, J. C. (1983). Violence in courtship relations: A southern sample. *Free Inquiry in Creative Sociology, 11,* 198-202.

Roscoe, B., & Benaske, N. (1985). Courtship violence experienced by abused wives: Similarities in patterns of abuse. *Family Relations, 34,* 419-424.

Roscoe, B., & Callahan, J. (1985). Adolescents' self-report of violence in families and dating relations. *Adolescence, 20,* 545-553.

Slaby, R. G., & Guerra, N. G. (1988). Cognitive mediators of aggression in adolescent offenders: 1. Assessment. *Developmental Psychology, 24,* 580-588.

Smith, J. P., & Williams, J. G. (1992). From abusive household to dating violence. *Journal of Family Violence, 7,* 153-165.

Stets, J., & Pirog-Good, M. (1987). Violence in dating relationships. *Social Psychology Quarterly, 50,* 237-246.

Walter, J. D. (1981). Police in the middle: A study of small city police intervention in domestic disputes. *Journal of Police Science Administration, 9,* 243-263.

Washburn, C., Frieze, I., & Knoble, J. (1979). *Some subtle biases of therapists toward women and violence* (Part of final report of Grant No.1 RO1 MH30193 to the National Institutes of Mental Health). Bethesda, MD: National Institutes of Mental Health.

Weinstein, N. (1988). Effects of personal experience on self-protective behavior. *Psychological Bulletin, 105,* 31-50.

PART II

HEALTH AND WORK

6

Life Contexts and Outcomes of Treated and Untreated Alcoholics

CHRISTINE TIMKO

R elatively little is known about ongoing processes of treatment selection and treatment outcomes among problem drinking individuals. This chapter begins with an overview of the problem of alcoholism and its links with conditions in the community. It then presents results from a longitudinal study of problem drinkers who were initially untreated. Collaborators on this study are John Finney, Rudolf Moos, and Keith Humphreys. The project is examining drinking and life context factors as predictors of treatment entry, treatment selection, and treatment outcomes. The chapter concludes by discussing possible roles of self-help and other community agencies in preventing and treating problem drinking.

AUTHOR'S NOTE: Preparation of this chapter was supported by NIAAA Grants AA02863 and AA06699, by the Department of Veterans Affairs Mental Health and Strategic Health Group, and by VA Health Services Research and Development Service funds. I thank Molly Kaplowitz for conducting data analyses and literature searches.

The Problem of Alcoholism

In a given year, about 18 million American adults experience problems resulting from alcohol use disorders. According to the Institute of
Medicine (IOM, 1990), alcohol problems, subsuming alcohol abuse and
alcohol dependence disorders, are ideally assessed in terms of three
domains: (a) the individual's use of alcohol (level, pattern, and history
of use), (b) signs and symptoms of alcohol use (tolerance to alcohol,
withdrawal symptoms when not using alcohol), and (c) consequences
of alcohol use (e.g., having medical, psychiatric, family, employment,
legal, and financial problems). Problem drinkers are very heterogeneous with respect to their status on these domains. For example,
more alcohol consumption is not necessarily related to more symptoms
and consequences of use. Problem drinkers are also heterogeneous with
respect to the etiology and course of their disorders (Schuckit, 1995).

The personal costs of alcohol abuse are substantial (cf. Moos, Finney,
& Cronkite, 1990). Alcohol abuse is associated with social problems
such as divorce, child abuse, and loss of employment; psychiatric
problems; neuropsychological deficits; medical complications of virtu-
ally all organ systems; and premature death. Societal costs of alcohol
problems are also substantial. For example, alcohol plays a role in 10%
of all deaths in the United States. A major societal response to the
growing awareness of alcohol abuse and its costs has been to expand
specialized alcoholism treatment services. Annually, more than 1 million people enter treatment for alcoholism, and the cost of alcoholism-
related health care services is more than $15 billion.

Community conditions that are associated with problem drinking
include reduced workplace performance and productivity, higher rates
of injury, and more criminal behavior (Weisner & Schmidt, 1995).
Workplace consequences of alcohol use include increased absenteeism
and impaired performance on the job (French, Zarkin, Hartwell, & Bray,
1995; Marmot, North, Feeney, & Head, 1993). Moreover, alcohol consumption and coming to work hungover have been shown to be related
to the overall number of work problems experienced by workers, as well
as to specific problems such as falling asleep on the job and conflicts
with supervisors (Ames, Grube, & Moore, 1997). Drinking also results
in more injury-related absences and injuries at work (Webb et al., 1994),
as well as more injuries sustained from falls and motor vehicle acci-
dents. Among patients presenting at a trauma center with injuries, prior

consumption of alcohol was highly associated with greater injury severity (Spaite et al., 1995).

Higher rates were found among alcoholic than nonalcoholic individuals for all types of criminal behavior, but especially for property and violent crimes; these results were independent of sociodemographic factors (Modestin, Berger, & Ammann, 1996). Similar to adults, teenagers who misused alcohol had higher rates of property and violent offenses than teenagers who did not misuse alcohol (Fergusson, Lynskey, & Horwood, 1996). Non-problem drinkers residing on college campuses housing large numbers of heavily drinking students more often were hit or assaulted, had their personal property damaged, and received unwanted sexual advances than non-problem drinkers on campuses with fewer heavily drinking students (Wechsler, Moeykens, Davenport, Castillo, & Hansen, 1995).

In addition to work and safety issues, problem drinking is associated with homelessness, a major concern within several communities. Alcohol abuse is more prevalent among homeless persons than in the general population (Heffron, Skipper, & Lambert, 1997; Segal, 1991), and homeless alcoholics have reported more severe and chronic disorders than have alcoholics with fixed residences (Castaneda, Lifshutz, Galanter, & Franco, 1993; Koegel & Burnam, 1988; Mavis, Humphreys, & Stoffelmayr, 1993).

A Longitudinal Study of Untreated Problem Drinkers

This chapter describes a longitudinal study of a sample of problem drinkers who, at the start of the project, had never received formal treatment for their alcohol problems. Only a few studies have followed untreated alcoholics to examine treatment selection processes and outcomes related to drinking and general functioning. Most studies of problem drinking have focused on treated individuals despite the fact that most people with drinking problems do not enter formal treatment (cf. Narrow, Regier, Rae, Manderscheid, & Locke, 1993; Sobell, Sobell, & Toneatto, 1992). We undertook the project to examine four main issues.

Study Issues

First, we used a stress and coping model to determine the factors that explain entering treatment for a drinking problem. Potential explanatory factors included severity of the drinking problem, the individual's general functioning (e.g., symptoms of depression), and chronic life stressors and stable social resources (the extent to which individuals experienced conflict with or felt supported by their spouses, friends, and coworkers).

Second, we examined what kind of treatment, if any, individuals selected. Why do some individuals go to formal alcoholism treatment programs, whereas others choose the self-help approach of Alcoholics Anonymous (AA)? Why do some enter inpatient or residential treatment programs, whereas others opt for outpatient treatment?

Third, we wanted to know whether individuals who received help for their drinking problems did better over time than individuals who remained untreated. This is the fundamental issue: whether or not treatment or AA "works." Specifically, is getting involved in AA more effective than not receiving any intervention? In assessing effectiveness, we examined several outcomes, including indexes of drinking-related behavior, general functioning, life stressors, and social resources.

Finally, we hoped to find out how different types of treatment were related to different outcomes. Put simply, this question concerns whether inpatient treatment, outpatient treatment, or AA is most effective when participants select the type of help they receive. We also examined whether amount of treatment or AA involvement was related to drinking, functioning, and stressor/resource outcomes. We were interested in whether more treatment results in better outcomes.

Sample

We collected baseline data from 631 individuals who had not received any prior inpatient or outpatient treatment for their problem drinking. These individuals contacted one of four alcohol information and referral centers (I&R) or one of three detoxification (detox) centers in the San Francisco Bay Area. One year later, we followed 515 of these individuals (82% of participants who were known not to have died). At 3 years, we followed 468 individuals who had completed the baseline assessment (77% of those who were known not to have died). At an 8-year follow-up, data were collected from 466 baseline participants (80% of individuals known not to have died during that period).

The initial data collection process varied, depending on whether a prospective participant was contacted at an I&R center or entered a detox program. At each I&R center, a staff member or volunteer approached individuals who were seeking help for drinking problems and had not had prior treatment, and briefly described the research project to them. If individuals were willing to be contacted by a member of the research group to be told more about the study, their names and telephone numbers were given to a project assistant who called them to describe the study. The baseline inventory was mailed to all individuals who agreed to participate. If the completed material was not received within 2 weeks, the person was called and encouraged to complete the inventory and to return it promptly. At each detox center, a staff member approached eligible clients when they were sufficiently detoxified to provide informed consent. At that time, the staff member explained the study and, if consent was obtained, administered the inventory on-site.

At baseline, the sample was almost evenly split between women (47%) and men (53%). Most participants were White (81%), were unmarried (79%), and reported some religious affiliation (76%). On average, participants were 35 years old and had 13 years of education, or 1 year of college.

One, 3, and 8 years after entering the study, participants were contacted by telephone when possible and then were mailed an inventory that was almost identical in content to the initial inventory. Participants did not receive any compensation for taking part in the study.

Measures of Drinking Patterns and Problems

At baseline and at follow-ups, participants were asked how much wine, beer, and hard liquor they usually drank on the days that they had consumed each type of alcoholic beverage during the past month. Responses were coded as ounces of ethanol and summed to obtain the average amount of ethanol consumed on drinking days (3 items; M [baseline] = 13.1; SD = 11.2). Participants also noted the extent to which they thought their drinking was a significant problem (1 = *no problem,* 5 = *serious problem; M* = 4.2; SD = 1.0), the number of days they were drunk or intoxicated during the past month (M = 13.7; SD = 10.8), and the extent to which they drank heavily during the past month (1 = *did not drink at all,* 4 = *fairly heavy drinking,* 6 = *occasional drinking binges;* M = 4.1; SD = 1.4). In addition, respondents indicated whether or not they had abstained from alcohol during the past 6 months (97.7% responded *no*).

An index of *problems arising from drinking* (e.g., health, job, money, family arguments) was taken from the Health and Daily Living (HDL) Form of Moos, Cronkite, and Finney (1990). Higher scores represented more drinking-related problems (9 items; M = 10.8; SD = 7.2; range = 0-36; Cronbach's alpha [baseline] = .80). Additionally, participants were categorized as having either no drinking-related problems or at least one such problem (94.6% had at least one problem).

Items from the Alcohol Dependence Scale that were identified by Skinner and Allen (1982) as focusing on withdrawal symptoms (e.g., had "shakes" when sobering up; had blackouts; had a craving for a drink the first thing after waking up) were used to assess *symptoms of alcohol dependence.* Higher scores represented more symptoms of alcohol dependence (11 items; M = 11.4; SD = 8.7; range = 0-44; alpha = .88). Items composing the *confidence in resisting alcohol* (alpha = .97) index were drawn from the Situational Confidence Questionnaire (Annis & Graham, 1988). Confidence was assessed in regard to four types of situations: (a) those involving negative emotions (8 items), (b) interpersonal conflict (9 items), (c) positive emotions (2 items), and (d) those testing one's self-control (one item). Scores could range from 0 (*not at all confident*) to 100 (*very confident*); M = 62.4; SD = 26.8.

Functioning Measures

Functioning was assessed in three areas. *Depression* was measured by using the HDL's measure of depressed mood, which was derived from Spitzer, Endicott, and Robins's (1978) Research Diagnostic Criteria. Higher scores represented more depressed mood (9 items, e.g., feeling sad or blue; feeling guilty, worthless, or down; thoughts about death or suicide; M = 21.4; SD = 8.8; range = 0-36; alpha = .92). Participants also completed Rosenberg's (1965) Self-Esteem Scale, on which higher scores represented more self-esteem (10 items, e.g., I feel that I have a number of good qualities; I am able to do things as well as most other people; $M = 16.4$; $SD = 5.8$; range = 0-30; alpha = .85). Last, participants were asked whether or not they were *employed* (40.4% were employed) and their *annual income* ($M = \$12,225$, $SD = \$11,664$).

Stressors and Resources

An adapted version of the Life Stressors and Social Resources Inventory (Moos & Moos, 1994) was used to assess chronic stressors and social resources; items were rated on a 5-point scale (0 = *never*, 4 = *often*). Chronic stressors were measured in the domains of work (sum of 6 items, e.g., supervisor criticizes minor things; have conflicts with coworkers; $M = 4.4$; $SD = 5.7$; alpha = .67), spouse/partner (5 items, e.g., spouse disagrees on important issues; $M = 6.2$; $SD = 5.8$; alpha = .81), relatives (3 items, e.g., relatives get on your nerves; $M = 5.3$; $SD = 3.2$; alpha = .79), and friends (4 items, e.g., friends disagree with you; $M = 5.8$; $SD = 2.7$; alpha = .73). *Negative events* was the count of 38 events (e.g., home burglarized, miscarriage) that the respondent had experienced in the past year ($M = 5.0$; $SD = 3.0$). Social resources were also measured in the domains of work (7 items, e.g., coworkers are friends with you; supervisor stands up for you; $M = 8.9$; $SD = 10.5$; alpha = .64), spouse/partner (10 items, e.g., count on spouse to help you; $M = 17.5$; $SD = 15.1$; alpha = .91), relatives (3 items, e.g., relatives respect your opinion; $M = 6.8$; $SD = 3.4$; alpha = .78), and friends (6 items, e.g., get along with friends; $M = 18.3$; $SD = 4.4$; alpha = .88).

Explaining Treatment Entry

One component of the longitudinal study consisted of applying a stress and coping model to determine the factors that explain entering treatment for a drinking problem. Specifically, it examined baseline factors that predicted participants getting help—either formal inpatient or outpatient treatment or AA—by the 1-year follow-up (see Finney & Moos, 1995, for a full report of this component). In the conceptual model on which this analysis was based, entering treatment was seen as a response enacted after other resources and responses had failed to alleviate a stressful situation. Specifically, the model hypothesized that treatment entry is prompted by the experience of hardship as a result of severe drinking and poor psychological functioning and by the accumulation of stressors. *Stressors* were defined as challenging life circumstances that, in contrast with hardship because of drinking, may or may not have been the result of an individual's drinking behavior; that is, they may occur independently of drinking behavior. In the model, both acute stressful life events and chronic strains were seen as factors precipitating an individual's contact with alcoholism treatment programs.

Prior studies found that, compared with individuals who did not seek treatment for their alcohol problems, individuals who entered treatment were likely to have more frequent and heavier alcohol consumption, more dependence symptoms, and more alcohol-related problems (e.g., work, legal, family, social); they were more likely to have comorbid depressive disorders, to be unemployed and have lower incomes, and to experience life stressors (Dawson, 1996; George & Tucker, 1996; Grant, 1996; Weisner, 1993). In addition, previous studies have found that, of the variables predicting hardship from drinking, the most powerful predictor of seeking help was the number of life areas negatively affected by drinking (Bannenberg, Raat, & Plomp, 1992; Pfeiffer, Feuerlein, & Brenk-Schulte, 1991). Consistent with these results, Helzer and Pryzbeck (1988) found that the presence of psychiatric diagnoses increased the likelihood of alcoholics seeking treatment. Findings of a relationship between hardship in various life areas and treatment entry are consistent with the beliefs of many treatment providers that alcoholic individuals seek treatment because of problems with one or more of the "four L's": liver, lover, livelihood, or the law (Weisner, 1986).

In addition to stressors, the conceptual model posits that *facilitative factors,* such as the individual's prior experience in seeking help from nonformal sources and/or being seen at a detox center where treatment is available on-site, should also increase the likelihood of treatment entry. In this view, prior experience in obtaining help, even if the intervention was unsuccessful, indicates a predisposition to seek help. On-site treatment involves shorter waiting periods for services, which are associated with greater referral success (Rees, Beech, & Hore, 1984).

Results of this project were that, once they had contacted an I&R or detox center, 76% of participants entered at least one form of help by the 1-year follow-up. Of individuals who sought help, 84% entered treatment or AA within 2 months of contacting the center.

Of the factors involving baseline drinking, functioning, and stressor/resource measures, individuals' perceived severity of their drinking problems played a central role in the treatment entry process. Participants were more likely to enter treatment if they perceived their drink-ing problems as more severe (mean of group that entered treatment = 4.32, mean of no-treatment group = 3.69, t = 5.86, p < .001; point-biserial correlation between perceived severity and treatment entry = .28, p < .001). As shown by additional t-test and correlational analyses (all ps < .05), other factors positively associated with treatment entry involved the other drinking, functioning, and stressor variables: having more alcohol-dependence symptoms, experiencing more adverse conse-quences as a result of drinking, having poorer psychological functioning (more symptoms of depression and lower self-esteem), experiencing more negative life events in the past year, and experiencing more chronic life stressors. Facilitative factors also related positively to treatment entry, in that people who had sought help for their drinking problems pre-viously or who were recruited into the study at a detox center that had treatment services on-site were more likely to enter treatment.

Perceived severity of the drinking problem, however, appeared to explain the connections between these other factors and help seeking. It was the most powerful predictor of treatment entry overall and was associated with the other predictor variables. Moreover, when perceived severity of the drinking problem was controlled in analyses, none of the other predictors that had a significant bivariate relationship with treat-ment entry continued to do so. Thus, poorer psychological functioning and more life stressors may facilitate help seeking by increasing peo-ple's perceptions of the severity of their drinking problems (Bardsley & Beckman, 1988).

Treatment Selection at 1 Year

Another component of our project examined the kinds of treatments, if any, individuals selected and why they selected AA or formal out-patient or inpatient treatment. It studied the proportions of previously untreated problem drinkers who received different types of help and exam-ined baseline sociodemographic characteristics, drinking patterns, and functioning of individuals who entered different types of treatments, comparing them with those who remained untreated (Timko, Finney, Moos, & Moos, 1995; Timko, Finney, Moos, Moos, & Steinbaum, 1993; Timko, Moos, Finney, & Moos, 1994).

Table 6.1
Types and Amounts of Treatment
at 1 Year for Three Treatment Groups

Treatment Group	Type of Treatment								
	Inpatient			*Outpatient*			*AA*		
	n	*%*	*M(SD)*	*n*	*%*	*M(SD)*	*n*	*%*	*M(SD)*
AA-Only (*n* = 95)									
No. of weeks							95	100	25.0(20.8)
No. of sessions							95	100	47.5(42.4)
Avg. no. of									
sessions/week							95	100	2.3(1.8)
Outpatient (*n* = 131)									
No. of weeks				131	100	24.5(25.0)	86	65.6	25.7(22.7)
No. of sessions				131	100	24.3(24.8)	86	65.6	49.2(43.1)
Avg. no. of									
sessions/week				131	100	1.2(0.9)	86	65.6	2.2(1.8)
Inpatient (*n* = 166)									
No. of weeks	166	100	12.7(13.1)	65	39.2	21.9(18.8)	113	68.1	34.4(20.0)
No. of sessions	166	100	— —	65	39.2	31.2(33.1)	113	68.1	72.7(36.0)
Avg. no. of									
sessions/week	166	100	— —	65	39.2	1.6(1.5)	113	68.1	2.5(1.4)

Treatment Selection. Participants' reports of alcoholism treatment at the 1-year follow-up placed them into one of four groups:

- *No-treatment group.* Fully 123 participants (24%) had not entered treatment for their drinking problems.
- *AA-only group.* A total of 95 individuals (18%) entered only AA or another self-help group for individuals with alcohol problems (see Table 6.1).
- *Outpatient group.* A total of 131 participants (25%) received outpatient treatment for their drinking problems (from a physician, psychiatrist, psychologist, counselor, outpatient treatment program, or clergy member). Of these, 86 also participated in AA.
- *Inpatient group.* Fully 166 participants (32%) received hospital inpatient or residential treatment (including halfway house or group home). Of these, 65 also received outpatient treatment, and 113 participated in AA.

In total, 57% of study participants attended AA, making AA the most commonly selected form of help. This is consistent with the finding in national surveys of alcoholic individuals (e.g., Room, 1989) that AA is the most common help modality for alcoholism among adults.

Treatment Amounts. Table 6.1 shows how much treatment individuals in each of the three helped groups received. On average, members of the AA-only group participated in AA for 25 weeks, for a total of almost 48 sessions, or about 2 meetings per week. (Because of rounding, the number of sessions per week is not precisely the quotient of number of sessions divided by the number of weeks.) Of the 131 individuals who had outpatient treatment, the treatment lasted an average of 24.5 weeks, for a total of 24 sessions, or about 1 session per week. Among outpatients who also attended AA, self-help participation lasted an average of 26 weeks and encompassed 49 meetings, or about 2 meetings per week.

Individuals in the inpatient/residential treatment group had an average of 13 weeks of treatment. Inpatients who also had outpatient treatment averaged 22 weeks of outpatient care and 31 sessions, or 1.6 sessions per week. Inpatients who also participated in AA did so on average for about 34 weeks and 73 meetings, or more than 2 meetings per week.

Predictors of Treatment Selection. We examined the baseline characteristics that predicted the type of help participants selected. The four groups—untreated, AA-only, outpatient, and inpatient—were compared on indexes of baseline sociodemographic characteristics, drinking, functioning, stressors, and resources. Specifically, chi-square tests and one-way analyses of variance (ANOVAs) were used to compare the four groups on sociodemographic variables. To compare the four groups on baseline drinking, functioning, and stressor/resource variables, we conducted analyses of covariance (ANCOVAs) that controlled for respondents' gender and marital status. Gender and marital status were controlled because they have been found in a number of studies to be related to treatment entry, selection, or outcome (cf. Timko et al., 1994). When the ANCOVAs found significant effects for group, Student-Newman-Keuls tests were used to compare group means.

The analyses of sociodemographic variables showed that, compared with men, women were somewhat more likely to enter each type of treatment. Non-White problem drinkers were less likely than White problem drinkers to enter AA-only or outpatient treatment but were more likely to be inpatients ($p < .05$). Marital status, religious affiliation, and age were unrelated to mode of treatment.

Table 6.2
Baseline Drinking Patterns and Functioning
of Four Help Status Groups (N = 515)

	1-Year Treatment Groups			
	No-Treatment	*AA-Only*	*Outpatient*	*Inpatient*
Baseline Drinking Indexes				
Perceived severity of				
drinking problem	3.7[a]	4.3[b]	4.1[b]	4.5[c]
Alcohol consumption	11.4[a]	12.1[a]	10.3[a]	16.1[b]
Days intoxicated	12.1[a]	12.8[a]	10.9[a]	15.7[b]
Heavy drinking pattern				
in past month	4.0[ab]	4.1[ab]	3.8[a]	4.3[b]
Drinking-related problems	9.1[a]	10.4[a]	8.5[a]	12.8[b]
Alcohol dependence	9.3[a]	11.3[a]	9.0[a]	13.5[b]
Confidence in resisting alcohol	67.1[a]	66.7[a]	68.9[a]	55.9[b]
Baseline Functioning Indexes				
Depression	18.9[a]	19.8[a]	19.8[a]	24.7[b]
Self-esteem	18.2[a]	17.0[a]	17.4[a]	14.2[b]
% Employed	45.5[a]	41.1[a]	61.1[b]	27.7[c]
Annual income				
(in thousands of dollars)	13.0[a]	12.7[ab]	16.5[b]	9.4[a]

NOTE: Means that do not share a superscript differ significantly. Analyses control for gender and marital status.

On the drinking indexes, we found that individuals who selected inpatient treatment had the most severe drinking problems at baseline (Table 6.2). They had the highest alcohol consumption (ounces of ethanol in a typical drinking day), number of days intoxicated in the past month, drinking-related problems (health, job, money, family problems because of drinking), and symptoms of alcohol dependence, and they had the least confidence in resisting alcohol. The AA-only and outpatient groups perceived their drinking problems as more severe at baseline than did the no-treatment group but did not differ on the other drinking indexes.

Individuals who entered inpatient treatment were also worse off on the functioning indexes at baseline (Table 6.2). They had more symptoms of depression, lower self-esteem, and the lowest employment rate. Individuals who selected outpatient treatment were the most likely to be employed and had the highest annual income of the groups. Not shown in the table, outpatients also were employed in jobs with higher occupational status and had the most education.

On chronic stressors and resources, few differences were found among the four groups at baseline. Those who chose inpatient treatment had significantly more negative events in the prior year and fewer friendship resources.

To summarize, individuals with more serious drinking problems, poorer functioning, and fewer financial resources more frequently sought help in inpatient or residential programs, whereas individuals with more education and higher income and occupational status were more likely to obtain outpatient treatment. These results are consistent with previous findings that alcoholic individuals with better psychosocial functioning tend to enter outpatient treatment and that those with poorer functioning tend to enter inpatient treatment (Bannenberg et al., 1992; Kern, Schmelter, & Fanelli, 1978). AA-only participants had less education and lower income and occupational status than outpatients but better drinking and functional status than inpatients. Or, put another way, individuals who sought AA as their only treatment shared the low socioeconomic status of inpatients and the overall higher functioning of outpatients.

Treatment Outcomes at 1 Year

We examined whether individuals who received help for their drinking problems did better at the 1-year follow-up than individuals who remained untreated. We also compared outcomes across the different types of treatment—AA-only, outpatient, and inpatient. Finally, we examined whether the amount of treatment or AA involvement was related to outcomes.

Change During 1 Year Among Treated and Untreated Individuals.
Paired *t* tests were used to examine each group's change from baseline to 1 year on each outcome. All four groups improved substantially on the drinking indexes during the year. Specifically, on average, all four groups viewed their drinking problems as less severe; consumed less alcohol in a typical drinking day; spent fewer days intoxicated in the previous month; drank more lightly in the past month; had higher abstinence rates for the past 6 months; and had fewer drinking-related

problems, fewer symptoms of alcohol dependence, and more confidence in their ability to resist drinking. All four groups also improved on the functioning indexes over the year. They had fewer symptoms of depression, higher self-esteem, better employment rates, and higher income levels (all $ps < .05$). On the whole, the four groups showed little improvement on the stressor and resource indexes during the year.

Whereas the helped groups might have been expected to improve over time, the improvement of the untreated group needs more explanation. The improvement of untreated alcoholics is often referred to as "spontaneous recovery." It is more likely among people whose alcoholism is less severe and chronic, which was characteristic of the sample in this study, given that participants had never sought help before. In addition, these untreated individuals had made contact with an alcoholism referral or detox service, and this initiative may have reflected a recognition of their drinking problems and some motivation to change. We return to the topic of spontaneous or natural recovery toward the end of the chapter.

Type of Help Related to Outcomes. Our next question was whether the amount of improvement among participants differed according to type of help received. Using ANCOVAs, we compared the four groups on the 1-year outcomes, controlling for the baseline value of the outcome being considered, as well as participants' gender and marital status. Results are shown in Table 6.3.

Focusing on whether the formally treated groups did better than the untreated group, we found that individuals who entered outpatient and/or inpatient treatment were superior to untreated individuals on drinking outcomes; that is, they consumed less alcohol, were less likely to drink heavily and were intoxicated for fewer days in the past month, and were more likely to have been abstinent during the past 6 months. Regarding how AA-only compared with no-treatment, at 1 year we found that AA-only participants were superior to untreated individuals in terms of spending fewer days intoxicated, having a lighter drinking pattern, and being abstinent.

Concentrating on formal inpatient or outpatient treatment in comparison with AA-only, the only difference was that individuals receiving inpatient or residential treatment were more likely to be abstinent than AA-only group members; nonetheless, inpatients continued to perceive their drinking problems as more severe than AA-only members. Other-

Table 6.3
Drinking Patterns and Problems
Four Help Status Groups at One Year (N = 515)

1-Year	*1-Year Treatment Groups*			
Drinking Index	*No-Treatment*	*AA-Only*	*Outpatient*	*Inpatient*
Perceived severity of drinking problem	3.1[a]	3.4[a]	3.4[a]	4.1[b]
Alcohol consumption	6.7[a]	4.7[ab]	3.6[b]	3.9[b]
Days intoxicated	5.1[a]	2.5[b]	2.4[b]	3.0[b]
Heavy drinking pattern in past month	2.8[a]	2.2[b]	2.0[b]	1.8[b]
Percentage abstinent for past 6 months	16.3[a]	41.0[b]	29.0[b]	52.0[c]
Drinking-related problems	4.3[a]	3.3[a]	3.2[a]	4.2[a]
Percentage with no drinking problems	38.2[a]	52.6[ab]	48.1[ab]	61.6[b]
Alcohol dependence	4.1[a]	3.3[a]	3.3[a]	4.5[a]
Confidence in resisting alcohol	73.9[a]	82.0[a]	79.6[a]	79.2[a]

NOTE: Means that do not share a superscript differ significantly. Analyses control for gender, marital status, and the baseline value of the outcome under consideration.

wise, AA was comparable with formal inpatient or outpatient treatment. Finally, comparisons of inpatients and outpatients found that, again, inpatients were more likely to be abstinent but nevertheless perceived their problems to be more severe. In contrast with results for the drinking indexes, we did not find any substantive differences among the four groups on the outcomes concerning employment, other functioning, stressors, or resources at the 1-year follow-up.

Amount of Treatment Related to Outcomes. Our final question at the 1-year follow-up was whether the amount of involvement in AA or the amount of formal treatment that individuals received was related to how much they improved. Regarding formal treatment, Miller and Hester (1986) and Mattick and Jarvis (1994) reviewed several randomized experimental studies comparing different lengths of inpatient or residential treatment for alcohol abuse. The consistent finding was no difference in outcome. In contrast, many naturalistic studies have found that patients who receive longer treatment for drinking problems tend to improve more, particularly in the areas of drinking, psychological functioning, and employment, than do patients with shorter treatment durations (McLellan, Luborsky, O'Brien, Woody, & Druley, 1982; Moos, Finney, & Cronkite, 1990; Welte, Hynes, Sokolow, & Lyons, 1981). To address this issue, we conducted multiple regression analyses to predict drinking outcomes at the 1-year follow-up from indicators of amount of participation, controlling for the baseline value of the outcome criterion being predicted and gender and marital status.

The first set of regressions was conducted on the AA-only group by using number of AA meetings attended since baseline as the indicator of AA involvement. Attending more AA meetings was associated with lighter drinking in the month prior to follow-up, being abstinent for the past 6 months, and having no drinking-related problems.

The second set of analyses was conducted on the outpatient group. Attending more outpatient sessions was a significant predictor of lighter drinking in the previous month and being abstinent for the past 6 months. For the outpatient group, attending more AA meetings was also associated with lighter drinking and abstinence.

The third set of analyses was conducted on the inpatient group. Being in inpatient or residential treatment longer was associated with lighter drinking in the past month, being abstinent for the past 6 months, having fewer drinking-related problems, having no drinking-related problems, and having fewer symptoms of alcohol dependence. More involvement in outpatient treatment was also associated with better drinking outcomes in this group, as was attending more AA meetings.

Summary of 1-Year Follow-Up. In general, individuals who entered AA or formal treatment within the first year of contacting an alcoholism service did so quickly and tended to be heavily involved in those interventions. At the 1-year follow-up, individuals who obtained help had improved since baseline on drinking and functioning outcomes. Although individuals who did not receive any intervention also improved, those who received help improved more, particularly on drinking-related outcomes.

Next, we examined treatment careers over a 3-year period for this sample of initially untreated problem-drinking individuals.

Table 6.4
Types and Amounts of Treatment at 3 Years
for Three Treatment Groups

				Type of Treatment					
		Inpatient			*Outpatient*			*AA*	
Treatment Group	*n*	*%*	*M(SD)*	*n*	*%*	*M(SD)*	*n*	*%*	*M(SD)*
AA-Only (*n* = 72)									
No. of weeks							72	100	56.9(63.6)
No. of sessions							72	100	155.7(225.5)
Avg. no. of sessions/week							72	100	2.7(2.5)
Outpatient (*n* = 126)									
No. of weeks				126	100	37.4(45.4)	91	72.2	40.2(47.0)
No. of sessions				126	100	41.4(54.9)	91	72.2	43.6(56.3)
Avg. no. of sessions/week				126	100	1.3(1.1)	91	72.2	1.4(1.1)
Inpatient (*n* = 189)									
No. of weeks	189	100	16.1(19.4)	96	51.0	41.4(50.3)	146	77.2	67.1(55.0)
No. of sessions	189	100	— —	96	51.0	57.5(69.5)	146	77.2	219.7(249.3)
Avg. no. of sessions/week	189	100	— —	96	51.0	1.6(1.8)	146	77.2	3.3(2.7)

Treatment Selection at 3 Years

We examined the kinds of treatments, if any, individuals had selected at 3 years. At 3 years, the no-treatment group consisted of 17% of the sample (*n* = 81). The AA-only group made up 15% of the sample (*n* = 72), the outpatient group 27% (*n* = 126), and the inpatient group 40% (*n* = 189) of the sample. Of the outpatients, 91 (72%) also went to AA; of the inpatients, 96 (51%) also received outpatient treatment and 146 (77%) participated in AA.

Treatment Amounts. Table 6.4 shows how much treatment individuals in each of the three helped groups had received by the 3-year follow-up. On average, members of the AA-only group participated in AA for 57 weeks, for a total of almost 156 sessions, or nearly 3 meetings per week. Of the 126 individuals who had outpatient treatment, the treatment lasted an average of 37 weeks, for a total of 41 sessions, or about 1 session per week. Among outpatients who also attended AA, self-help participation lasted an average of 40 weeks and encompassed 44 meetings, or about 1 meeting per week. Individuals in the inpatient/residential treatment group had an average of 16 weeks of treatment. Inpatients who also had outpatient treatment averaged 41 weeks of outpatient care and 57.5 sessions, or about 1.6 sessions per week. Inpatients who also participated in AA did so, on average, for about 67 weeks and 220 meetings, or more than 3 meetings per week.

Treatment Outcomes at 3 Years

We examined whether individuals who received help for their drinking problems did better at the 3-year follow-up than individuals who remained untreated. We also compared outcomes across treatment groups (AA-only, outpatient, and inpatient) and examined whether the amount of treatment or AA involvement was related to outcomes.

Change Over 3 Years Among Treated and Untreated Individuals. Using paired *t* tests, we examined change from baseline to the 3-year follow-up on the drinking outcomes. All four groups improved substantially on the drinking indexes during the 3 years. Specifically, on average, all four groups saw their drinking problems as less severe; consumed less alcohol in a typical drinking day; spent fewer days intoxicated in the previous month; drank more lightly in the past month; had higher abstinence rates for the past 6 months; and had fewer drinking-related problems and fewer symptoms of alcohol dependence. The three helped groups, but not the untreated group, gained in their confidence to resist alcohol and on their employment rates. All four groups also improved on the functioning indexes of depression, self-esteem, and income during the 3 years (all $ps < .05$).

On the whole, the four groups showed less change on the stressor and resource indexes during the 3 year period. At 3 years, all four groups reported fewer spouse/partner stressors and fewer negative events. Also at 3 years, inpatients reported more spouse/partner, relative, and friend support and fewer relative and friendship stressors than they had at baseline.

Type of Help and Outcomes. We compared the four groups on the 3-year outcomes, controlling for the baseline value of the outcome being considered, gender, and marital status. Table 6.5 shows the results.

Table 6.5
Drinking Patterns and Problems of Four Help Status
Groups at 3 Years ($N = 468$)

3-Year Drinking Index	*3-Year Treatment Status Group*			
	No-Treatment	*AA-Only*	*Outpatient*	*Inpatient*
Perceived severity of drinking problem	2.4[a]	2.8[a]	3.2[ab]	3.8[b]
Alcohol consumption	5.7[a]	2.4[b]	3.5[ab]	3.7[b]
Days intoxicated	3.3[a]	1.4[a]	3.3[a]	2.4[a]
Heavy drinking pattern in past month	2.6[a]	2.0[ab]	2.2[ab]	1.8[b]
Percentage abstinent for past 6 months	16.0[a]	45.8[bc]	35.7[b]	54.5[c]
Drinking-related problems	3.8[a]	1.9[a]	2.9[a]	4.2[a]
Percentage with no drinking problems	49.4[a]	68.1[a]	50.0[a]	58.7[a]
Alcohol dependence	2.6[a]	2.0[a]	3.3[a]	4.9[a]
Confidence in resisting alcohol	73.2[a]	88.2[b]	81.2[ab]	80.3[b]

NOTE: Means that do not share a superscript differ significantly. Analyses control for gender, marital status, and the baseline value of the outcome under consideration.

Focusing on whether the formally treated groups did better than the untreated group, we found that individuals who had inpatient or residential treatment were again superior to untreated individuals on drinking outcomes, including alcohol consumption, drinking pattern, abstinence during the past 6 months, and confidence in resisting drinking; despite their positive outcomes, inpatients still perceived their drinking problems as relatively severe. At 3 years, outpatients were also more likely to be abstinent than untreated individuals. Compared with individuals who obtained no help, individuals who entered AA-only were superior at 3 years on alcohol consumption, abstinence rate, and confidence in resisting drinking.

Focusing on formal inpatient or outpatient treatment in comparison with AA-only, AA was as effective as formal treatment. Individuals receiving inpatient or residential treatment perceived their drinking problem as more severe than AA-only group members. Finally, comparisons of outpatients and inpatients found, again, that inpatients were more likely to be abstinent. In contrast with these results for the drinking indexes, as we found at 1 year, no substantive differences were found at 3 years among the four groups on the outcomes regarding employment, other functioning, stressors, or resources.

Amount of Treatment and Outcomes. Again, we examined whether the amount of involvement in AA or formal treatment was related to amount of improvement. Regression analyses conducted on the AA-only group by using number of AA meetings attended between baseline and the 3-year follow-up as the indicator of AA involvement (and controlling for the baseline value of the outcome, gender, and marital status) showed that more AA involvement was associated with less alcohol consumption, fewer days spent intoxicated, a lighter drinking pattern, more confidence in resisting drinking, and a greater likelihood of 6-month abstinence.

The second set of regressions, conducted on the outpatient group, showed that attending more outpatient sessions was *not* related to drinking outcomes. For the outpatient group, attending more AA meetings *was* associated with better drinking outcomes—specifically, less alcohol consumption, fewer days intoxicated, a lighter drinking pattern, fewer symptoms of alcohol dependence, more confidence in resisting alcohol, greater 6-month abstinence, and fewer drinking-related problems.

The third set of regressions, conducted on the inpatient group, showed that being in inpatient or residential treatment longer was associated with less alcohol consumption, lighter drinking in the past month, and being abstinent for the past 6 months. For this group, more involvement in outpatient treatment showed no relationship with drinking outcomes. But again, attending more AA meetings was associated with better drinking outcomes, including less consumption; a lighter drinking pattern; fewer days intoxicated, drinking-related problems, and dependence symptoms; more confidence in resisting drinking; and a higher abstinence rate.

Summary of 1- and 3-Year Follow-Ups. At 1 and 3 years, all four groups of problem drinkers improved on the drinking and functioning outcomes but changed less on life stressors and social resources. Also at 1 and 3 years, inpatients, outpatients, and AA-only group members showed improvement superior to that of untreated participants. Benefits of AA or formal treatment were most apparent for drinking-related outcomes. These findings agree with those of other researchers, such as McLellan et al. (1982), who reported that people in treatment for substance abuse improve most on substance abuse outcomes and, to a lesser degree, on employment and psychological functioning. Treatment effects across life domains would probably be stronger if services for problem drinkers were more comprehensive and addressed broader needs, such as vocational rehabilitation and work training, family counseling, and training in coping skills oriented toward helping patients improve their life contexts.

We considered why AA and the two types of formal treatment did not differ more on effectiveness. Probably, effective alcoholism interventions have common elements, such as an emphasis on abstinence and the experience of a committed relationship with a therapist or sponsor. Findings suggest that alcoholism treatment systems should make different types of interventions available and facilitate clients' entry into the type of treatment they prefer.

It was striking that more AA attendance was associated with better drinking outcomes among AA-only participants, as well as outpatients and inpatients, especially at the 3-year follow-up. Importantly, most participants who received formal treatment did so early in their treatment careers, and so AA participation most likely served mainly as a maintenance factor. At 1 year and 3 years, more inpatient treatment was also associated with better drinking outcomes. These findings support clinicians in emphasizing the benefits of AA attendance and of completing formal treatment programs. Dropouts may need case management to make sure they obtain additional services, just as individuals do who are referred to treatment for the first time but do not follow through.

Although these results support the importance of getting help for many people with alcohol problems, they also showed that some problem drinkers improve without help. To understand better the processes by which individuals recover without formal alcoholism treatment, we undertook an investigation of "spontaneous" or natural recovery.

Two Pathways Out of Drinking
Without Formal Treatment

Using the same sample of initially untreated problem drinkers, Humphreys, Moos, and Finney (1995) focused on the groups that did not receive formal outpatient or inpatient services—that is, on the untreated and AA-only groups. Just under half (48%) of these individuals had become stably abstinent or had become stable moderate drinkers by the 3-year follow-up, and there appeared to be two distinct pathways out of problem drinking among them. The pathways reflected socioeconomic status and associated social and psychological factors.

At baseline, individuals who did not enter formal treatment *and later became abstinent* were of low socioeconomic status, had relatively little education, had severe drinking problems, and also perceived their drinking problem as very severe. They moved far into the course of alcohol abuse, "hitting bottom" before they decided that their drinking was problematic. Once they began their recovery, they relied heavily on AA as a maintenance factor.

In contrast, problem drinkers *who later became stable moderate drinkers* initially had higher levels of education and occupational status, higher self-esteem, and supportive relationships with family and friends. These individuals appeared to recognize early on that they had drinking problems, before they had lost their financial and social resources. It is commonly assumed that people fail to seek help for drinking until they hit bottom, but these people apparently sought help when they hit what in AA terminology is called "high bottom."

The Role of Community Agencies in Preventing and Treating Alcohol Problems

The Humphreys et al. (1995) study supports the notion that some individuals can remit or recover from drinking problems without professional treatment. Almost 20 years ago, an analysis of the alcoholism movement by Mulford (1979) suggested that community agencies should direct less effort at developing a formal treatment culture and more effort at accelerating natural recovery in the community. For example, agencies might attempt to improve problem drinking individuals' connections to family, friends, and self-help groups.

Humphreys and Moos (1996) analyzed the initially untreated sample of problem drinkers to determine the extent to which self-help groups are effective and cost-saving. They compared individuals who selected

AA as their initial source of help (n = 135) after contacting the I&R or detox center, with individuals who initially entered only outpatient treatment (n = 66). (These groups are not identical to the composition of the AA-only and outpatient groups identified earlier, which considered the entire 1-year or 3-year follow-up periods in classifying individuals.) By the 3-year follow-up, 24% of individuals in the initial AA group made at least one visit to a professional outpatient treatment provider, and 38% of individuals in the initial outpatient group attended at least one AA meeting.

The initial AA and initial outpatient groups were compared on average costs based on total use of care. These analyses suggested significant savings in the initial AA group, particularly in the first follow-up year. Specifically, per-person 3-year costs in the AA group were $2,251, which was 45% lower than 3-year costs in the initial outpatient group ($4,077). No differences were found between the groups on the 1- or 3-year outcome measures used in this study (alcohol consumption and dependence, number of days intoxicated in the past month, adverse consequences of drinking, depression symptoms). In addition, rates for admission to detox or inpatient/residential treatment were comparable for the initial AA and initial outpatient groups and involved few individuals.

Thus, although professional outpatient treatment produced no better 1- or 3-year outcomes than AA, it was associated with significantly higher substance-abuse-related health care costs. If these results are replicated, they suggest that efforts to increase involvement in alcohol self-help organizations may save money by reducing the demand on formal health care systems. Humphreys and Moos (1996) suggested it is highly unlikely that professional alcoholism treatment will ever be appealing, effective, and available for most or all alcoholic individuals at a cost they are willing to bear. Therefore, self-help and other community organizations may ameliorate this situation when individuals use them instead of seeking professional help.

In an extension of this work, Humphreys, Moos, and Cohen (1997) examined early AA participation as a predictor of outcomes at an 8-year follow-up. They found that more AA attendance in the first 3 years of follow-up was associated with a greater likelihood of remission, as well as less depression and more spouse/partner and friend support, at 8 years. Possibly, participation in AA is a predictor of long-term recovery because it is widely available, accessible, and provides a network of supportive people who do not use alcohol.

Mulford's (1979) ideas on the role of community agencies in alco-holism treatment, since supported by Humphreys et al.'s (1995, 1997) research, have been echoed by the Institute of Medicine (1990). The IOM recommended that people whose drinking problems are mild or moderate may be most appropriately helped, not within the specialized alcoholism treatment sector, but within community agencies that pro-vide general services to various populations. The specialized treatment sector is probably most appropriate for substantial or severe alcohol problems. To have a positive impact on the broad spectrum of alcohol problems, a collaborative effort between community agencies and the specialized treatment sector will be needed.

In this effort, community agencies would identify individuals with alcohol problems, provide therapeutic attention in the form of brief interventions to individuals with mild or moderate alcohol problems, and refer individuals with substantial or severe problems or those for whom brief interventions do not suffice to the specialized treatment sector for help. Routine screening for alcohol problems could take place in health care settings, social assistance agencies, educational settings such as colleges, occupational settings, and within the criminal justice system (Tam, Schmidt, & Weisner, 1996; Weisner & Schmidt, 1995). Community agencies could also help shape norms on alcohol consump-tion (through education programs, political activity, and prevention programs) to increase the likelihood that people will appraise their drinking as problematic early on (Humphreys et al., 1995).

Discussion

Our approach of evaluating programs in the real world has both limitations and strengths. In naturalistic evaluations, it is always possi-ble that outcome data for different types of interventions are affected by patient self-selection. Randomized clinical trials have somewhat similar limitations in that they typically employ numerous inclusion and exclusion criteria, including willingness to accept random assignment to treatment conditions; this procedure makes it difficult to know to what patient populations treatment effects may generalize. The advan-tage of not imposing such conditions in a study is that results more accurately reflect the real world of help seeking and service delivery.

We plan to continue our research using the 8-year follow-up data on this initially untreated sample of problem drinkers to examine treatment careers over the long term. We will attempt to develop and test broad and conceptually compelling models of selection processes among and within different types of interventions, as well as of the outcomes of these interventions. Such knowledge may be used to develop interventions by which community agencies can encourage more problem-drinking individuals to seek help and to obtain appropriate formal or informal help at critical points in their drinking careers.

References

Ames, G. M., Grube, J. W., & Moore, R. S. (1997). The relationship of drinking and hangovers to workplace problems: An empirical study. *Journal of Studies on Alcohol, 58,* 37-47.

Annis, H. M., & Graham, J. M. (1988). *Situational Confidence Questionnaire user's guide.* Toronto: Addiction Research Foundation.

Bannenberg, A. F. I., Raat, H., & Plomp, H. N. (1992). Demand for alcohol treatment by problem drinkers. *Journal of Substance Abuse Treatment, 9,* 59-62.

Bardsley, P. E., & Beckman, L. J. (1988). The health belief model and entry into alcoholism treatment. *International Journal of the Addictions, 23,* 19-28.

Castaneda, R., Lifshutz, H., Galanter, M., & Franco, H. (1993). Age at onset of alcoholism as a predictor of homelessness and drinking severity. *Journal of Addictive Diseases, 12,* 55-77.

Dawson, D. A. (1996). Correlates of past-year status among treated and untreated persons with former alcohol dependence: United States, 1992. *Alcoholism: Clinical and Experimental Research, 20,* 771-779.

Fergusson, D. M., Lynskey, M. T., & Horwood, L. J. (1996). Alcohol misuse and juvenile offending in adolescence. *Addiction, 91,* 483-494.

Finney, J. W., & Moos, R. H. (1995). Entering treatment for alcohol abuse: A stress and coping model. *Addiction, 90,* 1223-1240.

French, M. T., Zarkin, G. A., Hartwell, T. D., & Bray, J. H. (1995). Prevalence and consequences of smoking, alcohol use, and illicit drug use at five worksites. *Public Health Reports, 110,* 593-599.

George, A. A., & Tucker, J. A. (1996). Help seeking for alcohol-related problems: Social contexts surrounding entry into alcoholism treatment or Alcoholics Anonymous. *Journal of Studies on Alcohol, 57,* 449-457.

Grant, B. F. (1996). Toward an alcohol treatment model: A comparison of treated and untreated respondents with *DSM-IV* alcohol use disorders in the general population. *Alcoholism: Clinical and Experimental Research, 20,* 372-378.

Heffron, W. A., Skipper, B. J., & Lambert, L. (1997). Health and lifestyle issues as risk factors for homelessness. *Journal of the American Board of Family Practice, 10,* 6-12.

Helzer, J. E., & Pryzbeck, T. R. (1988). The co-occurrence of alcoholism with other psychiatric disorders in the general population and its impact on treatment. *Journal of Studies on Alcohol, 49,* 219-224.

Humphreys, K., & Moos, R. H. (1996). Reduced substance-abuse-related health care costs among voluntary participants in Alcoholics Anonymous. *Psychiatric Services, 47,* 709-713.

Humphreys, K., Moos, R. H., & Cohen, C. (1997). Social and community resources and long-term recovery from treated and untreated alcoholism. *Journal of Studies on Alcohol, 58,* 231-238.

Humphreys, K., Moos, R. H., & Finney, J. W. (1995). Two pathways out of drinking problems without professional treatment. *Addictive Behaviors, 20,* 427-441.

Institute of Medicine (IOM). (1990). *Broadening the base of treatment for alcohol problems.* Washington, DC: National Academy Press.

Kern, J. C., Schmelter, W., & Fanelli, M. (1978). A comparison of three alcoholism treatment populations: Implications for treatment. *Journal of Studies on Alcohol, 39,* 785-792.

Koegel, P., & Burnam, M. A. (1988). Alcoholism among homeless adults in the inner city of Los Angeles. *Archives of General Psychiatry, 45,* 1011-1018.

Marmot, M. G., North, F., Feeney, A., & Head, J. (1993). Alcohol consumption and sickness absence: From the Whitehall II study. *Addiction, 88,* 369-382.

Mattick, R. P., & Jarvis, T. (1994). In-patient setting and long duration for the treatment of alcohol dependence? Out-patient care is as good. *Drug and Alcohol Review, 13,* 127-135.

Mavis, B. E., Humphreys, K., & Stoffelmayr, B. E. (1993). Treatment needs and outcomes of two subtypes of homeless persons who abuse substances. *Hospital and Community Psychiatry, 44,* 1185-1187.

McLellan, A. T., Luborsky, L., O'Brien, C. P., Woody, G. E., & Druley, K. A. (1982). Is treatment for substance abuse effective? *Journal of the American Medical Association, 247,* 1423-1428.

Miller, W. R., & Hester, R. K. (1986). Inpatient alcoholism treatment: Who benefits? *American Psychologist, 41,* 794-805.

Modestin, J., Berger, A., & Ammann, R. (1996). Mental disorder and criminality. *Journal of Nervous and Mental Disease, 184,* 393-402.

Moos, R. H., Cronkite, R. C., & Finney, J. W. (1990). *Health and Daily Living Form manual* (2nd ed.). Palo Alto, CA: Consulting Psychologists Press.

Moos, R. H., Finney, J. W., & Cronkite, R. C. (1990). *Alcoholism treatment: Context, process, and outcome.* New York: Oxford University Press.

Moos, R. H., & Moos, B. S. (1994). *Life Stressors and Social Resources Inventory: Adult form manual.* Odessa, FL: Psychological Assessment Resources.

Mulford, H. A. (1979). Treating alcoholism versus accelerating the natural recovery process: A cost-benefit comparison. *Journal of Studies on Alcohol, 40,* 505-513.

Narrow, W. E., Regier, D. A., Rae, D. S., Manderscheid, R. W., & Locke, B. Z. (1993). Use of services by persons with mental and addictive disorders. *Archives of General Psychiatry, 50,* 95-107.

Pfeiffer, W., Feuerlein, W., & Brenk-Schulte, E. (1991). The motivation of alcohol dependents to undergo treatment. *Drug and Alcohol Dependence, 29,* 87-95.

Rees, D. W., Beech, H. R., & Hore, B. D. (1984). Some factors associated with compliance in the treatment of alcoholism. *Alcohol and Alcoholism, 19,* 303-307.

Room, R. (1989). The U.S. general population's experiences of responding to alcohol problems. *British Journal of Addiction, 84,* 1291-1304.

Rosenberg, M. (1965). *Society and the adolescent self-image.* Princeton, NJ: Princeton University Press.

Schuckit, M. (1995). *Drug and alcohol abuse: A clinical guide to diagnosis and treatment.* New York: Plenum.

Segal, B. (1991). Homelessness and drinking: A study of a street population. *Drugs and Society, 5,* 1-15.

Skinner, H. A., & Allen, B. A. (1982). Alcohol dependence syndrome: Measurement and validation. *Journal of Abnormal Psychology, 91,* 199-209.

Sobell, L. C., Sobell, M. B., & Toneatto, T. (1992). Recovery from alcohol problems without treatment. In N. Heather, W. R. Miller, & J. Greely (Eds.), *Self-control and addictive behaviors* (pp. 198-242). New York: Macmillan.

Spaite, D. W., Criss, E. A., Weist, D. J., Valenzuela, T. D., Judkins, D., & Meislin, H. W. (1995). A prospective investigation of the impact of alcohol consumption on care costs in bicycle-related trauma. *Journal of Trauma, 38,* 287-290.

Spitzer, R. L., Endicott, J., & Robins, E. (1978). Research diagnostic criteria: Rationale and reliability. *Archives of General Psychiatry, 35,* 773-782.

Tam, T. W., Schmidt, L., & Weisner, C. (1996). Patterns in the institutional encounters of problem drinkers in a community human services network. *Addiction, 91,* 657-660.

Timko, C., Finney, J. W., Moos, R. H., & Moos, B. S. (1995). Short-term treatment careers and outcomes of previously untreated alcoholics. *Journal of Studies on Alcohol, 56,* 597-610.

Timko, C., Finney, J. W., Moos, R. H., Moos, B. S., & Steinbaum, D. P. (1993). The process of treatment selection among previously untreated help-seeking problem drinkers. *Journal of Substance Abuse, 5,* 203-220.

Timko, C., Moos, R. H., Finney, J. W., & Moos, B. S. (1994). Outcome of treatment for alcohol abuse and involvement in Alcoholics Anonymous among previously untreated problem drinkers. *Journal of Mental Health Administration, 21,* 145-160.

Webb, G. R., Redman, S., Hennrikus, D. J., Kelman, G. R., Gibberd, R. W., & Sanson-Fisher, R. W. (1994). The relationships between high-risk and problem drinking and the occurrence of work injuries and related absences. *Journal of Studies on Alcohol, 55,* 434-445.

Wechsler, H., Moeykens, B., Davenport, A., Castillo, S., & Hansen, J. (1995). The adverse impact of heavy episodic drinkers on other college students. *Journal of Studies on Alcohol, 56,* 628-634.

Weisner, C. (1986). The social ecology of alcohol treatment in the United States. In M. Galanter (Ed.), *Recent developments in alcoholism* (Vol. 5, pp. 203-243). New York: Plenum.

Weisner, C. (1993). Toward an alcohol treatment entry model: A comparison of problem drinkers in the general population and in treatment. *Alcoholism: Clinical and Experimental Research, 17,* 746-752.

Weisner, C., & Schmidt, L. (1995). The Community Epidemiology Laboratory: Studying alcohol problems in community and agency-based populations. *Addiction, 90,* 329-341.

Welte, J., Hynes, G., Sokolow, L., & Lyons, J. P. (1981). Effect of length of stay in inpatient alcoholism treatment on outcome. *Journal of Studies on Alcohol, 42,* 483-491.

7

Promoting Health and Well-Being Through Work
Science and Practice

STEWART I. DONALDSON
LAURA E. GOOLER
RACHEL WEISS

Most adults spend the majority of their waking hours engaged in work-related activities. If the definition of work is broadened to include children and adolescents pursuing educational goals (often in direct pursuit of paid employment), child rearing, homemaking, and volunteerism, it is clear that work is the central

AUTHORS' NOTE: This work was supported, in part, by research grants from The California Wellness Foundation to Dr. Stewart I. Donaldson, Principal Investigator. The authors thank Work and Health Initiative Evaluation Team members (in alphabetical order) Bryan Baldwin, Dr. Thomas Horan, Lynette Probst, Dr. Michael Scriven, Rachel Vecchiotti, and Christine Webster Moore for their various contributions toward the design of the initiative evaluation. Special thanks to Gary Yates, Tom David, Dr. Ruth Brousseau, and Lucia Corral of the California Wellness Foundation; Paul J. Vandeventer, Albert Fong, and Wendy Lazarus of the Computers in Our Future Program; Sharon Rowser and Dr. Richard H. Price of the Winning New Jobs Program; and Drs. Helen Schauffler and E. Richard Brown of the Health Policy Program for designing, leading, and supporting programs to promote health and well-being through work. The authors also thank the Pasadena Consortium evaluation team of Robert McKenna, Elisa Grant-Vallone, and Juliet Evans for their efforts to extend health promotion opportunities to traditionally underserved employee populations.

activity of modern life. In fact, Freud (1930) argued that "work had a more powerful effect than any other aspect of human life to bind a person to reality" (cited in Quick, Murphy, Hurrell, & Orman, 1992, p. 3). He also said that "the life of human beings has a twofold foundation: The compulsion to work, created by external necessity, and the power of love" (cited in Quick, Murphy, Hurrell, & Orman, 1992, p. 3).

Subsequently, much research has shown that work is of primary importance, both socially and personally, for individuals throughout the world. For example, work not only contributes to one's economic well-being but also establishes patterns of social interaction, imposes a schedule on people's lives, and provides them with structure, a sense of identity, and self-esteem (Donaldson & Weiss, 1998). Work also provides others with a means of judging one's status, skills, and personal worth. Therefore, it should be no surprise that the nature of one's work (e.g., presence or absence of work, conditions of work) is most often a major determinant of a person's health status, well-being, and overall quality of life (cf. Dooley, Fielding, & Levi, 1996; Karasek & Theorell, 1990; Keita & Sauter, 1992; Levi, 1994).

Defining Health and Well-Being

The World Health Organization (1948, Preamble) defines *health* as "a state of complete physical, mental, and social well-being and not merely the absence of disease or infirmity." A similar conceptualization views health on a continuum ranging from death (the lowest point), through disability, symptoms of illness, absence of disease, to wellness (Donaldson & Blanchard, 1995; Everly & Feldman, 1984; see Figure 7.1). The midpoint along the continuum is absence of illness or disease, which is often considered to be the neutral point and is the focus of traditional medicine. Health promotion interventions typically are designed to prevent illness factors toward the lower end of the continuum and to promote wellness factors toward the upper end. The *American Journal of Health Promotion* provided the following definition:

> Health promotion is the science and practice of helping people change their lifestyle to move toward a state of optimal mental and physical health. Lifestyle (broadly defined) can be facilitated through a combina-

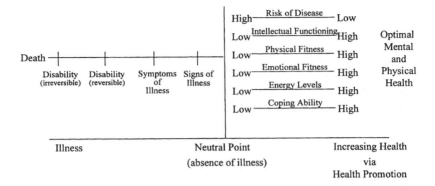

Figure 7.1. The Illness-to-Wellness Continuum
SOURCE: Reprinted by permission from Everly and Feldman (1984, p. 15).

tion of efforts to enhance awareness, change behavior, and create environments that support good health practices. Of the three, supportive environments will probably have the greatest impact in producing lasting changes. (O'Donnell, 1989, p. 5)

Community Problems, Health, and Work

Various events, behaviors, and situations get defined as community problems because they threaten the health and well-being of the individual exhibiting the problem behavior and/or the people affected by that individual. We argue that many interventions targeted at modern community problems can be viewed as a form of health promotion—for example, interventions designed to prevent various types of violence, juvenile delinquency and criminal behavior, alcohol and drug abuse, teenage pregnancy and parenthood, child neglect and abuse, and learning disabilities. If these interventions are successful, they prevent illness or promote wellness factors or both not only for program recipients but also for members of the larger community. Although it is true that many interventions are designed in response to crisis or health-threatening events, one intention underlying most community-based efforts is prevention of problems, or health promotion.

Most interventions designed to address community problems are based on research or assumptions about the etiology of the specific problem. Most community problems are thought to be caused by multiple and complex sets of events. Although any given problem has a unique set of causal agents, some risk factors are robust and seem to affect a variety of modern social ills. We assert that the nature of work—specifically, the presence or absence of work and the conditions of work—is one such robust causal agent that can affect many community problems. That is, when one asks where the lion's share of the variance lies in predicting today's social problems, quite often the conditions of employment are a significant predictor. For example, it can be argued that the need for many popular child and adolescent social programs (e.g., Head Start, adolescent substance abuse prevention or treatment programs, juvenile delinquency programs) arises, in part, because parents or caregivers do not have favorable employment conditions or opportunities.

This chapter aims to expand the domain of work site health promotion by describing innovative community applications. To build a foundation for our perspective, we begin by summarizing the traditional work site health promotion literature. Challenges posed by this research paradigm naturally lead us into discussing interventions designed to promote health and well-being "through work" (vs. "at work"); for example, programs to reach traditionally underserved employee populations, and a statewide initiative designed to understand the rapidly changing nature of work and health, to increase access to high-quality employment, and to improve conditions of work.

Work Site Health Promotion

Work site health promotion (WHP) programs traditionally consist of a combination of activities—diagnostic or screening, educational, and behavior-change activities—initiated, endorsed, and supported by an employing organization and designed to support the attainment and maintenance of employee health and well-being (see Donaldson, 1995; Matteson & Ivancevich, 1988). WHP programs have typically been driven by theories and research from the disciplines of epidemiology, public health, and preventive medicine and have focused largely on "controllable lifestyle" or behavioral risk factors linked with the leading causes of mortality and morbidity in modern societies (cf. U.S. Department of Health and Human Services [DHHS], 1991). For example, health risk appraisal, cancer screening, programs for physical fitness, weight management, smoking cessation, injury prevention, back care, and stress management are commonly reported WHP activities (Fielding & Piserchia, 1989; DHHS, 1993).

During the past decade, WHP activities have become commonplace in corporate America. By 1992, national survey data showed that 81% of companies with 50 or more employees offered at least one health promotion activity (DHHS, 1993).

Prior to 1991, reviewers of the WHP effectiveness literature were quite critical. It was a common conclusion that many claims made about the benefits of WHP were not based on sound scientific evidence (see Falkenberg, 1987; Gebhardt & Crump, 1990; Matteson & Ivancevich, 1988; Terborg, 1986; Warner, 1987; Warner, Wickizer, Wolfe, Schildroth, & Samuelson, 1988). Pelletier (1991), however, reviewed 26 evaluations of WHP programs implemented in large corporate contexts and concluded that a growing body of evidence demonstrated WHP to be both health- and cost-effective. Ironically, in the same year and same journal, Conrad, Conrad, and Walcott-McQuigg (1991) argued that "a careful examination of the literature reveals that claims about the effectiveness of work site health promotion programs are, in general, based on flawed studies containing serious threats to validity" (p. 112). Subsequently, Pelletier (1993) reviewed 48 peer-reviewed WHP evaluations and found convergent evidence of improved health outcomes and a positive return on company investment (also see Stokols, Pelletier, & Fielding, 1995). Although sorting out this apparent contradiction in the literature about WHP effectiveness is beyond the scope of this chapter, we highlight some key insights to be gleaned from two decades of WHP research.

The dominant orientation of WHP is to view the work site as a setting, outside the standard health care delivery system, that is ideal for the implementation of health promotion and disease prevention services. Work sites tend to provide stable and "captive" audiences for health promotion practitioners. WHP promises to prevent illnesses and diseases that account for a large percentage of corporate health care costs (Stokols et al., 1995).

This approach, however, requires *active* participation from employees, making employees responsible for changing or maintaining prescribed health practices. A serious limitation of health promotion or wellness programs "at work," to date, has been the apparent lack of employee willingness or ability to make these rather dramatic (in some cases) changes toward living a "healthful lifestyle." One of the most consistent findings in the existing WHP literature is that employee participation in WHP programs tends to be exceptionally low. Estimates of participation in WHP programs typically range from 15% to 30% for white-collar populations and only 3% to 5% for blue-collar populations (Gebhardt & Crump, 1990).

A second major challenge has been the inability to substantiate the promise that WHP leads to organizationally valued outcomes (e.g., improved job performance, morale, employee health and well-being; reduced health care costs, absenteeism, and turnover). This challenge has been particularly difficult outside the confines of tightly constrained efficacy trials. Two aspects of this problem for WHP are the dose-response curve and methodological dilemmas posed by organizational settings.

First, changing health practices can require much time and effort on the part of employees. Even for those who do make and sustain positive behavioral changes, health and productivity gains may not be immediate (there is a delayed response curve). Much basic research suggests that the benefits of leading a healthful lifestyle may be rather distal (e.g., reduced morbidity, mortality, and disability later in life). In the light of the recent trend toward careers that span several employers, Warner (1987) argued that effects of successful WHP activities may be realized by future employers, not necessarily by current employers. In his articulation of the "abuses of the economic argument" for WHP, Warner also noted the organizational disadvantage of having employees who live longer (e.g., they may cost employers more in pension funds and health care costs later in life). Even in the short term, however, some research shows that WHP efforts may initially increase employer health care costs by encouraging more employees to seek treatment for health risks identified during health screenings (e.g., Gibbs, Mulvaney, Henes, & Reed, 1985). For the typical organization deciding whether to invest in WHP, the financial benefits, particularly in the short term, are not clear-cut.

Second, WHP researchers face the common challenges of conducting research in organizational contexts. For example, because it is not feasible to maintain strict experimental control and is difficult to routinize high-quality data collection procedures and to inspire participation rates that uphold the strength and integrity of WHP interventions, evaluators must often rely on quasi-experimental or measurement designs. These designs make it difficult to rule out plausible rival hypotheses (e.g., self-selection, attrition, diffusion of treatment effects, compensatory rivalry; Conrad et al., 1991; Donaldson, 1995; Warner et al., 1988). Some practical realities also inhibit WHP evaluation research, including severe time and resource restrictions and lack of cooperation with research requirements by employees and employers. Additionally, because stakeholder livelihoods are often perceived to be threatened by negative findings from WHP research, some of the most difficult challenges to overcome are biases of involved personnel who need to view WHP as effective and the motivation of participants to look good at work. A more detailed examination of these methodological challenges and of recommendations for addressing them can be found in Donaldson (1995).

Other emerging themes in the WHP literature are a call for evaluating comprehensive, multifaceted programs, for improving access to hard-to-reach populations, and for integrating WHP with the medical care system, managed care, and corporate benefit plans (cf. Donaldson, 1995; O'Donnell & Harris, 1994; Stokols et al., 1995). We extend this list by suggesting a reformulation of WHP to encompass and encourage community and corporate-focused interventions designed to promote health and well-being "through work," in addition to the standard corporate approach of lifestyle enhancement "at work."

In addition to work being a setting for providing prevention services, the nature of work itself can be a powerful determinant of one's health and well-being. Sloan (1987) noted that the dominant paradigm of WHP, which focuses on employee health practices, severely limits a broader understanding of how best to promote healthy and effective functioning. Specifically, the dominant WHP paradigm does not consider the system of work in which employees are embedded to be a health-promoting factor.

Promoting health and well-being through work expands the traditional WHP focus to include an emphasis on providing favorable working conditions for employees and access to meaningful employment, particularly for disadvantaged groups, in addition to health-related behavior change activities and work environments that support these activities.

This conceptualization has two definitive advantages. First, this approach dramatically increases the chances that people in most need will be reached by WHP. A disconcerting criticism has been that most

WHP activities are provided to highly educated and well-paid employees working for large corporations (Donaldson & Blanchard, 1995). Given that education and income are highly correlated with leading a healthful lifestyle (DHHS, 1991), one can argue that WHP typically is available to those who will have good health practices regardless of whether or not their employer provides WHP resources. There is much more room for improvement and more opportunity for impact when employees who have poor health practices and unfavorable working conditions are reached by WHP.

Second, a major limitation of traditional WHP has been that all the responsibility for health and well-being has rested with employees. This newer approach shifts some responsibility for health and well-being from employees to the employer and related human service organizations, who become active agents in creating better working conditions. From the worker's perspective, WHP becomes a combination of "active" and "passive" WHP interventions (Williams, 1982), which promise to be much more effective in the long run (see Rosen & Berger, 1991; Stokols, 1992). WHP programs based solely on the active participation or behavior change of employees have been plagued with dismal participation rates, as mentioned earlier. Below, we illustrate some opportunities for promoting health through work by discussing (a) the potential for improving psychosocial working conditions, (b) strategies for reaching the underserved, and (c) a statewide initiative designed to promote health and well-being through work, in the light of the changing nature of work in California.

Psychosocial Working Conditions

The field of occupational health and safety has traditionally concentrated its efforts on physical working conditions and related safety concerns. In recent years, however, research on the link between psychosocial working conditions and employee health and well-being has been increasing (see Karasek & Theorell, 1990; Stokols, 1992). Now, a solid body of evidence shows that the nature of an employee's psychosocial working conditions can have a strong effect on her or his well-being and performance (cf. Eisenberger, Fasolo, & Davis-LaMastro, 1990; Greiner, 1996; Keita & Sauter, 1992; Levi, 1994; Murphy, Hurrel, Sauter, & Keita, 1995; Quick, Murphy, & Hurrell, 1992; Sauter &

Murphy, 1995). The fields of organizational psychology and, more recently, occupational health psychology have advanced theory and research illustrating the value of quality of worklife factors and interventions. Although a comprehensive review of this literature is beyond the scope of this chapter, it may be helpful to provide examples of poor and favorable psychosocial working environments.

Imagine if your job were characterized in the following way:

Poor psychosocial working conditions: Low pay; no benefits; no opportunities for advancement; no control over your schedule or work tasks; high job insecurity; no input into major decisions; excessive demands and stress; no organizational support for family demands and responsibilities; a group of coworkers you despise; and the cruelest boss imaginable.

It should be easy to imagine that working under these conditions for long periods of time would threaten almost anyone's health and well-being. In contrast, imagine a job that provides the following working conditions:

Favorable psychosocial working conditions: Great pay; comprehensive benefits; optimal control over your schedule and work; high job security; input into all major decisions; great opportunities for career advancement; organizational support for family demands and responsibilities; a group of coworkers you respect and admire; and the kindest and most effective boss imaginable.

Obviously, this characterization is an ideal, and it may not be feasible to achieve such an environment in any given work situation. Nevertheless, these rather extreme characterizations of potential psychosocial work environments illustrate the type of factors over which employers have some control and that could be targeted in WHP efforts to promote health and well-being through work.

Strategies for Reaching the Underserved

Although traditional WHP services are fairly common among well-paid and well-educated white-collar employees working in Fortune-500-type companies, the vast majority of U.S. employers, employees, and their families still do not have easy access to these services (see

Kaiser, 1988). Similarly, Fielding (1991) reported that most research on WHP interventions was in work sites with 500 to 5,000 employees even though the majority of the workforce was employed at work sites with fewer than 50 employees. One main finding of the 1992 National Survey of WHP was the pressing need for strategies to provide WHP to employees working in small and medium-size businesses.

Some research that has been conducted on WHP issues at small and underserved work sites seems promising. For example, Erfurt and Holtyn (1991) demonstrated the effectiveness of WHP in small companies, showing that great opportunities existed for personalized health feedback and goal setting. Donaldson and Blanchard (1995) showed that employee health practices predicted proximal wellness (vitality, psychological well-being, good attendance) and illness status (anxiety, depression, lack of self-control, physical illness) among those working in small and underserved work sites. Finally, Stokols and his colleagues have developed a strategy using Web sites to provide health information to small businesses, and they are currently engaged in a major research effort that aims to develop and test a workplace wellness program for small and medium-size businesses that is based on a social-ecological model (e.g., Stokols, 1992, 1996; Wells, Stokols, McMahan, & Clitheroe, in press).

Although some externally funded research efforts are focused on small businesses, by themselves small employers typically cannot afford to invest in efforts that meet public health objectives (improving employee health) but reduce their organizational profitability. Further, because almost all small businesses are community-rated for their health insurance premiums, they have practically no financial incentive to reduce health care costs. Traditional WHP strategies (e.g., company-sponsored in-house programs) are usually not considered to be cost-effective for small and most medium-size businesses (see Every & Leong, 1994).

In response to these dilemmas, Donaldson and Klien (1997) designed and implemented a community/industry/university consortium model to meet the needs of currently underserved employee populations, particularly ethnically diverse workforces in small and medium-size businesses. In the model, a wide variety of community organizations, medical and mental health treatment providers, management consultants, local foundations, and academically based field researchers teamed up to provide low-cost WHP services to small and medium-size businesses. This innovative WHP delivery system is currently providing services to more than 4,000 southern Californians. Unlike other WHP models, psychosocial working conditions, as well as employee lifestyle factors, are being targeted. A detailed discussion of this delivery system and preliminary findings about how to engage underserved employees in WHP are provided by Donaldson and Klien (1997).

Another strategy for reaching the underserved is to provide services to those with inadequate employment or employment opportunities. Dooley et al. (1996) discussed research linking unemployment, underemployment, and job-loss with poor health outcomes. Interventions designed to provide requisite skills for the unemployed and underemployed and to reduce the adverse effects of job-loss also hold great promise for promoting health and well-being through work. Below, we describe a strategic initiative that is partially designed to increase employment opportunities for disadvantaged youths and young adults and reduce the impact of job-loss on negative health outcomes and that addresses some shortcomings of past WHP programs.

The Work and Health Initiative

In 1995, The California Wellness Foundation launched a 5-year, $20 million statewide Work and Health Initiative to promote the health and well-being of California workers and their families through work. The mission of the Work and Health Initiative is to improve the health of Californians by designing and systematically evaluating interventions related to employment. Fundamental to this initiative is the perspective that a variety of important relationships between work and health are being shaped by an evolving California economy.

The goals of the initiative are (a) to understand the rapidly changing nature of work and its effects on Californians, (b) to increase access to high-quality employment for all Californians, (c) to improve conditions of work for employed Californians, and (d) to expand the availability of WHP programs and benefits, with particular emphasis on employer-sponsored health insurance. The means of achieving these goals are (a) by gaining a better *understanding* of the links among economic conditions, work, and health and their effects on employees, employers, and the community; (b) by *demonstrating* the relationship(s) between work and health for employees, potential employees, employers, and the larger community; (c) by *influencing* corporate and governmental policymakers to improve working conditions for individuals in California; (d) by *establishing* a self-sustaining network of researchers and practitioners to advance the work and health agenda; and (e) by *evaluating* the process and impact of all funded projects aimed at improving the work and health of Californians.

To accomplish these objectives, The California Wellness Foundation funded four interrelated programs (see Figure 7.2). The *Future of Work and Health* and the *Health Insurance Policy Program* are research-driven programs designed to build a new understanding of how the nature of work is being transformed and how that change will affect the health and well-being of Californians. Current statewide trends related to health and health insurance within California are being examined through extensive survey research on an annual basis. In addition, researchers throughout California are being engaged to analyze system-atically the changing nature of work and health and to search for ways to improve health with the focus on the changing California workplace. On the demonstration project side, *Winning New Jobs* aims to help workers regain employment lost because of downsizing, reengineering, and other aspects of the dramatic changes in the California workplace and thereby put an end to the adverse health consequences that most workers experience as a result of unemployment. Finally, *Computers in Our Future* aims to enable youths and young adults from low-income communities to learn computer skills and to improve their education and employment opportunities, thereby improving their own future health, as well as the health and well-being of their families and communities.

The California Wellness Foundation is also deeply committed to the science of promoting health and well-being through work. As part of this commitment, systematic evaluation research is being used to guide the strategic management of each program in the initiative, as well as to inform the direction of the entire initiative. The initiative evaluator is serving as an integrating, synthesizing force in evaluating goals, objectives, strategies, and outcomes central to the long-term impact of the initiative (see Figure 7.2). Cross-cutting goals and synergies are being identified, enhanced, and evaluated in an effort to maximize the overall impact of the initiative (the whole is expected to be greater than the sum of the parts). In addition, the initiative evaluator is developing evaluation systems that provide responsive assessment data for each program; these data will be used to continually improve program effec-tiveness, as well as to evaluate long-term outcomes. The evaluation component of the initiative promises to enhance dramatically the impact of the initiative, as well as to document the effectiveness of these approaches to promoting health and well-being through work.

Work and Health Initiative

The mission of the Work and Health Initiative is to understand the rapidly changing nature of work and its effects on the health of Californians and to improve health through improving conditions of work, access to employment, and the caliber of health insurance available to the state's workforce.

Evaluator's Role

The mission of the Initiative Evaluator is to serve as an as an integrating, synthesizing force in evaluating goals, objectives, strategies and outcomes central to the long-term impact of the Initiative. In addition, the Initiative Evaluator will consult on the design of each program's evaluation by helping to (1) define the evaluation goals, (2) evaluate strategies and progress, and (3) analyze findings from data collection efforts.

Cross-cutting Goals & Synergies	•Raise public awareness of work and health issues in California •Replicate successful components of California initiative		•Develop additional funding for initiative sustainment •Affect policy making community	
	Future of Work and Health	**Health Insurance Policy Program**	**Winning New Jobs**	**Computers in Our Future**
Goals	• Create new knowledge and allow researchers to focus on work and health issues • Engage business leaders in implementing improved work practices • Recommend changes to public policy and raise public awareness • Build lasting structures for cooperative action	• Conduct analysis on the relationships between employment, insurance coverage, health & risk status, and preventive services utilization • Provide policy analysis on barriers to CA health insurance reform that are problems for small & mid-size businesses • Foster integration of health promotion and disease prevention approaches	• Implement JOBS program in three training sites • Build community support for program including financing support for project continuation • Identify "best practices" in program design and implementation and widely disseminate information • Influence policy change and spending	• Build computer literacy programs in ten low- income communities enabling residents to improve education and access to employment • Modify public and corporate policies, creating support for community technology learning models • Create local advocacy groups to empower residents to participate in policy making
Targets	• Applied research targeting business leaders	• Annual study focused on small & mid-size businesses	• Community-level program aimed at unemployed adults	• Community-level program aimed at unemployed young adults

Figure 7.2. Overview of the California Wellness Foundation's Work and Health Initiative

As part of the evaluation effort, major trends and changes in the California context that determine the core challenges and opportunities facing each initiative program have been analyzed. Below, we summarize these trends and then present some key findings from each of the initiative programs during their first year of operation.

The California Workplace

The California workplace is being reshaped by profound and potentially permanent changes, such as large-scale restructuring and downsizing that have left many workers with reduced wages or unemployed; a surging growth in part-time, temporary, and nonbenefited employment; rapid technological advances; and an increasingly globalized economy. Simultaneously, the composition of the workforce is changing. The consequences of such change have affected nearly all Californians; however, the greatest impact tends to fall on those who are the least skilled and the least educated.

Workforce Diversity

The U.S. workforce is becoming more diverse in terms of ethnicity, age, and gender (Jarratt, Coates, Mahaffie, & Hinnes, 1995; London & Greller, 1991; Stenberg & Colman, 1994; U.S. Bureau of the Census, 1992). For example, by the year 2000, it is expected that women will make up about 47% of the workforce. Similarly, ethnic minority groups together (African American, Asian, Native American, and Latino) accounted for 11% of the U.S. population in 1960, but by 2020, they will likely reach or exceed 38%.

California's population composition is projected to be uniquely affected by these demographic shifts. It is predicted that, between 1990 and 2005, at least two out of three new California residents will be Latino, African American, or Asian (Center for the Continuing Study of the California Economy, 1993). The Latino population is growing the most rapidly, however, totaling 18.8 million in 1987 and expected to reach 67.7 million by 2030. Currently, Latinos make up 25% of the state's population (U.S. Bureau of the Census, 1993) and have become the largest group in places like Los Angeles County (42.5% Latino vs. 34.2% European Americans in 1997; Los Angeles County Internal Services Department, 1993). Further, the Latino population has a younger median age than non-Latino populations, which means that Latinos will account for a disproportional number of future entry-level workers. The largest contributing factor to California's population growth between 1995 and 2005 is expected to be births, especially among the rapidly growing Latino population (Jarratt et al., 1995).

Another significant trend is the "graying" of the U.S. workforce. In 1960, 9.2% of the population was over age 65; by 2020, this figure is projected to grow to 16.6%. In California, however, the high birth rate and the young age of many immigrants have caused a bimodal change in the age of its residents. Whereas most of the United States is aging, California is experiencing growth in the numbers of both children and the elderly (Walters, 1996). Fast growth in these two age-groups means increasing pressures on the working-age population to support a larger number of individuals, either personally or through taxation.

Advances in Information Technology

Many experts believe that advances in computer and information technologies are having, and will continue to have, a profound impact on the way employees work and live (cf. Hakken, 1993; Howard, 1995). Some scholars suggest that we are witnessing the demise of the Industrial Revolution and the beginnings of the Information Revolution. For example, computer literacy is fast becoming a prerequisite to gainful employment, and knowledge workers are no longer tightly constrained by the geographic location of the traditional office (e.g., Tomaskovic-Devey & Risman, 1993).

Communication technology has made it possible for organizations to develop more flexible methods of production, to disperse their operations, and to tap global pockets of expertise. Technologies support new patterns of communication and information access and facilitate higher levels of participative work styles and greater reductions in bureaucratic management methods and hierarchical structures of control (Sproull & Kiesler, 1991). For example, information technology can enable telecommuting and computer-mediated cooperative work. California's organizations are also struggling to adapt to the dramatic impacts of these technological and demographic changes.

On the negative side, some authors point to the rapid advance and spread of information technology as the primary factor responsible for such things as widening income inequality, the emergence of a two-class society, and massive future unemployment (Rifkin, 1995); wasteful competition within global, winner-take-all markets (Frank & Cook, 1995); and the obsolescence of urban centers and the flight of wealthy, educated, technology-savvy individuals (Jarratt et al., 1995). In fact, the replacement of labor-intensive work with "knowledge work" as the primary source of business value and growth has been accompanied by a widening income disparity, with the top 20% of all households now earning 55% of all income. The factor most responsible for this growing earnings disparity, it has been argued, is technology access and mastery. If these predictions are correct, technological literacy will divide the population into a two-class society—technology "haves" and "have nots."

Indeed, statistics show that 27% of Americans in 1994 had personal computers (PCs) in their homes; of these, 60% had graduated from college and 50% had household incomes of $50,000 or more. In contrast, within the general population, only 21% held college degrees and only 15% had annual household incomes over $50,000 (Schroth & Mui, 1995). The picture is particularly bleak for ethnic minorities. In 1994, only 13% of Latinos and 14% of African Americans had PCs in their homes, in comparison with 29% of European Americans. Further, 29% of Latinos and 36% of African Americans used PCs on their jobs, as compared with almost 50% of all European American employees (Tomas Rivera Center, 1996). In Southern California, twice the number of non-Latino Whites own computers as do Latinos (Harmon, 1996). Further, schools are often unable to compensate for these differences by providing low-income communities with sufficient computer access. It is important to note, however, that the two best predictors of computer access are education and income and that there are few differences between ethnic groups at high-income levels.

Job Churning

According to predictions, the movement toward even more service-oriented and information-intensive work will continue, with the fastest growing occupations being in such areas as communications and computers, health care, and entertainment. Furthermore, a decade of "rightsizing" and downsizing has resulted in the single biggest job-creator industry being temporary employment businesses (Aley, 1995). The shift toward "contingent work" (temporary work and migrant managers), the sequential career (changing professions every few years), and jobs requiring new and different skills will continue (London & Greller, 1991). These trends together have been referred to as "job churning."

New Psychological Contract

During the past decade, many California workers have lost stable, well-paying jobs because of structural economic changes and, in particular, defense spending cuts (e.g., Friedman, 1994). In the midst of all the restructuring and downsizing, something more subtle has been lost, or rather transformed: the psychological contract. In fact, the reengineering movement has been most harshly criticized for ignoring the human side of the organizational change process (e.g., Grey & Mitev, 1995). We now see the results manifested in some unexpected and detrimental ways for employees and their employers (Rousseau, 1996).

The traditional *psychological contract,* a type of unwritten commitment based on trust between employees and employers, facilitated employee loyalty and effort in return for wages, security, and reasonable working conditions. According to Rogers (1995), this mutual understanding has been "blasted out of existence" in recent years, with perceived employer greed and unethical leadership contributing to a growing cynicism in the workplace. Although saving many organizations, some reengineering and downsizing strategies have left many loyal, hardworking employees jobless and have fundamentally redefined the psychological work contract. This contract is now often characterized by self-interest, career (rather than organizational) commitment, and mistrust on the part of the employee.

Not only the job-losers suffer negative emotional and psychological consequences. A 1991 survey found that the survivors of downsizing, too, were afraid of losing their jobs and suffered from guilt, anger, and sadness over the loss of colleagues and from increased anxiety and job insecurity (cited in Houston, 1992). *Job insecurity,* which is a sense of uncertainty and powerlessness to maintain one's desired level of current and future job continuity, can lead to stress-related illnesses, higher levels of depression, reduced work effort, a greater propensity to leave the organization, and lower job involvement, job satisfaction, and trust in management (Borg & Elizur, 1992; Hearney, Israel, & House, 1994). Although moderate levels of job insecurity are not always harmful (Brockner, Grover, Reed, & Dewitt, 1994), high levels may have long-term detrimental consequences.

Continuous Training

For the employee, it is becoming increasingly important to embrace continuous learning or training to ensure high-quality employment in this turbulent workplace. For many employers, this importance will mean their workforces will need assistance in developing new and evolving work behaviors. Furthermore, training aimed at instilling a sense of self-efficacy can lead to the most positive outcomes (e.g., McDonald & Siegall, 1992).

Currently, some underdeveloped skills in the labor force require attention: (a) *enabling skills,* such as literacy, arithmetic, and generic job-related skills; (b) *technical skills* particular to occupations; and (c) *integrative skills,* which involve the use of complex and diverse information (Stenberg & Colman, 1994). More and more, computer literacy must be included within the category of enabling skills. For example, more than half of California's new jobs require some form of technology literacy (Lazarus & Lipper, 1996).

In fact, the basic skill level required of many entry-level employees is a large challenge facing California employers (California Economic Strategy Panel, 1996). In many ways, the California population is becoming increasingly mismatched to the needs of employers. The skills that many employers believe are lacking in a large proportion of new hires include basic arithmetic, computational skills, and English literacy. While California is witnessing an evolution in high-tech and globally competitive industries, it is also experiencing a growth in the size of undereducated, unskilled, and immigrant populations who are not prepared for the jobs available in many high-growth sectors (Brady, Mungen, Renwick, & Stassel, 1996; Mazmanian, 1995). Despite the rising number of African American, Asian, Latino, and female workers, these groups are still underrepresented in California's high-skill, high-tech, and managerial occupations (e.g., Hayghe & Comartie, 1991).

In summary, the demographic and organizational forces outlined above have led to significant and potentially permanent changes in California, with a new diversity in the workforce and new conditions under which work is accomplished. The following key findings from programs in the Work and Health Initiative illustrate the potential that community-based approaches have for addressing this changing environment and for improving health and well-being through work.

Year 1 Findings

Future of Work and Health

The aim of The Future of Work and Health (TFWH) program is to build a new understanding of how the nature of work is being trans-formed and how this change will affect the health and well-being of Californians. During the first year of operation, TFWH supported several projects to examine the links between work and health in California. One project was a telephone survey of California adults carried out by The Field Institute using random digit dialing and probability sampling methods (The Field Institute, 1996). A total of 2,310 California adults were interviewed by telephone in English or Spanish; of them, 1,410 reported being employed either full- or part-time. With results closely mirroring official government labor force statistics, the Field Institute poll found that 36% of all California adults were out of the labor force. Of adults who were in the labor force, 75% were employed full-time, 18% were employed part-time, and 7% were unemployed. Although many authors see low unemployment as a sign of economic improvement, it should be noted that more than one in three (34%) respondents who were officially counted as "out of the labor force" said they wanted employment.

To understand the nature of current psychosocial working conditions experienced by employed Californians, the Field Institute poll explored the existence of job-related problems such as inadequate compensation and limited opportunities for advancement. Similarly, employed Californians were also surveyed about their health and well-being. Disturbingly, nearly one half of employed Californians (46%) reported having serious job-related problems. Slightly more employed Californians (53%) reported having serious health-related problems. On closer examination, the most frequently reported job problems included having no medical insurance (22%); having no opportunities for advancement (15%); having a household income less than 125% of the poverty level (12%); losing a job in the past year (9%); being "very" financially insecure (8%); and believing that one's job "very likely" will be lost in the next year (5%). In turn, the most frequently cited health-related problems included serious back problems (22%); cigarette smoking (20%); emotional problems that kept workers from fully accomplishing their work (15%); depression (11%); physical problems that kept workers from fully accomplishing their work (10%); and alcohol problems (10%).

Consistent with previous research, this study also showed that underserved populations were experiencing the highest levels of serious job problems. These problems were most prevalent among Latinos and noncitizens, younger workers, part-time workers, and those with less formal education. For example, 62% of Latinos, 46% of African Americans, and 41% of Asians/others reported having serious job-related problems, as compared with 39% of the non-Latino White population. With respect to age, more than half of workers under age 30 reported having serious job problems (60% of the 18- to 24-year-olds; 54% of 25- to 29-year-olds), compared with less than 40% of those age 40 and older (39% of those ages 40-49 and 37% of those 50 years and older). In addition, nearly three fourths of those having less than high school educations (74%) and over half of those with high school diplomas (52%) reported having serious work-related problems, whereas fewer individuals with some college (40%) or college degrees (26%) reported having these problems. Similarly, this higher incidence of serious job-related problems was also more prevalent among employees who worked in small companies (fewer than 50 employees), had low annual incomes (less than $20,000), were in blue-collar jobs, and worked in manufacturing, construction, or agricultural industries.

In its examination of the relationship between current work conditions and health issues among employed Californians, the Field Institute poll offered new evidence that negative working conditions, such as having serious job-related problems, are linked with poor health outcomes. For example, workers with serious job-related problems were more likely to report having serious health-related problems (61%) than were workers who did not have serious job problems (46%). Unfortunately, the cross-sectional nature of this study did not allow tests of causality. Therefore, more research is needed to identify how and which types of working conditions contribute most to poor health outcomes. Interestingly, this study suggests that people do not appear to be cognizant of the connection between negative work conditions and their well-being; that is, despite evidence demonstrating a negative impact of job problems on health, few people with these problems appear to see connections among their work, health, and productivity.

To examine further the changing nature of work and its impact on employee well-being, the Field Institute poll also examined Californians' perceptions about job and financial security. Overall, results were mixed. One in five California workers (21%) reported fear of losing their jobs within the upcoming year. In contrast, 39% believed that they would likely get promotions. With respect to financial security, nearly two thirds believed that they were either worse off (29%) or essentially in the same financial situation (29%) that year, compared with the previous year, and only 42% reported being better off financially.

With respect to job skills, a lack of perceived security over job skills was associated with an increased prevalence of serious job-related problems. For instance, workers who reported being concerned about their job skills becoming outdated and those who did not use computers were more likely to report having serious job-related problems. With respect to skill base, those who rated themselves as very concerned about skill obsolescence were much more likely than those who were unconcerned to report having serious job-related problems (71% vs. 37%). Furthermore, 70% of workers who do not use computers reported having job problems, compared with 44% of computer "beginners," 39% of comfortable users, and 31% of sophisticated users.

When asked what they blamed most for job insecurity, the top two factors identified by California workers were organizational restructuring and/or personnel practices. More specifically, 65% of workers blamed company mergers, downsizing, and/or relocation; 42% blamed company practices of hiring temporary employees ("temps") instead of permanent workers. Other factors that were blamed for job insecurity included a lack of worker job training (32%); foreign competition (31%); government laws and policies (31%); technical advances (30%); and new immigrants (28%).

Health Insurance Policy Program

The goal of the Health Insurance Policy Program (HIPP) is to support the development of state policy to increase access to health insurance for employees and their dependents—insurance that not only is affordable and comprehensive but also emphasizes the promotion of health and the prevention of disease. Recently, the HIPP published a comprehensive report, *The State of Health Insurance in California, 1996* (Schauffler, Brown, & Rice, 1997), which is the first in a series of annual reports based on statewide surveys of representative samples of the population under age 65 and employers, as well as all HMOs, major health insurers, and purchasing cooperatives operating in California.

Overall, results of the HIPP report reinforced our view that work may have enormous potential for positively affecting the health and well-being of individuals. Most adult Californians, for example, got their health insurance through work. Work was also the primary vehicle through which health promotion opportunities were available.

A large proportion of the California population, however, nearly one person in four, continue to go without health insurance coverage, even when governmental programs like Medi-Cal are available. In 1994, 6.6 million Californians—23% of the population under age 65—were uninsured. This figure included 1.8 million children—one out of five in the state. Contrary to some beliefs, the uninsured were largely *working* families and adults. They were also predominantly low income and non-White. More than 8 in every 10 uninsured persons in California (84%) were either workers or in families headed by workers, including 6 in 10 (61%) who were full-time employees or their dependents. Also, nearly half of all uninsured employees (48%) worked full-time for the full year. With respect to race and ethnicity, a disproportionate number of Latinos (36%), African Americans (20%), and Asians (23%) were uninsured. In contrast, fewer non-Latino Whites (16%) were uninsured. In addition, two thirds of all uninsured Californians had low family incomes, and two thirds of all uninsured adult employees made less than $15,000 per year. Furthermore, individuals working in firms with fewer than 50 employees were much less likely to have health benefits available to them than those working in firms with more than 1,000 employees (66% vs. 95%).

When asked why they are uninsured, more than half of uninsured adults (54%) cited job-related reasons for their lack of health insurance coverage—for example, their employers did not offer coverage, or they were without coverage because they lost or changed jobs. Indeed, most non-elderly Californians did get their health insurance through employment (57%), with the best health insurance coverage received by families in which at least one adult was employed full-time for the full year. In contrast, only a small share of the population below age 65 (4%) purchased health insurance plans in the private market—that is, purchased insurance independent of any employment group. In general, job-based coverage usually provided broader benefits and smaller deductibles and copayments than privately purchased insurance.

A second major reason cited for being uninsured was the high cost of health coverage. One in five uninsured adults cited the high cost of insurance as the main reason they were uninsured. Employers reported that the main reasons they did not offer health benefits to their workers were the high cost of premiums (73%), and financial considerations such as uncertain profits (62%) or future costs (48%).

Lack of health insurance coverage is especially problematic because it deprives many people of both medical care for their current health problems and preventive care that could help reduce their health risks. Results from this study showed that uninsured adults aged 18 to 64 in California had poorer health status, higher rates of preventable health risks, and less access to preventive care than did insured adults. More than one third of uninsured adults in California (37%) did not go to the doctor in 1996, even when they needed medical care, because of the cost.

In contrast with estimates from 1992 national survey data, which suggest that 81% of companies with 50 or more employees offered at least one health promotion activity (DHHS, 1993), the HIPP report revealed a much lower prevalence of company-sponsored WHP programs in California in 1996. Only 31% of California companies with 1,000 or more employees were found to offer such programs, compared with about 15% of mid-size firms (200-1,000 employees), 13% of companies with 51 to 199 employees, and only 3% of small firms (those with 5-50 employees). This apparent sharp decline or marked regional difference in traditional WHP programs requires further thorough investigation. With respect to types of WHP programs offered, small firms tended to have only programs in exercise-related and weight loss programs, whereas larger firms tended to provide the most health benefits. Among the largest firms, the most common WHP benefits were stress management, exercise-related programs, weight management, and smoking cessation.

Compared with the low rate of company-sponsored WHP programs in California, almost two thirds (65%) of HMOs surveyed subsidized work site health promotion programs. In contrast, only 30% of PPO/indemnity plans provided subsidies. HMO-sponsored programs included preventive screening, health risk appraisals, and exercise facilities. About one third of health plans offering work site programs required a minimum group size, usually 50 employees. Thus, an important barrier to work site health promotion for small employers is that many health plans have policies against offering work site programs to small firms.

Consistent with past research, this study found that very few workers with work site and/or HMO-sponsored health promotion programs available to them used these programs. Only 5% of adults under age 65 in California reported that they participated in WHP programs, and only 2% of the sample reported having participated in health promotion programs offered through their health plans. In general, participation in WHP programs was highest among those with insurance coverage provided by their employers, those working in large firms (500 or more employees), and those who had been working for more than 5 years at the same job. Participation was low among individuals who purchased their own insurance and those who were covered through Medi-Cal. Not surprisingly, uninsured individuals participated the least (1%). Despite the adoption of work site wellness programs, particularly by large employers, the low use rate may limit their potential impact on health improvement among adults in California.

Winning New Jobs

Many displaced workers remain unemployed for long periods, suffering a variety of negative psychosocial and physical health consequences. Searching for a new job can be a long-term, uncertain, coping activity that requires substantial self-control and self-efficacy. The Winning New Jobs (WNJ) program seeks to help unemployed workers avoid depression, anxiety, and adverse health behaviors while they are seeking reemployment. Specifically, the program is building training capacities within three community organizations to provide job-search training to 6,500 Californians. These individuals will represent a mix of California's job-losers across categories of income, job classification, industry, ethnicity, and gender. The content delivered through WNJ has been shown, by rigorous scientific studies, to enhance quality reemployment and psychological well-being (see Price, van Ryn, & Vinokur, 1992; Vinokur, van Ryn, Gramlich, & Price, 1991).

As the intervention has been designed, each site follows basic eligibility parameters during the recruitment of potential participants in an effort to select those for whom the intervention has been shown to be most effective. Specifically, participants should (a) be at least 18 years of age, (b) have been employed in the past for at least 6 months, (c) be seeking a job, and have either lost or left a job within the past year, (d) be literate in the language in which training is provided, and (e) not be experiencing high levels of depression (as measured by the Hopkins Symptom Checklist) at the time of enrollment. This procedure will ensure that the program is reaching the intended target population, as well as minimizing the possibility of negative consequences for persons who would be better served by a different type of intervention or training. To address the problem of workers who lack the fundamental skills necessary for high-quality employment, grantee organizations will provide either referrals or training services to participants who lack the requisite job skills.

Implementing innovative programs such as WNJ presents numerous challenges (e.g., Lorig, 1986; Scheirer, 1981). The implementation process is complex, and many problems can occur. Innovations fail for a variety of reasons, including resistance to change by individuals, organizations, the community, or the intended beneficiaries (Rothman, Erlich, & Teresa, 1976; Zaltman, Duncan, & Holbek, 1984). In addition, innovative programs may fail if the program itself is not sound (Fullan, 1982), if persons responsible for implementation do not understand the context into which the new programs are introduced (Sarason, 1972), or if program developers fail to involve the persons delivering the program during implementation and adoption phases (Oppewal, 1992).

Typically, innovations are not adopted instantaneously by organizational decision makers. They infiltrate organizations, moving between social units and passing through several phases, including awareness, evaluation, adoption, utilization, and institutionalization (Beyer & Trice, 1978; Daft, 1982; Ettlie & Vallenga, 1979). The earliest phase of implementation and program adoption is what Berman (1981) refers to as *mobilization*. Mobilization involves the preparation for change; it consists of making the decision to adopt an innovation and planning the innovation's implementation. The success of an innovation is determined by how well management acquires, allocates, and uses its personnel, facilities, equipment, supplies, and cash (Zelman, McLaughlin, Gelb, & Miller, 1985).

To ensure the greatest possible success for the demonstration components of the Work and Health Initiative, much effort has focused on assessing organizational readiness to adopt and deliver innovative programs. Although some authors have written about readiness as it applies to individuals (e.g., Armenakis, Harris, & Mossholder, 1993), less is known about the specific aspects of readiness as it applies to organizations. Careful attention has been given to indicators of organizational readiness while selecting WNJ sites and implementing the program.

The WNJ site selection and implementation phases have afforded an opportunity to learn about organizational preparation and program adoption. Of particular interest is the sites' ability to mobilize financial and human resources. Site selection was a multistage process that began by identifying potential communities and that resulted in the selection of six California counties. Specifically, the community assessment process involved several criteria, including size of the unemployed population, projected changes in the local labor markets, geographic diversity, and ethnic and racial diversity. Within the targeted counties, 300 organizations were identified as working with the unemployed and received the request for proposal. Proposals from responding organizations were reviewed, and site visits were conducted in an effort to determine "organizational readiness" to adopt WNJ. Organizational readiness assessments were based on numerous criteria, including the following:

Indicators of organizational capacity (e.g., size, age, financial resources, history and nature of programs and services, characteristics of the community served)

Indicators that the organization was not duplicating services offered nearby

Evidence of collaboration among agencies (where appropriate) and the ways such partnerships would strengthen the ability to meet program goals

Efficacy of the WNJ client recruitment plan

Provision of extra support and services for job-search and employment needs

Compatibility of the organization's mission and WNJ goals

WNJ is currently being implemented within three separate types of organizations (a private industry council, educational institution, and community-based organization). The intention in sampling organizations included in different service systems is to facilitate later dissemination of the program. Furthermore, it enables greater learning through comparative research of the program as it operates in unique settings and serves different populations. For example, with the multicultural diversity of California communities, this project will allow us to explore the ways WNJ may affect groups differently. Also, this design provides an opportunity to examine the tension that always exists between maintaining program fidelity and making the adaptations to serve unique populations. Currently, we are learning about the ways implementation speed is related to organizational type, including differences in administrative structures, organization size, and staffing patterns.

As workplace trends suggest, Californians may increasingly experience temporary work and a sequential career. As those individuals face more frequent career transitions, finely honed job-search skills, such as those acquired through WNJ, may be crucial for the maintenance of employability and for increasing the long-term quality of work life.

Computers in Our Future

With the growing demand in work settings for technology literacy, community computing centers in low-income communities are a potentially powerful resource for fostering technology access and literacy, developing life skills, and increasing employability. In particular, the development of culturally sensitive programming within such communities should increase the possibility of reaching and effectively serving "at-risk" populations—in particular, youths and young people who might otherwise succumb to the negative life events in their community environments.

The Computers in Our Future (CIOF) program aims to help youths and young adults from low-income communities learn computer skills to improve their education and employment opportunities—thereby improving their own future health, as well as the health and well-being of their families and communities. This program is creating computer learning centers within community service organizations in 11 low-income areas where residents have had very limited access to the latest information technologies. The goal is to teach computer literacy to thousands of youths and young adults in participating communities— individuals who currently do not have access to information technology.

Overall, the CIOF program model is designed to achieve four positive outcomes. First, it seeks to provide *access for residents of low-income communities.* Centers will offer periods of largely unrestricted use of computers to residents of low-income communities who would otherwise lack access to computer technology. Second, the program emphasizes *education and skills development for youths and young adults.* Centers will use computers to teach skills that enhance employment and educational opportunities, specifically for youths and young adults in the 14- to 23-age range. Third, the program provides *service to the wider community as a technology resource.* Centers should have linkages with, and serve as a vital computer technology resource for, important organizations in the broader community, such as businesses, schools, and community-based organizations. Last, the program seeks to serve as *a respected community voice in support of technology access.* The leadership of each center will include a broadly represented Community Technology Advisory Committee (CommTAC) composed of local, governmental, and business leaders. This group will guide development of the center, build support for the center's work, and assist in articulating and advocating policies that ensure equitable technology access for low-income communities.

The CIOF program includes a unique and multifaceted emphasis on employability, community organizing, broad policy advocacy, and corporate sponsorship. Additionally, CIOF seeks to create a model, capable of replication and adaptation, for introducing technology literacy in low-income communities and to encourage development of public and corporate policies that support the community technology learning model. The program will depend on close partnerships and corporate sponsorship. This will allow not only for cost-effective technology procurement but also for insight into the skill needs of California's employers.

As discussed earlier in the section on Winning New Jobs, developing and implementing an innovative program are often fraught with challenges and potential pitfalls. To ensure the greatest possible success for CIOF, much like WNJ, careful attention was given to the assessment of organizational readiness of potential sites. Significant time and resources were expended in an effort to assess carefully each site's capabilities and to identify potential organizational level indicators of readiness to develop and deliver the innovative CIOF program. Examples of questions asked to assess readiness are listed below:

What is the overall quality of the applicant organization or partnership?
Is the applicant relevant and accessible to its served community?
Is there a good fit between CIOF and the applicant? How suitable is the identified program site?
What is the quality of key staff?
What is the applicant's commitment to evaluation and demonstration?
What is the applicant's capability for running a technology program?
What is the quality of the employment component of the program?
What are the applicant's prospects for long-term sustainability?
What is the quality of the proposed CIOF program? What special features are offered by this applicant?

One key lesson learned during the site selection process was that the CIOF program model is very ambitious relative to most community-based organizations. The selection process provided a means of verifying our assessment of organizational readiness and capacity among applicant organizations. The applicant organizations varied in their ability to address and integrate various components of the CIOF program model. Applicants tended to focus more on describing strategies for developing CIOF centers and programs and less on developing strategies for influencing policy and providing a technology resource to their community. These areas ultimately will enable a broader impact on their communities.

One implication is that the sites' need for technical assistance will be greater than originally anticipated. After the sites are funded, initial site visits will be held to identify (a) where the needs are greatest—for instance, in providing technology-oriented education, serving as a community resource, influencing policy, and evaluating programs—and (b) how these needs can be met most effectively.

A second implication concerns developing site capability to achieve the CIOF program objectives. To support site capacity building, sites will be allowed to adopt a "phased implementation" approach to program objectives; that is, each CIOF center will focus on providing community access to technology and technology training during Years 1 and 2. In Years 3 and 4, each center will go beyond the access and education components and work toward the goals of serving as a community resource and as a voice for improving technology opportunities. In addition, the California Wellness Foundation decided to increase the overall amount of funding and to "front-load" the funding (provide a greater proportion of funding earlier in the grant period); this funding is aimed at ensuring that sufficient resources are available early on to support site program development, implementation, and evaluation.

Concluding Remarks

We have attempted to expand the domain of work site health promotion by including the science and practice of promoting health "through work," as well as "at work." Much of the discussion has focused on understanding and responding to new links between work and health in a changing workplace. We posited that the nature of work itself, including psychosocial working conditions and access to quality employment, is perhaps the most powerful vehicle for improving people's health and well-being in modern societies. Systematic efforts toward improving the conditions of work, guided by rigorous evaluation research, seem to hold great promise for promoting individuals' health, well-being, and productivity, as well as for preventing social and community problems. It is our hope that the issues presented in this chapter stimulate other scientists and practitioners to consider the nature of work in their efforts toward preventing and solving community problems.

References

Aley, J. (1995). Where the jobs are. *Fortune, 132,* 53-56.

Armenakis, A. A., Harris, S. G., & Mossholder, K. W. (1993). Creating readiness for organizational change. *Human Relations, 46,* 681-703.

Berman, P. (1981). Educational change: An implementation paradigm. In R. Lehming & M. Kane (Eds.), *Improving schools: Using what we know.* Beverly Hills, CA: Sage.

Beyer, J. M., & Trice, H. M. (1978). *Implementing change: Alcoholism policies in work organizations.* New York: Free Press.

Borg, I., & Elizur, D. (1992). Job insecurity: Correlates, moderators, and measurements. *International Journal of Manpower, 13,* 13-26.

Brady, D. E., Mungen, D., Renwick, L., & Stassel, S. (1996, June 12). Round table: A discussion of poverty in the valley. *Los Angeles Times*, p. B1.

Brockner, J., Grover, S., Reed, T. F., & Dewitt, R. L. (1994). Layoff and surviving employees: The relationship between job insecurity and work effort. *Stores, 76*, RR10-11.

California Economic Strategy Panel. (1996). *Collaborating to compete in the new economy: An economic strategy for California.* Sacramento: California Trade and Commerce Agency.

Center for the Continuing Study of the California Economy. (1993). *California county projections.* Palo Alto: Author.

Conrad, K. M., Conrad, K. J., & Walcott-McQuigg, J. (1991). Threats to internal validity in worksite health promotion program research: Common problems and possible solutions. *American Journal of Health Promotion, 6*, 112-122.

Daft, R. L. (1982). Bureaucratic versus nonbureaucratic structure and the process of innovation and change. *Research in the Sociology of Organizations, 1*, 129-166.

Donaldson, S. I. (1995). Worksite health promotion: A theory-driven, empirically based perspective. In L. R. Murphy, J. J. Hurrell, S. L. Sauter, & G. P. Keita (Eds.), *Job stress interventions* (pp. 73-90). Washington, DC: American Psychological Association.

Donaldson, S. I., & Blanchard, A. L. (1995). The seven health practices, well-being, and performance at work: Evidence for the value of reaching small and underserved worksites. *Preventive Medicine, 24*, 270-277.

Donaldson, S. I., & Klien, D. (1997). Creating healthful work environments for ethnically diverse employees working in small and medium-size businesses: A nonprofit industry/community/university collaboration model. *Employee Assistance Quarterly, 13*, 17-32.

Donaldson, S. I., & Weiss, R. (1998). Health, well-being, and organizational effectiveness in the virtual workplace. In M. Igbaria & M. Tan (Eds.), *The virtual workplace.* Harrisburg, PA: Idea Group.

Dooley, D., Fielding, J., & Levi, L. (1996). Health and unemployment. *Annual Review of Public Health, 17*, 449-465.

Eisenberger, R., Fasolo, P., & Davis-LaMastro, V. (1990). Perceived organizational support and employee diligence, commitment, and innovation. *Journal of Applied Psychology, 75*, 51-59.

Erfurt, J. C., & Holtyn, K. (1991). Health promotion in small business: What works and what doesn't work? *Journal of Occupational Medicine, 33*, 66-73.

Ettlie, J. E., & Vallenga, D. B. (1979). The adoption time period for some transportation innovations. *Management Science, 25*, 429-443.

Everly, G. S., & Feldman, R. L. (1984). *Occupational health promotion: Health behavior in the workplace.* New York: John Wiley.

Every, D. K., & Leong, D. M. (1994). Exploring EAP cost-effectiveness: Profile of a nuclear power plant internal EAP. *Employee Assistance Quarterly, 10*, 1-12.

Falkenberg, L. E. (1987). Employee fitness programs: Their impact on the employee and the organization. *Academy of Management Review, 12*, 511-522.

Fielding, J. E. (1991). The challenges of workplace health promotion. In S. M. Weiss, J. E. Fielding, & A. Baum (Eds.), *Perspectives in behavioral medicine: Health at work* (pp. 13-28). Mahwah, NJ: Lawrence Erlbaum.

Fielding, J. E., & Piserchia, P. V. (1989). Frequency of worksite health promotion activities. *American Journal of Public Health, 79*, 16-20.

The Field Institute. (1996). *The work and health of Californians.* Report submitted to the

California Wellness Foundation, Woodland Hills, CA.

Frank, R. H., & Cook, P. J. (1995). *The winner-take-all society.* New York: Free Press.

Freud, S. (1930). *Civilization and its discontents* (J. Riviere, Trans.). London: Hogarth.

Friedman, D. (1994). *The new economy project.* Report for the New Vision Business Council of Southern California, Los Angeles.

Fullan, M. (1982). *The meaning of educational changes.* New York: Columbia University Teachers College.

Gebhardt, D. L., & Crump, C. E. (1990) Employee fitness and wellness programs in the workplace. Special issue: Organizational psychology. *American Psychologist, 45,* 262-272.

Gibbs, J. O., Mulvaney, D., Henes, C., & Reed, R. W. (1985). Worksite health promotion: Five-year trends in employee health care costs. *Journal of Occupational Medicine, 27,* 826-830.

Greiner, B. A. (1996). *Psychological work factors and health: Building bridges between disciplines* (pp. 1-38). Background paper for The California Wellness Foundation, Woodland Hills.

Grey, C., & Mitev, N. (1995). Reengineering organizations: A critical appraisal. *Personnel Review, 24,* 6-18.

Hakken, D. (1993). Computing and social change: New technology and workplace transformation, 1980-1990. *Annual Review of Anthropology, 22,* 107-132.

Harmon, A. (1996, October 7). With the digital era, age-old social schisms take on a new gravity. *Los Angeles Times, Business,* pp. D1, D4.

Hayghe, H., & Comartie, S. W. (1991). *Working women: A chartbook.* Washington, DC: U.S. Department of Labor, Bureau of Labor Statistics.

Hearney, C. A., Israel, B. A., & House, J. S. (1994). Chronic job insecurity among automobile workers: Effects on job satisfaction and health. *Social Science and Medicine, 38,* 1431-1437.

Houston, P. (1992). Surviving the survivor syndrome. *Working Women, 17,* 56-60.

Howard, A. (1995). A framework for work change. In A. Howard (Ed.), *The changing nature of work* (pp. 1-44). San Francisco: Jossey-Bass.

Jarratt, J., Coates, J. F., Mahaffie, J. B., & Hinnes, A. (1995). Focusing on the future. *Association Management, 47,* 16-30.

Kaiser, J. (1988). Still on the sidelines: Health promotion has missed the mark with blue-collar workers. *Health Action Managers, 2,* 5-10.

Karasek, R., & Theorell, T. (1990). *Healthy work: Stress, productivity, and the reconstruction of working life.* New York: Basic Books.

Keita, G. P., & Sauter, S. L. (Eds.). (1992). *Work and well-being: An agenda for the 1990s.* Washington, DC: American Psychological Association.

Lazarus, W., & Lipper, L. (1996). *America's children and the information superhighway: An update.* Santa Monica, CA: Children's Partnership.

Levi, L. (1994). Work, worker, and well-being: An overview. Special issue: A healthier work environment. *Work & Stress, 8,* 79-83.

London, M., & Greller, M. M. (1991). Invited contribution: Demographic trends and vocational behavior: A 20-year retrospective and agenda for the 1990s. *Journal of Vocational Behavior, 28,* 125-164.

Lorig, K. (1986). Development and dissemination of an arthritis patient education course. *Family & Community Health, 9,* 23-32.

Los Angeles County Internal Services Department. (1993). Los Angeles: Southern California Association of Governments, Urban Research Section, Information Technology Services.

Matteson, M. T., & Ivancevich, J. M. (1988). Health promotion at work. In C. L. Cooper & I. T. Robertson (Eds.), *International review of industrial and organizational psychology: 1988.* Chichester, UK: Wiley.

Mazmanian, D. A. (1995). *Clear vision, clean skies: A new epoch in air pollution control for the Los Angeles region.* Claremont, CA: Claremont Graduate School.

McDonald, T., & Siegall, M. (1992). The effects of technological self-efficacy and job focus on job performance, attitudes, and withdrawal behaviors. *Journal of Psychology, ·126,* 465-475.

Murphy, L. R., Hurrell, J. J., Jr., Sauter, S. L., & Keita, G. P. (Eds.). (1995). *Job stress interventions.* Washington, DC: American Psychological Association.

O'Donnell, M. P. (1989). Definition of health promotion: 3. Expanding the definition. *American Journal of Health Promotion, 3,* 5-6.

O'Donnell, M. P., & Harris, J. S. (Eds.). (1994). *Health promotion in the workplace.* Albany, NY: Delmar.

Oppewal, S. R. (1992). Implementing a community-based innovation: Organizational challenges and strategies. *Family & Community Health, 15,* 70-79.

Pelletier, K. R. (1991). A review and analysis of the health and cost-effective outcome studies of comprehensive health promotion and disease prevention programs. *American Journal of Health Promotion, 5,* 311-315.

Pelletier, K. R. (1993). A review and analysis of the health and cost-effective studies of comprehensive health promotion and disease prevention programs at the worksite: 1991-1993 update. *American Journal of Health Promotion, 8,* 50-62.

Price, R. H., van Ryn, M., & Vinokur, A. D. (1992). Impact of a preventive job-search intervention on the likelihood of depression among the unemployed. *Journal of Health and Social Behavior, 33,* 158-167.

Quick, J. C., Murphy, L. R., & Hurrell, J. J., Jr. (Eds.). (1992). *Stress and well-being at work: Assessments and interventions for occupational mental health.* Washington, DC: American Psychological Association.

Quick, J. C., Murphy, L. R., Hurrell, J. J., Jr. & Orman, D. (1992). The value of work, the risk of distress, and the poser of prevention. In J. C. Quick, L. R. Murphy, & J. J. Hurrell, Jr. (Eds.), *Stress and well-being at work: Assessments and interventions for occupational mental health.* Washington, DC: American Psychological Association.

Rifkin, J. (1995). *The end of work: The decline of the global labor force and the dawn of the postmarket era.* New York: Tarcher/Putnam.

Rogers, R. (1995). The psychological contract of trust: Part I. *Executive Development, 8,* 15-19.

Rosen, R., & Berger, L. (1991). *The healthy company: Eight strategies to develop people, productivity, and profits.* Los Angeles: Tarcher.

Rothman, J., Erlich, J. L., & Teresa, J. G. (1976). *Promoting innovation and change in organization and communities: A planning manual.* New York: John Wiley.

Rousseau, D. M. (1996). Changing the deal while keeping the people. *Academy of Management Executive, 10,* 50-59.

Sarason, S. B. (1972). *The creation of settings and the future societies.* San Francisco: Jossey-Bass.

Sauter, S. L., & Murphy, L. R. (Eds.). (1995). *Organizational risk factors for job stress.* Washington, DC: American Psychological Association.

Schauffler, H. H., Brown, E. R., & Rice, T. (1997). *The state of health insurance in California, 1996.* Los Angeles: University of California, Center for Health Policy Research.

Scheirer, M. A. (1981). *Program implementation: The organizational context.* Beverly Hills, CA: Sage.

Schroth, R., & Mui, C. (1995). Ten major trends in strategic networking. *Telecommunications, 29,* 33-42.

Sloan, R. P. (1987). Workplace health promotion: A commentary on the evolution of a paradigm. *Health Education Quarterly, 14,* 181-194.

Sproull, L., & Kiesler, S. (1991). *Connections: New ways of working in the networked organization.* Cambridge: MIT Press.

Stenberg, C. W., III, & Colman, W. G. (1994). *America's future workforce: A health and education policy issues handbook.* Westport, CT: Greenwood.

Stokols, D. (1992). Establishing and maintaining healthy environments: Toward a social ecology of health promotion. *American Psychologist, 47,* 6-22.

Stokols, D. (1996). Bridging the theoretical and applied facets of environmental psychology. *American Psychologist, 51,* 1188-1189.

Stokols, D., Pelletier, K. R., & Fielding, J. E. (1995). Integration of medical care and worksite health promotion. *Journal of the American Medical Association, 273,* 1136-1142.

Terborg, J. R. (1986). Health promotion at the worksite: A research challenge for personnel and human resources management. In K. M. Rowland & G. R. Ferris (Eds.), *Research in personnel and human resources management* (pp. 225-267). Greenwich, CT: JAI.

Tomaskovic-Devey, D., & Risman, B. J. (1993). Telecommuting innovation and organization: A contingency theory of labor process change. *Social Science Quarterly, 74,* 367-385.

Tomas Rivera Center. (1996). *Latinos and information technology: Perspectives for the 21st century.* Claremont, CA: Author.

U.S. Bureau of the Census. (1992). *Statistical abstract of the United States.* Washington, DC: U.S. Department of Commerce.

U.S. Bureau of the Census. (1993). Current population reports. *Hispanic Americans today* (pp. 23-183). Washington, DC: Government Printing Office.

U.S. Department of Health and Human Services (DHHS). (1991). *Healthy people 2000: National health promotion and disease prevention objectives* (DHHS Publication No. PHS 91-50212). Washington, DC: Government Printing Office.

U.S. Department of Health and Human Services (DHHS). (1993). 1992 national survey of worksite health promotion activities: Summary. *American Journal of Health Promotion, 7,* 452-464.

Vinokur, A. D., van Ryn, M., Gramlich, E. M., & Price, R. H. (1991). Long-term follow-up and benefit-cost analysis of the JOBS program: A preventive intervention for the unemployed. *Journal of Applied Psychology, 76,* 213-219.

Walters, D. (1996, May 7). Age gap is growing into a political issue. *Fresno Bee, Telegraph,* p. A3.

Warner, K. E. (1987). Selling health promotion to corporate America: Uses and abuses of the economic argument. *Health Education Quarterly, 14,* 39-55.

Warner, K. E., Wickizer, T. M., Wolfe, R. A., Schildroth, J. E., & Samuelson, M. H. (1988). Economic implications of workplace health promotion programs: Review of the literature. *Journal of Occupational Medicine, 10,* 106-112.

Wells, M., Stokols, D., McMahan, S., & Clitheroe, C. (in press). Evaluation of a worksite injury and illness prevention program: Do the effects of the REACH OUT training program reach the employees? *Journal of Occupational Health Psychology.*

Williams, A. F. (1982). Passive and active measures for controlling disease and injury: The role of health psychologists. *Health Psychology, 1,* 399-409.

World Health Organization (WHO). (1948). *Constitution of the World Health Organization.* Geneva, Switzerland: WHO Basic Documents.

Zaltman, G., Duncan, R., & Holbek, J. (1984). *Innovations and organizations.* Malabar, FL: Krieger.

Zelman, W. N., McLaughlin, C. P., Gelb, N., & Miller, E. (1985). Survival strategies for community mental health organizations: A conceptual framework. *Community Mental Health Journal, 21,* 228-236.

8

Job-Loss and Work Transitions in a Time of Global Economic Change

RICHARD H. PRICE
DANIEL S. FRIEDLAND
JIN NAM CHOI
ROBERT D. CAPLAN

We live in an era of dramatic economic, political, and technological change. In the United States, manufacturing industries are rapidly shrinking, and the service economy is growing. At the same time, in other parts of the world, planned economies are giving way to market economies (Porter, 1990). Technology is changing rapidly, and jobs that used to be done with strong backs are now being taken over by automated systems (Reich, 1990). All of these changes are producing economic restructuring on a global scale (see Figure 8.1), which in turn is producing dramatic transformations in the nature of jobs and work (Thurow, 1992).

AUTHORS' NOTE: Work on this chapter was supported by NIMH grants 5P30MH38330 and R10MH52913 to the Michigan Prevention Research Center, as well as by the California Wellness Foundation through Manpower Demonstration Research Corporation (96-90).

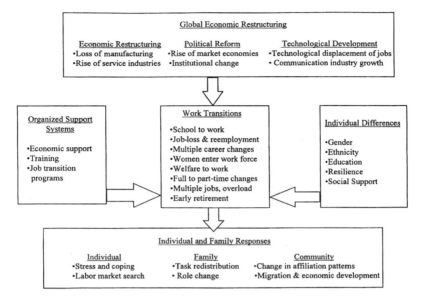

Figure 8.1. Global Economic Change, Work Transitions, and Individual and Family Response

Traditional jobs, involving a mutual commitment between worker and employer for full-time work in exchange for pay over the course of a working life, are rapidly disappearing. Downsizing, job displacement, the rise of a temporary workforce (Belous, 1989), and demographic changes, both in the United States and elsewhere, are producing job-loss and work transitions of unprecedented scope and variety. These work transitions not only involve job-loss and reemployment but also reflect changes in the nature of work and careers as women enter the workforce and as students strive to make the transition from school to work. At the same time, welfare support to families now involves a work require-ment, which is producing new transitions from welfare to work (Bane & Ellwood, 1994). Many workers faced with low pay rates in the service economy (Danziger & Gottschalk, 1995) are taking on multiple jobs and are experiencing substantial work overload as a consequence. Finally, workers who have lost their jobs toward the end of their working life are facing the possibility of early retirement, often with the prospect of continuing economic insecurity. How individuals and families cope with these work transitions will depend heavily on where they are located in the social structure in terms of education, ethnicity, and gender. Individual differences in psychological resilience and in levels of social support will have an important impact as well (Dew, Penkower, & Bromet, 1991).

How individuals and families respond to these work transitions will depend heavily on the organized support systems available to them (Price, 1992). In most Western industrialized nations, some form of economic support and training is available to workers facing work transitions. Nevertheless, we believe that carefully designed programs to aid individuals and families in successfully coping with the transitions they face continue to be an important unmet need—not only in the United States but also in many other countries. Individuals and families will face continued periods of stress and coping in the process of negotiating work transitions. Many of these transitions will require new forms of family adaptation, including changes in family roles and responsibilities. Finally, work transitions such as job-loss and reemployment will also have important impacts on communities—in some cases, stimulating migration patterns and local efforts at economic development, and in others, changing patterns of friendship and work-family relationships in communities.

Necessity, Invention, and Reinvention

We believe that these myriad work transitions and their often deleterious effects present a compelling necessity for the invention of more effective organized support systems for individuals and families. In this chapter, we describe one important dimension of that compelling *necessity*—the impact of job-loss and economic hardship on individuals, families, and communities. We then describe one such *invention*—the JOBS program, developed by the Michigan Prevention Research Center—and we document the program's impact on reemployment, psychological well-being, and other outcomes. Even proven programs of organized support, however, are not automatically adopted and implemented where they are needed. Therefore, we examine three paradigms for the diffusion of innovations and conclude that innovations such as JOBS will, necessarily, require *reinvention*—mutual adaptation between the host organization or community and the innovation itself. Finally, we argue that a theory of the intervention is an essential guide to the process of mutual adaptation and for the accumulation of new knowledge.

Necessity: Job-Loss Impact on
Individuals, Families, and Communities

Since the pioneering work of Jahoda, Lazarsfeld, and Zeisel (1933), job-loss has been a topic of research in social science. Research findings have documented the psychological and social costs of job-loss for the unemployed person, for individual members of the person's family, and for the family as a whole (Dew et al., 1991). In what follows, we review that research, with special emphasis on how job-loss and economic hardship have effects that influence individual, family, and community well-being.[1]

Impact of Job-Loss on Mental Health. Job-loss has adverse effects on social and psychological functioning (Vinokur, Caplan, & Williams, 1987). Research indicates that job-loss leads to increased depressive symptoms (Catalano, 1991; Catalano & Dooley, 1977; Kessler, Turner, & House, 1988, 1989), increased anxiety (Catalano, 1991), decreased subjective perceptions of competence (Warr, Jackson, & Banks, 1988), and decreased self-esteem (Jackson & Warr, 1984). Job-loss is also associated with increased risk of suicide attempts (Platt & Kreitman, 1985), increased risk of alcohol abuse (Catalano, Dooley, Wilson, & Hough, 1993), and increased propensity for violent behavior (Catalano, Dooley, Novaco, Wilson, & Hough, 1993). Several studies have demonstrated that job-loss produces mental health problems that are significantly more extensive than any prior problems (Dooley, Catalano, & Wilson, 1994; Kessler, Turner, & House, 1987).

The Role of Economic Hardship. Studies have identified economic hardship as a key mediating influence between job-loss and depressive symptomatology (e.g., Kessler et al., 1987; Price, van Ryn, & Vinokur, 1992; Vinokur, Price, & Schul, 1995). Furthermore, substantial evidence suggests a relationship between economic hardship and health outcomes more generally (Umberson, Wortman, & Kessler, 1992).

Impact of Job-Loss on Family Members. Job-loss also affects members of the job-seeker's family (Dew et al., 1991; Elder & Caspi, 1988). The job-seeker's increased propensity for aggressive and sometimes violent behavior often manifests itself in the context of the family. Positive correlations have been found between job-loss and both spousal abuse (Windschuttle, 1980) and child abuse (Gil, 1970; Parke & Collmer, 1975). Research also indicates that the wives of job-losers have a higher prevalence of psychiatric disorders than wives of people who remain employed (Bebbington, Hurry, Tennant, Stuart, & Wing, 1981). Finally, job-loss has been linked with marital and family dissolution (Liem & Liem, 1988). The deprivation associated with economic hardship may affect physical health and general well-being of family members, both because of negative effects on nutrition and because of loss of access to health care. Poor nutrition because of economic hardship has its own radiating set of consequences on well-being. Poor nutrition can make both children and adults more susceptible to physical illness (Beasley, 1991). Malnourished children show lower levels of school achievement (Pollitt, 1994), increasing the likelihood of continued downward social mobility in later generations.

Because, in the United States, health insurance is frequently tied directly to paid employment, one of the most immediate consequences of job-loss is diminished access to health care for family members of the job-loser. Price (1990) has observed that families will often reallocate limited benefits among family members. For example, a family may seek treatment for children while neglecting acute conditions among adults. Individuals may fail to seek either preventive services or care for acute and chronic conditions. In these circumstances, acute conditions can become chronic, and chronic conditions may deteriorate still further (Price, 1990). These health effects, of course, also influence the capacity of unemployed persons to seek new employment that might reverse the flow of negative health and unemployment effects.

Impact of Job-Loss on Family Relationships. Still another set of findings implicates economic hardship and family dynamics in increasing the risk of poor mental health. Several studies suggest that the distress displayed by job-losers affects the well-being of their spouses (Liem & Liem, 1988; Penkower, Bromet, & Dew, 1988), as well as their children (Elder & Caspi, 1988; Justice & Duncan, 1977; Steinberg, Catalano, & Dooley, 1981). Recent results reported by Vinokur, Price, and Caplan (1996) implicate additional couple dynamics in influencing the mental health of the unemployed person. Their analyses suggest that economic hardship increases depressive symptoms in both the job-loser and the spouse. The depressed spouse or partner then withdraws social support from, and increases undermining behaviors toward, the unemployed person. Both reduced support and increased undermining by the spouse then increase the depression and reduce the marital satisfaction of the unemployed person. These findings suggest that economic hardship associated with job-loss in a family has direct effects on the spouse or partner, which in turn erodes her or his capacity to support the job-loser, with predictable effects on the job-loser's mental health.

Finally, job-loss disrupts one's sense of identity, mastery, and competence in valued social roles as provider, spouse, and parent (Thoits, 1991). This role disruption takes several forms. Job-loss introduces new and pressing agendas into the family, including coping with financial hardship and mobilizing to find reemployment, and these can disrupt previously stable household role allocations and relationships (Conger et al., 1990; Menaghan, 1991). When role reallocation involves shifts in authority and status in the family, the resulting shift in power dynamics can lead to conflicts that threaten the short-term stability of the couple relationship (Atkinson, Liem, & Liem, 1986). Such a realignment can undermine the self-confidence of the job-seeker and partner in coping with job-loss, both individually and as a couple (Howe, Caplan, Foster, Lockshin, & McGrath, 1995; Vinokur et al., 1987).

Job-Loss and Community Processes. The impact of job-loss on community processes has been well documented in numerous studies, beginning with the classic study of Marienthal by Marie Jahoda et al. (1933) during the Great Depression. Jahoda and her colleagues found that unemployment influenced a wide variety of aspects of community life, including friendship patterns, how people structured their time, and their sense of identity and well-being. Job-loss may also alter an individual's network of friendships and social support. Loss of a job may result in loss of a primary source of contact with friends (Bolton & Oatley, 1987). Because friendships often arise and are maintained by proximity (Whyte, 1956), bonds of friendship are more difficult to maintain when people are no longer employed by the same organization. Over time, the frequency of contact with friends from the previous job decreases (Atkinson et al., 1986). Loss of friendship networks can erode mental health. Kessler et al. (1988) found that being integrated into an affiliative network reduced the impact of unemployment on anxiety,

depression, somatization, and physical illness of job-losers. Their findings underline the importance of supportive friendships for identity and
well-being.

Invention: The JOBS Program of Research
on the Psychology of Job-Search

In 1982, researchers at the Institute for Social Research at the
University of Michigan began a new program of research on the problems facing unemployed persons and their families. This continuous
program of research conducted over the last 15 years has produced
detailed information on the problems facing unemployed persons and their
families, particularly those associated with job-search (Caplan, Vinokur,
Price, & van Ryn, 1989), economic hardship (Vinokur et al., 1996), and
family difficulties (Howe et al., 1995; Price, 1992). After a series of
studies documenting these problems and analyzing the needs of unemployed workers and their families, the Michigan Prevention Research
Center (MPRC) developed and evaluated the JOBS program to aid
unemployed workers in effectively seeking reemployment and coping
with the multiple challenges and stresses of unemployment and
job-search (Caplan, Vinokur, & Price, 1997; Price & Vinokur, 1995).

The positive impact of the JOBS program has been documented and
replicated in randomized trials (Caplan et al., 1989; Vinokur et al.,
1995). New related programs have been developed for helping couples
cope with job-loss and job-search (Howe et al., 1995) and with economic hardship (Vinokur et al., 1995). In a promising new development,
private and public agencies in California, Finland, Israel, and China are
investing in research and development and are adopting and replicating
the JOBS program to respond to their own unique problems and needs
in the area of job-loss and reemployment.

What Is the JOBS Program?

JOBS is a program for recruitment into, delivery of, and evaluation
of a job-search, skill-enhancement workshop for unemployed job-seekers.
The JOBS model has the dual goals of promoting reemployment and
enhancing coping capacities for the unemployed and their families. The
intervention workshop itself consists of five intensive half-day sessions
held over a 1- to 2-week period. These sessions focus on identifying

effective job-search strategies, improving participant job-search skills, and increasing the self-esteem, confidence, and motivation of participants to engage in and persist in job-search activities until they become reemployed. JOBS is delivered by two trainers to groups of job-seekers consisting of 12 to 20 participants.

The program has five essential components:

1. *Job-search skills training.* Participants are invited to acquire and rehearse job-search skills in a safe and supportive learning environment, which is crucial for effective learning of new skills (Caplan et al., 1989).

2. *Active teaching and learning methods.* Trainers use nondidactic, active-learning methods to engage participants in job-search training. These methods use the knowledge and skills of the participants themselves as part of the learning process—elicited through small- and large-group discussions, role-playing exercises, and other activities (Caplan et al., 1997).

3. *Skilled trainers.* Workshop trainers are carefully chosen and rigorously trained to build trust and to work together in pairs to facilitate group processes that promote the learning of skills and the ability to cope with job-search tasks.

4. *Supportive learning environment.* In the workshops, trainers model and reinforce supportive behavior and work to create a positive learning environment through exercises that provide opportunities for participants to learn from and support each other. Social support is a key ingredient for new learning and facing challenges in the job market (Price & Vinokur, 1995).

5. *Inoculation against setbacks.* Program participants are provided with a problem-solving process to help them cope with the stress related to unemployment and the job-search process and the inevitable setbacks they will encounter. Part of the group problem-solving process involves identifying or anticipating possible barriers to success and advance preparation of solutions to overcome them. Inoculation against setbacks is fundamental to effective coping with an inherently stressful job-search process (Vinokur & Schul, in press).

What Is the Impact of JOBS?

A summary of studies on the impact of JOBS is presented in Table 8.1. The JOBS program has been evaluated and replicated in randomized

Table 8.1
Impact of the MPRC JOBS Program:
Major Findings (1989-1997)

Major Findings	Research Report
JOBS I	
- More rapid reemployment	Caplan, Vinokur, Price, & van Ryn (1989). *Journal of Applied Psychology.*
- Stronger search motivation	
- Better mental health	
- Higher earnings	
- Favorable benefit-cost ratio	Vinokur, van Ryn, Gramlich, & Price (1991). *Journal of Applied Psychology.*
- Impact greater with more exposure to program	Vinokur, Price, & Caplan (1991). *American Journal of Community Psychology.*
- Job-search self-efficacy key factor in impact	van Ryn & Vinokur (1992). *American Journal of Community Psychology.*
- Reduces risk of depressive episodes in high-risk participants	Price, van Ryn, & Vinokur (1992). *Journal of Health and Social Behavior.*
JOBS II	
- Replicates major JOBS I findings	Vinokur, Price, & Schul (1995). *American Journal of Community Psychology.*
- Improves mastery for all participants	
- Reduces depression in high-risk participants	
- Reduces depression by reducing economic hardship	Vinokur & Schul (in press). *Journal of Consulting and Clinical Psychology.*
- Inoculates against depression from second job loss	

trials involving thousands of unemployed workers and their partners (Caplan et al., 1989; Vinokur et al., 1995). The program returns unemployed workers to new jobs more quickly, produces reemployment in jobs that pay more (Vinokur, van Ryn, Gramlich, & Price, 1991), and reduces mental health problems associated with prolonged unemployment (Vinokur et al., 1995), particularly among those most vulnerable to mental health problems (Price et al., 1992). In addition, the program has been shown to inoculate workers against the adverse effects of subsequent job-loss (Vinokur & Schul, in press). In comparison with control group counterparts, program participants who regained employment and suffered a second job-loss did not experience the same discouragement and increased depressive symptoms that afflicted control group participants who had the same labor market experience. The JOBS program inoculates participants against subsequent job-loss setbacks because they gain an enhanced sense of mastery over the challenges of job-search (Vinokur & Schul, in press).

Reemployment, Improved Mental Health and Cost-Benefit. In the initial series of outcome studies of the JOBS program, Caplan et al. (1989) found that JOBS participants showed higher job-search motivation, were reemployed more rapidly, and showed better mental health outcomes than control participants. These findings suggested that the JOBS program was achieving its goals of enhancing participants' motivation and skill, leading to reemployment and better mental health. In a subsequent study, Vinokur, van Ryn, et al. (1991) also found that participants in the JOBS program had, on average, higher earnings than those who did not participate and that the JOBS program demonstrated substantial cost-benefit effectiveness because higher earnings led on average to higher tax revenues for governments.

Higher Practical Impact. As in all social programs, not all people invited to the JOBS program attended. When analyses were confined only to those people who actually attended the JOBS program, the actual amount of impact of the program was shown to be approximately twice as large as it was for all invitees in the randomized trial (Vinokur, Price, & Caplan, 1991). This finding is particularly important because it suggests that the practical impact of the JOBS program is much larger than the conservative lower-bound estimates provided by strict adherence to the randomized-trial evaluation design.

High-Risk People Benefit Most. MPRC researchers suspected that not all participants benefited equally from the JOBS program, particularly in terms of mental health outcomes. What about those most vulnerable to the effects of job-loss? Were those most at risk able to benefit from the program? Price et al. (1992) conducted a series of analyses to identify those at highest risk for depression and found that elevated depressive symptoms, increased economic hardship, and low social assertiveness were key risk factors for subsequent episodes of depression. When they later conducted analyses to identify how groups exhibiting these risk factors fared, they found that high-risk participants benefited most from participation in the JOBS program, particularly in terms of reduced risk for episodes of depression.

Enhanced Job-Search Self-Efficacy. The mechanisms by which JOBS had its impact on reemployment also needed to be identified. Van Ryn and Vinokur (1992) conducted a series of analyses to identify those psychological factors, influenced by the JOBS program, that were responsible for positive outcomes. Their analyses indicated that an enhanced sense of job-search self-efficacy was a key factor responsible for positive impacts of the program.

Enhanced Mastery and Inoculation Against Setbacks. A second major replication of the JOBS program was conducted that replicated many of the initial findings and revealed other important outcomes. JOBS II replicated all major JOBS I findings and showed that mastery was enhanced for all participants and that high-risk participants benefited most in terms of reduced risk for later depression (Vinokur et al., 1995). JOBS II also provided an opportunity for further exploration of the mechanisms by which the innovation has its effects. Vinokur and Schul (in press) conducted a series of analyses to uncover the mechanisms by which the JOBS program has its effect on mental health. Their analyses make it clear that the beneficial mental health effects of the JOBS program are consequences of reduced economic hardship associated with reemployment for program participants.

New Focus on Couples and Economic Hardship. Additional studies by researchers in the Michigan Prevention Research Center have demonstrated that economic hardship and strain represent a major stressor for unemployed workers and their spouses (Vinokur et al., 1996). As a result, MPRC scientists have embarked on further research and program development aimed at enhancing family coping with economic stressors. At the same time, a related line of research by MPRC scientists has shown that the stresses of unemployment produce additional stresses in couple and family relationships (Howe et al. 1995; Vinokur et al., 1996). A program of research in collaboration with colleagues at George Washington University has begun another set of large-scale, randomized trials aimed at enhancing the coping resources and skills of couples facing job-loss.

JOBS Implementation in Diverse Settings. As the JOBS program has become more widely known, foundations, state governments, and governments in other countries have begun to invest in the JOBS program and have sought to implement JOBS in their own home settings. Under the sponsorship of the California Wellness Foundation, the Michigan Prevention Research Center is collaborating with the Manpower Demonstration Research Corporation to launch the "Winning New Jobs" project in three communities in California. The program is being implemented for 6,500 Californians who were recently unemployed. The 5-year project uses the JOBS intervention program in three distinctly different communities and service systems. In each case, the program involves existing community organizations, which receive funds, staff training, and technical assistance from the Michigan Prevention Research Center and the Manpower Demonstration Research Corporation to implement the JOBS program. Adoption and implementation of the program will be documented to provide concrete implementation lessons for adoption in other locations.

In addition, in collaboration with the Finnish Institute of Occupational Health, the JOBS program is being implemented and evaluated in Finland. The program is cosponsored by the Finnish Social Security Agency, the Finnish Department of Labor, and other agencies in Finland. Similarly, in collaboration with researchers at Tel Aviv University and with the support of the U.S.-Israel Binational Science Foundation, the MPRC has undertaken a program of research that will result in a randomized field experiment testing the effectiveness of the JOBS program in the existing service system for unemployed workers provided by the Israeli Ministry of Labor and Welfare. Finally, in collaboration with colleagues in China, we have begun a new program of research for implementation of the JOBS program. The MPRC will collaborate actively with Chinese scientists and service system administrators to adapt the JOBS program to the special cultural, social, and economic needs and circumstances of unemployed Chinese workers and their families, for whom the program is being developed.

Reinvention: Three Paradigms

Program models like JOBS that are based on extensive research showing evidence of their efficacy still represent only the first step on

Table 8.2
Implementing Social Innovations:
Three Perspectives

Paradigm	Assumption About Nature of Innovation	Assumption About Organization	Scenario for Implementation	Definition of Success
Technology Transfer	Fixed and constant technology; immutable	Passive recipient of innovation	Technology-dominant process; local and process conditions largely irrelevant	Adoption is sufficient
Perfect Replication	Ideal model is available from previous controlled research	Error-prone; bounded rationality	Strive for match between program as designed and local version	Minimum deviation from original design
Mutual Adaptation	Cannot exist independent of implementing organization	Organization is active shaper of innovation through internal and external exchange	Negotiated reinvention of prototype	Local ownership is valued as much as client impact

the route to establishing effective programs in the community. A large gap exists between developing a promising program model and establishing the model in practice. Embry (1984) has observed that "the field is littered with corpses of proven innovations. Solving a problem is usually not enough to ensure that the solution will be widely implemented" (p. 82). Price and Lorion (1989) have argued that implementation is an organizational process involving the orchestration of both external and internal organizational resources and requiring continuous negotiation with the environment of the organization. The implementing organization must also have the capacity to monitor and adjust aspects of the model program once it has been implemented. Successful implementation of an innovation like JOBS is a substantial organizational achievement.

Research and theory on social innovations reflect an evolution of ideas about the fundamental nature of the implementation. Indeed, the large literature on diffusion of innovations (Rogers, 1995) offers no single, clear-cut theoretical approach to guide research and action. Instead, several dominant paradigms have evolved (see Table 8.2). Each paradigm makes claims about the essential nature of innovating organizations and offers an implicit scenario for implementation. Furthermore, each paradigm has its own definition of success. These conceptual and operational paradigms influence the thinking of both researchers and practitioners. We believe that making the paradigms and their underlying assumptions explicit can be of great value in advancing scientific understanding, as well as actual practice.

Implementation as Technology Transfer

Perhaps the oldest and still-dominant paradigm involves the idea of *technology transfer.* As researchers worked in such fields as agriculture—where the innovation might be, for example, a new strain of seed corn—the innovation itself was viewed as a fixed and constant technology (Berman, 1981). The technology transfer paradigm also made strong assumptions about the nature of the adopting organization. In this view, the organization was essentially a passive recipient of the innovation and would fairly automatically adjust itself to the new process or product. Implementation was regarded as a mechanical process dominated by the technology itself. Local conditions and local organizational processes were regarded as largely irrelevant. Furthermore, the technology transfer perspective assumed that the implementation process was fairly automatic and error-free. As a consequence, the technology transfer paradigm defines success largely in terms of the adoption of the innovation. Indeed, much of the early research assumed that adoption was largely sufficient for successful implementation, and it paid little attention to the process of implementing the innovation that was adopted (Berman, 1981).

The prescription for implementing JOBS according to the technology transfer paradigm is fairly clear. Effort should be invested in promoting the adoption of JOBS by a wide range of organizations and communities. Conditions that promote adoption, such as credibility, relevance, trialability, and relative advantage (Rogers, 1995), should be enhanced and supported. Once adopted, actual implementation of JOBS would be fairly automatic, and evaluating the success of JOBS would be largely a matter of counting instances of adoption of the program.

Implementation as Perfect Replication

Reports of disquieting and inexplicable failures of innovations began to emerge in the field, and the view slowly emerged that adoption was clearly not enough for successful implementation (McGrew, Bond, Dietzen, & Salyers, 1994). Instead, evidence showed that, once adopted, innovations tended to be implemented quite differently in different organizations or failed to be implemented at all. This observation led some researchers to argue that implementing organizations should strive for *perfect replication* of the innovation as it emerged from the research process (Blakely et al., 1987). The argument was that an ideal model based on previous research was already available and that no deviation from the original model should be allowed. It is worth noting that implicit in the perfect replication paradigm was the idea that previous research had already revealed what was needed for effective implementation. Frequently, however, innovations are developed and tested in a limited range of circumstances, and their range of effectiveness, as well as the conditions necessary for their implementation in the field, are only imperfectly understood.

Nevertheless, the perfect replication paradigm assumes that the implementing organization is error-prone and subject to "bounded rationality" (March, 1981). The scenario for implementation is clear here. Organizations should strive for a match between the program as it was originally designed and the local version. In this paradigm, *success* is defined as a minimum deviation from the original design in implementation. If one were to apply the perfect replication paradigm to implementing JOBS, the plan would focus on creating local versions of the programs that were faithful copies of JOBS in all its original features. Detailed documentation would be established, including manuals and procedures. Training of local practitioners would be intensive and would focus on minimizing deviations from prescribed practices. Program evaluation would focus on detailed observations of the program delivery and would measure deviations from the prescribed standard. Incentives and controls would be created to encourage conformity to the original model.

Implementation as Mutual Adaptation

Both the technology transfer and the perfect replication paradigms minimize the role of the adopting organization as an active agent in the implementation process. The implementing organization is regarded either as irrelevant, in the technology transfer view, or as a source of errors to be controlled, in the perfect replication paradigm. Increasingly, however, the role of the implementing organization as an active agent began to be recognized, and researchers realized what practitioners had always known—that a social innovation cannot exist independent of the organization implementing it (Sproull & Hofmeister, 1986). Indeed, the innovation is enacted through the organization that adopts and implements it. How it succeeds or fails and, indeed, why it is regarded as a success or a failure depend heavily on the motives, values, organizational arrangements, and exchanges of actors within the organization itself and in its environment. Furthermore, as the innovation is implemented, new demands on the resources and relationships in the adopting organization emerge, requiring changes in the organization. This suggests a third paradigm, involving *mutual adaptation* (Berman, 1981; Price, Friedland, & Choi, 1996).

The mutual adaptation paradigm holds that the organization is both actively shaping and being shaped by the innovation. Consequently, the scenario for implementation involves the negotiated reinvention of the innovation prototype. Because organizational actors are motivated agents, each with its own goals, values, and bases of power, the innovation is "reinvented" during its implementation. The idea of reinvention was first introduced by Rice and Rogers (1980), and it emphasizes that all social innovations must be reinvented by local agents who negotiate various features of the innovation, depending on local conditions.

A largely unexplored aspect of the field of social innovation has to do with the nature and extent of change *in the adopting organization itself* (Price et al., 1996) that occurs as a consequence of implementation. The mutual adaptation perspective also implies that a different definition of success will be adopted. Here, the sense of ownership by the organization itself is a criterion that may supplement whatever other intended outcomes the organization may have had in adopting and implementing the innovation.

The mutual adaptation paradigm's prescription for implementing JOBS would be quite different from either the technology transfer or perfect replication approach. It would recognize that the local organization has strengths and capacities that could be of value in implementing JOBS. The local organization would be seen as an active agent, rather than as a passive recipient or conforming replicator. Considerable attention would be paid to the potential changes required in the implementing organization and their costs and benefits. In addition, changes in JOBS would be seen as inevitable or even as desirable local inventive adaptations. Evaluation of JOBS would focus on the strength of local ownership, as well as on the benefits of the local version for the clients being served.

Theory as a Guide to Reinvention

The Problem With "Black Box" Interventions. Kurt Lewin (1951) noted that there is nothing so useful as a good theory. We argue that, in translating a proven research model into community practice, there is nothing so useful as a theoretically driven intervention model. But, as Koepsell et al. (1992) observed, even proven interventions previously tested in randomized control trials may be "'black boxes' whose overall effects may be detectable, but whose contents are obscure" (p. 33). Lipsey (1990) has elaborated on this theme, describing "black box interventions" as ones where the inputs and outputs can be observed but the connecting processes are not readily visible.

The black box issue is a major problem in the implementation of community-based interventions. Substantial resources and effort may have been devoted to testing whether the intervention actually had the anticipated effects. In the absence of a theory about the intervention, however, researchers can do little other than recommend the "perfect replication" strategy to implementers. We have already noted that organizations that adopt a new program model will not replicate it perfectly, preferring to place their own stamps of ownership on the model through selective adoption and modification. Furthermore, lack of a theory about the intervention will reduce the chances of new learning in the process of implementation. As Koepsell et al. (1992) and Lipsey (1990) have observed, intervention theory can play a crucial role in disentangling results that are attributable to inadequate evaluation methods, poor treatment ideas, or inadequate treatment implementation.

Intervention Theories as Blueprints for Successful Implementation. Researchers in the fields of public health (Koepsell et al., 1992), program evaluation (Chen & Rossi, 1983), applied social research (Lipsey, 1990), and prevention (Price, 1987) have all argued that intervention theories can play a crucial role in solving the black box problem. The minimum elements of an intervention theory would specify (a) the inputs of the intervention in terms of knowledge, skill, training, and resources; (b) the outputs of the program, such as improved client outcomes and improved service systems; and (c) the causal sequence of mediating events or processes that connect the inputs and the outputs. These mediating processes are a crucial part of the causal account of the intervention. In addition, a well-specified treatment theory may state conditions that moderate the strength of the relationship between inputs and mediating processes or outcomes.

The JOBS Program as a Theory of Intervention. Figure 8.2 uses the JOBS program as an example of a theory of intervention. This model incorporates research findings from previous investigations of the JOBS program that were reviewed above. At the same time, the model introduces elements that have not yet been tested explicitly but that represent hypotheses about ingredients necessary for strong impacts of the JOBS program. The program model shown in Figure 8.2 specifies *outcomes* of the program in terms of reemployment, reduced economic hardship, and improved mental health. It is supported by already existing empirical findings (Vinokur & Schul, in press) that show a mediational process by which JOBS increases reemployment rates, which in turn reduce economic hardship for participants, thus improving their mental health. At the same time, the model specifies *inputs* of the JOBS program in terms of job-search skills that are important for its success. These include the capacity for participants to learn perspective taking—that is, to "think like an employer" in order to understand what employers value in making decisions about job candidates. Other skills include networking to identify job openings and anticipatory problem-solving skills that will help inoculate participants against the inevitable setbacks in the job-search process. The model also specifies *mediating processes* that are changed for participants as a consequence of participation in the program. These key mediators have been documented in previous research and include job-search, self-efficacy (van Ryn & Vinokur, 1992), and inoculation against setbacks (Vinokur & Schul, in press).

Finally, the theory of the JOBS intervention presented in Figure 8.2 adds a fourth crucial element to the model. The model specifies an active learning process as a crucial *moderating* condition that strengthens the relationship between teaching job skills and job-search self-efficacy for participants. Caplan et al. (1997) have described the active learning process and its hypothesized role in the JOBS program in considerable

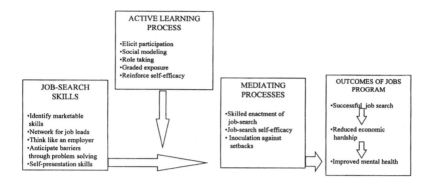

Figure 8.2. Theory of Intervention for the JOBS Program

detail. The model incorporates already-established research findings that provide a more reliable guide to implementation. At the same time, it incorporates elements, such as the active learning component, that represent working hypotheses to be tested in future studies of the JOBS program. Program models like the JOBS model represent an intermediate level of theoretical abstraction that readily allows translation from theory to practice and vice versa. As Koepsell et al. (1992) have observed, the model should be specified at a level that is not so abstract as general frameworks such as exchange theory but also that is not a rigidly specified set of concrete procedures with little capacity for generalization.

Advantages of a Theory-Driven Approach. The theory-driven approach has some advantages over black box approaches or rigid attempts at perfect replication. First, a working program theory provides a "common language" with the potential to bridge diverse groups of practitioners, researchers, policymakers, and community groups, all of whom may be engaged in reinventing a program model. This is no small advantage; each of these groups represents stakeholders with different needs, values, and goals in the implementation process. Second, the theory-driven approach provides a "cognitive blueprint" for action and a focus for coordinated activity. Third, a theory of the program establishes theoretically and empirically based priorities among those elements of a program that are important for effective implementation. These "core elements" (Price & Lorion, 1989) must be specified in the process of reinvention. Finally, theory-driven models, measured appropriately, can contribute to the development of theory and organizational learning, as well as to improved practice in the community.

Conducting Research on the Mutual Adaptation Model

Successful adoption and adaptation of a program such as JOBS will require involvement of stakeholders who are drawn from multiple levels. Those levels range from interorganizational to individual. Although a significant literature on the impacts of these different levels already exists (e.g., Damanpour, 1991; Goes & Park, 1997; Kanter, 1990; Klein & Sorra, 1966; Price & Lorion, 1989), much remains to be discovered about the roles that different stakeholders should play to promote successful program implementation. In addition, little is known about how the process of implementing innovations affects the influence of the organizations involved. What follows are some illustrations of the array of questions that might be considered at different levels of analysis and some research designs that might help answer those questions.

Interorganizational Processes: Linkages and Mutual Benefits. The processes of dissemination and implementation invariably involve multiple organizations playing roles as sponsor, broker, and implementer. Once two or more organizations are embarked on the process of mutual adaptation, what characteristics of interorganizational linkages are likely to promote continued and successful adaptation? For example, what effect does the mix of organizations with varying goals have on the success of such linkages when one considers such characteristics as organizational size, public/private or profit/nonprofit status, and whether the organizations are involved in competition for the same resources? It is also interesting to explore hypotheses about the unintended collateral effects on organizational relationships that emerge as a result of collaborating in the implementation process. Under what conditions do mutual benefits emerge?

Case studies can be valuable in suggesting hypotheses regarding these effects. Designs that study clusters of organizations longitudinally can test such hypotheses by comparing the effects of such linkages as they vary among multiple networks or organizations involved in the implementation of programs such as JOBS. Koepsell et al. (1992) discuss statistical issues in multicommunity designs. Field experiments in which the unit of analysis is the interorganizational network can directly test prescriptive theories of what works best while providing an opportunity to generate theories regarding *how* to initiate and maintain such networks and the circumstances under which they will be mutually beneficial.

The Power of Legitimacy and Sanction. Some organizations, professional and governmental, have the capacity to sanction or certify service programs (D'Aunno & Price, 1986). Such control is carried out either by licensing or by certification that staff members have completed standardized training or that the service provider meets accreditation standards. Contract-awarding organizations may also sanction by specifying the process standards a provider must meet to qualify for funding. In cases where such sanctions are effective, what are the effects on the willingness and success of mutually adaptive partnerships between the host organization and other organizational actors likely to be? Among the research designs that might be considered to answer these questions are quasi-experimental, interrupted time-series designs in which certification is implemented and measurement occurs before and after certification.

Organizational Dynamics: Developmental Processes Over Time. As noted earlier, the process of mutual adaptation is likely to progress in overlapping phases. The process may begin with a period of mutual exploration aimed at reaching a decision about whether to proceed to actual implementation and adaptation. A phase of mutual adaptation may follow, after which a phase involving institutionalization of the adaptive process may occur. In this case, the host organization retains the flexibility to adapt to changing resources, client populations, and the coming and going of other complementary client services.

Research questions at this level have a strong developmental character. For example, what elements of the mutual adaptation process at each phase are most crucial in determining the success of later phases? At the stage of mutual exploration, is it important that the host organization has opportunities to observe the program elsewhere, to try out the innovation in a pilot format, and to make use of a stakeholder-based method for deciding to proceed with implementation (e.g., Heller, 1996)? Do such opportunities have an impact on whether later phases of adaptation and implementation succeed?

To address such questions, the research must use methods of data collection and analysis that generate a developmental understanding of the mutual adaptation process. Research designs should permit longitudinal multivariate modeling. Such models might include predictor terms that represent the implementation of specific processes and the achievement of specific states at a range of times in the history of the collaborative partnership. Such models might also allow for the likelihood that different collaborative partnerships will proceed at different speeds, depending on the resources, skills, and competing agendas that confront the potential host organization and the researcher/consultant. At the same time, the models will need to take into account the amount of time spent in periods of exploration, adaptation, and implementation. Time's main effects and interaction effects with other components of each antecedent period may predict the quality of what is achieved in a particular later period.

Hierarchy and Developmentally Sensitive Timing. To prevent adaptation failure and to promote implementation success during mutual adaptation, what is the optimal role of actors in different levels of the organizational hierarchy? Will the answer depend on the phase of the collaboration between various organizational actors and the host organizations? For example, in early phases of the mutual adaptation process, how crucial is it that the top members of the organization be involved in supporting exploration and loose coupling to allow experimentation to occur in a rapid and flexible manner? Once adaptation has been largely completed, how important is recontact with the top of the hierarchy to tighten the coupling and to ensure some permanence, as well as fidelity to program principles (e.g., Greenwood & Hinings, 1996)? As with the study of time, methods of modeling the dynamics of moving up and down the hierarchy can help extract the dynamic signal that promotes the successful process of mutual adaption.

Individuals and Teams Within Organizations: Selection for Effectiveness. Through replicated, independent launchings of JOBS, criteria have been identified that make it possible to select effective trainers (Curran, 1992). Each replication of JOBS, in effect, constituted a case study in the use of such selection procedures. Nevertheless, a rigorous scientific determination is needed of which characteristics of job applicants best predict their success as trainers. Consequently, studies are needed to determine the characteristics of good trainers, including formal training, knowledge skills, and abilities, and also to determine the best methods for selecting for those characteristics. For example, how do observation of "thin slices of behavior" (Ambady & Rosenthal, 1992), role-playing evaluations, and biographical questions (e.g., Mumford & Stokes, 1992) compare as valid methods of selection? Research is needed that includes formal job analysis (e.g., Harvey, 1992) conducted with the use of subject matter experts and followed up with appropriate validation studies.

Such validation studies can be of two types. One type would be the study of incumbent trainers to determine whether potential selection devices can distinguish among them in terms of competency. A second type would involve a prospective study using new applicants for positions as job transition trainers. Follow-up research could be conducted at several stages to monitor the predictive validity of the proposed selection techniques. As a result, a theory of selection could be developed, aimed at predicting the likelihood of future trainer performance at multiple key points in the job tenure of the trainer.

Benefits and Costs of Trainer Teams. An important part of the JOBS program is the human infrastructure of trainer teams and supportive supervisors and reinforcement of that infrastructure. Teams have been used under the untested assumption that a pair of trainers minimizes drift from the principles of JOBS because each trainer (a) serves as a source of social sanction to maintain fidelity to the protocol, (b) can provide support to the other trainer when lapses occur, and (c) can provide feedback so that corrective action can be taken. These assumed benefits have not yet been systematically studied. Benefit-cost research could determine whether the cost of using two trainers, rather than one, to deliver an intervention is outweighed by the benefits that are generated. We know that JOBS has generated substantial economic benefits that cover its costs (Vinokur, van Ryn, et al. 1991). We do not know, however, what the benefit-cost ratio would look like if only single trainers used it. Research might randomly assign trainers to work in teams or alone within organizations. Multiple organizations, which might be selected to vary in staff size, resources, client population, or other contextual parameters that the research hypothesized, could specify the effects of trainer pairing and could also generate practical knowledge regarding the generalizability of the benefit-cost findings for trainer teams.

Conclusion

Continuing turbulence in the world economy will produce an increasing number and variety of work transitions, many of which will influence the well-being of individuals and families. Organized support systems such as the JOBS program are essential to help individuals and families cope with, and adapt to, these changes. Large-scale implementation of such innovations will require theory-guided reinvention of these innovations to ensure both local acceptance and program impact. There is, indeed, nothing so useful as a good theory (Lewin, 1951). Theories not only guide practitioners and researchers in their work but also provide the most useful medium for accumulating, cataloging, and transmitting research knowledge (Price, 1997). In the turbulent world that is currently emerging, that cumulative knowledge may be more valuable than ever before.

Note

1. Earlier versions of the material on job-loss appeared in Price, Friedland, and Vinokur (in press) and Price, Vinokur, and Friedland (in press).

References

Ambady, N., & Rosenthal, R. (1992). Thin slices of expressive behavior as predictors of interpersonal consequences: A meta-analysis. *Psychological Bulletin, 111,* 256-274.

Atkinson, T., Liem, R., & Liem, J. (1986). The social costs of unemployment: Implications for social support. *Journal of Health and Social Behavior, 27,* 317-331.

Bane, M. J., & Ellwood, D. T. (1994). *Welfare realities: From rhetoric to reform.* Cambridge, MA: Harvard University Press.

Beasley, J. D. (1991). *The betrayal of health: The impact of nutrition, environment, and lifestyle on illness in America.* New York: Times Books.

Bebbington, P., Hurry, J., Tennant, C., Stuart, E. Y., & Wing, J. K. (1981). Epidemiology of mental disorders in Camberwell. *Psychological Medicine, 11,* 561-579.

Belous, R. S. (1989). *The contingent economy: The growth of the temporary, part-time, and subcontracted workforce.* Washington, DC: National Planning Association.

Berman, P. (1981). Educational change: An implementation paradigm. In R. Lehming & M. Kane (Eds.), *Improving schools: Using what we know* (pp. 251-286). Beverly Hills, CA: Sage.

Blakely, C. H., Mayer, J. P., Gottschalk, R. G., Schmitt, N., Davidson, W. S., Roitman, D. B., & Emshoff, J. G. (1987). The fidelity adaptation debate: Implications for the implementation of public-sector social programs. *American Journal of Community Psychology, 15,* 253-268.

Bolton, W., & Oatley, K. (1987). A longitudinal study of social support and depression in unemployed men. *Psychological Medicine, 17,* 453-460.

Caplan, R. D., Vinokur, A. D., & Price, R. H. (1997). From job-loss to reemployment: Field experiments in prevention-focused coping. In G. W. Albee & T. P. Gullotta (Eds.), *Primary prevention works: Issues in children's and families' lives* (Vol. 16, pp. 341-379). Thousand Oaks, CA: Sage.

Caplan, R. D., Vinokur, A. D., Price, R. H., & van Ryn, M. (1989). Job seeking, reemployment, and mental health: A randomized field experiment in coping with job-loss. *Journal of Applied Psychology, 74,* 759-769.

Catalano, R. (1991). The health effects of economic insecurity. *American Journal of Public Health, 81,* 1148-1152.

Catalano, R., & Dooley, D. (1977). Economic predictor of depressed mood and stressful life events in a metropolitan community. *Journal of Health and Social Behavior, 18,* 292-307.

Catalano, R., Dooley, D., Novaco, R., Wilson, G., & Hough, R. (1993). Using ECA survey data to examine the effect of job layoffs on violent behavior. *Hospital and Community Psychiatry, 44*(9), 874-879.

Catalano, R., Dooley, D., Wilson, G., & Hough, R. (1993). Job-loss and alcohol abuse: A test using data from the Epidemiologic Catchment Area project. *Journal of Health and Social Behavior, 34,* 215-225.

Chen, H. T., & Rossi, P. H. (1983). Evaluation with sense: The theory-driven approach. *Evaluation Review, 7,* 283-302.

Conger, R. D., Elder, G. H., Lorenz, F. O., Conger, K. J., Simons, R. L., Whitbeck, L. B., Huck, S., & Melby, J. N. (1990). Linking economic hardship to marital quality and instability. *Journal of Marriage and the Family, 52,* 643-656.

Curran, J. (1992). *JOBS. A manual for teaching people successful job-search strategies.* Ann Arbor: University of Michigan, Institute for Social Research, Michigan Prevention Research Center.

Damanpour, F. (1991). Organizational innovation: A meta-analysis of effects of determinants and moderators. *Academy of Management Journal, 34,* 555-590.

Danziger, S., & Gottschalk, P. (1995). *America unequal.* New York: Russell Sage.

D'Aunno, T., & Price, R. H. (1986). Linked systems: Drug abuse and mental health services. In W. R. Scott & B. L. Black (Eds.), *The organization of mental health services: Societal and community systems.* Beverly Hills, CA: Sage.

Dew, M. A., Penkower, L., & Bromet, E. J. (1991). Effects of unemployment on mental health in the contemporary family. *Behavior Modification, 15,* 501-544.

Dooley, D., Catalano, R., & Wilson, G. (1994). Depression and unemployment: Panel findings from the Epidemiologic Catchment Area Study. *American Journal of Community Psychology, 22,* 745-765.

Elder, G. H., Jr., & Caspi, A. (1988). Economic stress in lives: Developmental perspectives. *Journal of Social Issues, 44*(4), 25-45.

Embry, D. D. (1984). The safe-playing kit: A standardized intervention package. In S. C. Paine, G. L. Bellamy, & B. Wilcox (Eds.), *Human services that work: From innovation to standard practice* (pp. 79-92). Baltimore, MD: Brooks.

Gil, D. G. (1970). *Violence against children: Physical abuse in the United States.* Cambridge, MA: Harvard University Press.

Goes, J. B., & Park, S. H. (1997). Interorganizational links and innovation: The case of hospital services. *Academy of Management Journal, 40,* 673-696.

Greenwood, R., & Hinings, C. R. (1996). Understanding radical organizational change: Bringing together the old and new institutionalism. *Academy of Management Journal, 21,* 1022-1054.

Harvey, R. J. (1992). Job analysis. In M. D. Dunnette & L. M. Hough (Eds.), *Handbook of industrial and organizational psychology* (pp. 71-163). Palo Alto, CA: Consulting Psychologists Press.

Heller, K. (1996, May). Models of community adoption in prevention research. In *5th National NIMH Conference on Prevention Research,* Tysons Corner, VA.

Howe, G. W., Caplan, R., Foster, D., Lockshin, M., & McGrath, C. (1995). When couples cope with job-loss: A research strategy for developing preventive intervention. In L. R. Murphy, J. J. Hurrell, Jr., S. L. Sauter, & G. P. Keita (Eds.), *Job stress interventions* (pp. 139-158). Washington, DC: American Psychological Association.

Jackson, P. R., & Warr, P. B. (1984). Unemployment and psychological ill-health: The moderating role of duration and age. *Psychological Medicine, 14,* 605-614.

Jahoda, M., Lazarsfeld, P. F., & Zeisel, H. (1933). *Marienthal: The sociography of an unemployed community* (English translation, 1971). Chicago: Aldine.

Justice, B., & Duncan, D. F. (1977). Child abuse as a work-related problem. *Corrective and Social Psychiatry and Journal of Behavior Technology, Methods and Therapy, 23,* 53-55.

Kanter, R. M. (1990). When a thousand flowers bloom: Structural, collective, and social conditions for innovation in organizations. In B. M. Staw & L. L. Cummings (Eds.), *The evolution and adaptation of organizations.* Greenwich, CT: JAI.

Kessler, R., Turner, J., & House, J. (1987). Intervening processes in the relationship between unemployment and health. *Psychological Medicine, 17,* 949-961.

Kessler, R. C., Turner, J. B., & House, J. S. (1988). The effects of unemployment on health in a community survey: Main, modifying, and mediating effects. *Journal of Social Issues, 44*(4), 69-86.

Kessler, R. C., Turner, J. B., & House, J. S. (1989). Unemployment, reemployment, and emotional functioning in a community sample. *American Sociological Review, 54,* 648-657.

Klein, K. J., & Sorra, J. S. (1996). The challenge of innovation implementation. *Academy of Management Review, 21,* 1055-1080.

· Koepsell, T. D., Wagner, E. H., Cheadle, A. C., Patrick, D. L., Martin, D. C., Diehr, P. H., Perrin, E. B., Kristal, A. R., Allan-Andrilla, C. H., & Dey, L. J. (1992). Selected methodological issues in evaluating community-based health promotion and disease prevention programs. *Annual Review of Public Health, 13,* 31-57.

Lewin, K. (1951). *Field theory in social science: Selected theoretical papers.* New York: Harper.

Liem, R., & Liem, J. H. (1988). The psychological effects of unemployment on workers and their families. *Journal of Social Issues, 44*(4), 87-105.

Lipsey, M. W. (1990). Theory as method: Small theories of treatment. In L. Sechrest, E. Perrin, & J. Bunker (Eds.), *AHCPR Conference Proceedings, Research Methodology: Strengthening causal interpretations of nonexperimental data* (DHHS Publication No. PHS. 90-3454, pp. 33-51). Rockville, MD: U.S. Department of Health and Human Services.

March, J. G. (1981). Footnotes to organizational change. *Administrative Science Quarterly, 26,* 563-577.

McGrew, J. H., Bond, G. R., Dietzen, L., & Salyers, M. (1994). Measuring the fidelity of implementation of a mental health program model. *Journal of Consulting and Clinical Psychology, 62,* 670-678.

Menaghan, E. G. (1991). Work experiences and family interaction processes: The long reach of the job. *Annual Review of Sociology, 17,* 419-444.

Mumford, M. D., & Stokes, G. S. (1992). Developmental determinants of individual action: Theory and practice in applying background measures. In M. D. Dunnette & L. M. Hough (Eds.), *Handbook of industrial and organizational psychology* (pp. 61-138). Palo Alto, CA: Consulting Psychologists Press.

Parke, R., & Collmer, C. (1975). *Review of child development research: Child abuse. An interdisciplinary review.* Chicago: University of Chicago Press.

Penkower, L., Bromet, E., & Dew, M. (1988). Husbands' layoff and wives' mental health: A prospective analysis. *Archives of General Psychiatry, 45,* 994-1000.

Platt, S., & Kreitman, N. (1985). Parasuicide and unemployment among men in Edinburgh, 1968-1982. *Psychological Medicine, 15,* 113-123.

Pollitt, E. (1994). Poverty and child development: Relevance of research in developing countries to the United States. Special Issue: Children and poverty. *Child Development, 65,* 283-295.

Porter, M. E. (1990). *The competitive advantage of nations.* New York: Free Press.

Price, R. H. (1987). Linking intervention research and risk factor research. In A. Steinberg & M. M. Silverman (Eds.), *Preventing mental disorders: A research perspective* (DHHS Publication No. ADM 87-1492, pp. 48-56). Washington, DC: Government Printing Office.

Price, R. H. (1990). Strategies for managing plant closings and downsizing. In D. Fishman & C. Cherniss (Eds.), *The human side of corporate competitiveness* (pp. 127-151). Newbury Park, CA: Sage.

Price, R. H. (1992). Psychosocial impact of job-loss on individuals and families. *Current Directions in Psychological Science, 1,* 9-11.

Price, R. H. (1997). In praise of a cumulative prevention science. *American Journal of Community Psychology, 25,* 169-176.

Price, R. H., Friedland, D. S., & Choi, J. (1996). *An approach to evaluating implementation in the Winning New Jobs Project.* Ann Arbor: University of Michigan, Institute for Social Research, Michigan Prevention Research Center.

Price, R. H., Friedland, D. S., & Vinokur, A. D. (in press). Job-loss: Hard times and eroded identity. In J. Harvey (Ed.), *Perspectives on loss: A source book.* Washington, DC: Taylor & Francis.

Price, R. H., & Lorion, R. P. (1989). Prevention programming as organizational reinvention: From research to implementation. In D. Shaffer, I. Phillips, & N. B. Enzer (Eds.), *Prevention of mental disorders, alcohol and drug use in children and adolescents* (Prevention Monograph #2, DHHS Publication No. ADM 89-1646, pp. 97-123). Rockville, MD: Office of Substance Abuse Prevention and American Academy of Child and Adolescent Psychiatry.

Price, R. H., van Ryn, M., & Vinokur, A. (1992). Impact of a preventive job-search intervention on the likelihood of depression among the unemployed. *Journal of Health and Social Behavior, 33,* 158-167.

Price, R. H., & Vinokur, A. D. (1995). Supporting career transitions in a time of organizational downsizing: The Michigan JOBS program. In M. London (Ed.), *Employees, careers, and job creation: Developing growth-oriented human resource strategies and programs* (pp. 191-209). San Francisco: Jossey-Bass.

Price, R. H., Vinokur, A. D., & Friedland, D. (in press). The job-seeker role as resource: Achieving reemployment and enhancing mental health. In *NIH workshop on social conditions, stress, resources and health.*

Reich, R. B. (1990). *The work of nations: Capitalism in the 21st century.* New York: Knopf.

Rice, R. E., & Rogers, E. M. (1980). Reinvention in the innovation process. *Knowledge, 1,* 499-514.

Rogers, E. M. (1995). *Diffusion of innovations.* New York: Free Press.

Sproull, L. S., & Hofmeister, K. R. (1986). Thinking about implementation. *Journal of Management, 12*(1), 43-60.

Steinberg, L. D., Catalano, R., & Dooley, D. (1981). Economic antecedents of child abuse and neglect. *Child Development, 52,* 975-985.

Thoits, P. A. (1991). On merging identity theory and stress research. *Social Psychology Quarterly, 54,* 101-112.

Thurow, L. (1992). *Head to head.* New York: Morrow.

Umberson, D., Wortman, C., & Kessler, R. (1992). Widowhood and depression: Explaining long-term gender differences in vulnerability. *Journal of Health and Social Behavior, 33*(1), 10-24.

van Ryn, M., & Vinokur, A. D. (1992). How did it work? An examination of the mechanisms through which an intervention for the unemployed promoted job-search behavior. *American Journal of Community Psychology, 20,* 577-597.

Vinokur, A., Caplan, R. D., & Williams, C. C. (1987). Attitudes and social support: Determinants of job-seeking behavior and well-being among the unemployed. *Journal of Applied Social Psychology, 17,* 1007-1024.

Vinokur, A. D., Price, R. H., & Caplan, R. D. (1991). From field experiments to program implementation: Assessing the potential outcomes of an experimental intervention program for unemployed persons. *American Journal of Community Psychology, 19,* 543-562.

Vinokur, A. D., Price, R. H., & Caplan, R. D. (1996). Hard times and hurtful partners: How financial strain affects depression and relationship satisfaction of unemployed persons and their spouses. *Journal of Personality and Social Psychology, 71,* 166-179.

Vinokur, A. D., Price, R. H., & Schul, Y. (1995). Impact of the JOBS intervention on unemployed workers varying in risk for depression. *American Journal of Community Psychology, 23,* 39-74.

Vinokur, A. D., & Schul, Y. (in press). Mastery and inoculation against setbacks as active ingredients in the JOBS intervention for the unemployed. *Journal of Consulting and Clinical Psychology.*

Vinokur, A. D., van Ryn, M., Gramlich, E., & Price, R. H. (1991). Long-term follow-up and benefit-cost analysis of the JOBS program: A preventive intervention for the unemployed. *Journal of Applied Psychology, 76,* 213-219.

Warr, P. B., Jackson, P. R., & Banks, M. H. (1988). Unemployment and mental health: Some British studies. *Journal of Social Issues, 44*(4), 47-68.

Whyte, W. H., Jr. (1956). *The organization man.* New York: Simon & Schuster.

Windschuttle, K. (1980). *Unemployment: A social and political analysis of the economic crisis in Australia.* Ringwood, Victoria, Australia: Penguin.

PART III

COMMUNITY EMPOWERMENT

9

The Art of Social Change
Community Narratives as Resources for Individual and Collective Identity

JULIAN RAPPAPORT

T his chapter is about the relationship between community narratives and individual lives. My intention is to illustrate the proposition that narratives, expressed in various forms, are powerful resources for personal and social change. My examples are from the worlds of art, autobiography, and history, as well as psychology, especially highlighting some ways in which assumptions about race and class are reproduced in the narratives of mainstream social institutions, including universities, children's books, and historical accounts. But I argue that narratives are powerful regardless of their form and that they are powerful, in part, because they cut across levels of analysis, linking individual experience and social process.

Among the most interesting and perplexing issues for the fields of community and applied social psychology are matters concerning levels of analysis. Conceptual, philosophical, methodological, and analytic problems are encountered when a field attempts to cross levels of analysis by examining the mutual influence process between individual minds and social forces (see, e.g., Altman & Rogoff, 1987; Kenny & La Voie, 1985; Shinn, 1990). This is both an interesting theoretical problem and a practical one in the context of identity development and social change, the topic of concern here.

Narratives (as defined below) create memory, meaning, and identity among individuals, even as they are expressions of a social and cultural context. Social context, in turn, is created by individuals who construct rituals, performances, activities, and symbols in language, in art, and in behavioral routines. I argue that psychologists, social scientists, and helping professionals who understand the reciprocal and continuous creation (and re-creation) of cultural context and individual identity can participate as collaborators with artists, writers, and other social activists and citizens in the pursuit of a common interest in social change.

Spanning Levels of Analysis: Theoretical Assumptions

Underlying my analysis are theoretical assumptions about the psychology of identity development and change. Because these assumptions inform my understanding of the artistic, biographical, and historical narratives used as examples here, it is useful to make them explicit. I do not attempt to review the evidence that supports these assumptions, although I do cite considerable relevant literature.

I use the concept of *narrative* as a way to span levels of analysis, making the assumption that all communities have narratives about themselves and that these narratives have powerful effects on their members. For example, the community of university professors, or members of a particular discipline who organize themselves into a professional society, hold a shared sense of what it means to be a professor or a member of a particular discipline, such as a psychologist, a lawyer, a social worker, or a historian. The same holds for graduate students in a particular field. Although no single person is a perfect embodiment of the shared story of the professor or the graduate student, this communal identity is no less powerful than the identity that people experience as members of a particular religious tradition such as Mormons, Catholics, Presbyterians, or, in some cases, a particular church community (see, e.g., Rappaport & Simkins, 1991). The same could be said for membership in an ethnic group (Deaux, 1993) or in a wide variety of social organizations, including self-help and mutual-help groups (Mankowski & Rappaport, 1995; Rappaport, 1993). In the modern world, many people belong to more than one such community, perhaps crossing ethnic, neighborhood, professional, or religious identities, although this is easier and more likely to the extent that one has the economic, educational, and mobility advantages of higher rather than lower socioeconomic status.

As noted above, I also assume that the influence of social context and individual identity is reciprocal, particularly with respect to local culture (Geertz, 1973). Put simply, people both receive and create their narratives—although again, it is somewhat easier to create a narrative to the extent that one has economic and social capital. Psychology as a discipline has sometimes had difficulty construing social context as more than a confounding variable, or something that exists outside the person and that should be "accounted for" rather than studied. Some psychologists insist that individual personalities are best understood as biological or temperamental stabilities, separate from lived experience in social arrangements. Other social scientists often argue exactly the opposite. But the distinction between levels of analysis is more of a social science fiction than an experienced reality (Rappaport & Stewart, 1997). Although it may be convenient for analytic purposes (a way to remind ourselves of the many different influences on human behavior), this is not the way people actually experience their lives.

For researchers driven by the search for a universal human psychology, individual personality, identity, and sense of self are understood as conveniently contained within the person, quite independent of their changing social and historical contexts. Although sociologists and anthropologists are often better at grasping the power of community and culture to create meaning and personal identity, they tend to ignore individual variation. A somewhat different approach is suggested by Shweder and his colleagues in what they call "cultural psychology" (Stigler, Shweder, & Herdt, 1990). As Shweder (1990) put it,

> no sociocultural environment exists or has identity independent of the way human beings seize meanings and resources from it, while every human being has her or his subjectivity and mental life altered through the process of seizing meanings and resources from some sociocultural environment and using them. (p. 2)

In adopting this point of view, I want to emphasize that communities are resources. They also distribute resources, including identity narratives, to their members. In the modern world, many people belong to more than one community. But like most other resources, the number (and more important, the choice) of communities and stories available to any individual tends to be, for reasons mentioned above, positively related to economic and social class.

The medium through which community narratives operate is cognitive representations of individual and collective identity. I assume that such cognitive representations have both emotional and behavioral implications. This is easily illustrated in everyday life by advertisements that capitalize on depicting celebrity or team identity. Ultimately, identity representations that people choose or acquire without conscious choice have political implications—again visible in everyday observations such as how people respond to a national symbol like a flag or to a school logo or to a gang sign. Even people who do not consider themselves to be patriotic will often be surprised by their heightened awareness of a collective identity when visiting another country.

The general psychological processes involved in this analysis are very well documented (see, e.g., Bruner, 1990). But this chapter is not a review. Rather, it is intended to illustrate how some of these processes operate in the world of social action. Below, I provide a working definition of *narrative* and other related terms, which are discussed in more detail elsewhere (Mankowski & Rappaport, 1995; Rappaport, 1993, 1995; Thomas & Rappaport, 1996). I argue that our knowledge about basic psychology has clear implications for those of us who value progressive social change—the kind that is empowering, in the sense defined below. Consequently, we ought to help amplify the voices of those whom we say we wish to serve; and we ought to point out the negative consequences of oppressive narratives even (or perhaps especially) when they are perpetuated by the most powerful stakeholders in our own communities.

Many psychologists (e.g., Sarbin, 1986) see the concept of *narrative* as a "root metaphor" for psychology. Schank (1990) and Schank and Abelson (1995) argue that all important knowledge is obtained in storied form. Stories told and retold are indexed in memory. These indexes (like headlines in a newspaper) are shorthand devices that enable people to recall many details that would otherwise be forgotten. (See, e.g., Bower & Clark, 1969, for a study contrasting learning by list or in story form.) Similarly, art in its various forms (visual, performance, verbal, ritual) serves a recall function for the collective: It indexes the important stories of a society. Art is the keeper of a society's memory. What is allowed to be remembered both creates our shared history and provides resources for our personal identity stories. It can also, like other forms of narrative, tell us who is in the group and who is not.

As a practical matter, our knowledge of psychological processes adds up to this conclusion: Stories are powerful resources. How these resources are used by social policymakers, clinicians, social activists, administrators, reporters, teachers, and others to construe "reality" has serious practical and political consequences. Despite our individualistic culture, the experience of collective identity is unavoidable. Everyone adopts community narratives (e.g., religious, fraternal, professional, ethnic, neighborhood) into his or her personal life story. For those of us interested in social justice and the links between personal and social change, this raises certain central questions. Where do community narratives come from? Which narratives will be available to whom? And who gets to tell their own stories? For many people, particularly the least powerful, least well-off economically, or least educated, the only stories available for adoption are those I refer to as "dominant cultural narratives" (see the discussion below). One way that psychologists can contribute to social change is by helping people discover, create, and make available to each other alternative narratives.

Narratives and Stories Are Resources for Empowerment

One of my concerns as a community psychologist has been how to locate, understand, and help create contexts that make it more likely rather than less likely for people to experience genuine empowerment. Because *empowerment* is now a word used by people who hold many divergent political aims, a definition is useful. The one I have adopted was offered by the Cornell University Empowerment Group (1989):

> Empowerment is an intentional, ongoing process, centered in the local community, involving mutual respect, critical reflection, caring and group

participation, through which people lacking an equal share of valued resources gain greater access to and control over those resources. (p. 2)

The part of this definition of interest here is its emphasis on access to resources. I regard stories about me and my community as resources for personal and social stability and change. I intend the word *story* to be understood exactly as it is understood in everyday language. A story is a description of events over time. It usually has a beginning, a middle, and an end. It often has a point. Sometimes the point is obvious; sometimes the point needs to be figured out by the listener, reader, or observer. *Story* may be defined in other, more technical ways that depend on one's purpose and the sort of analysis one is doing (e.g., linguistic discourse analysis, cognitive processes in memory, thematic descriptive analysis), but these details need not concern us here. A story need not be in words. It can be told in a ritual, in a picture, or even in architecture as noted below (see Thomas & Rappaport, 1996, for a broader analysis of the role of the arts in narrative communities). Pictures can "index" a story that is well known; that is, a picture can efficiently remind people of stories preserved in memory (Salzer, 1997; Schank, 1990; Thomas & Rappaport, 1996; Wyer, 1995).

With respect to the link between a community identity and a personal identity, we may use the term *story* to refer to an individual's cognitive representation or social communication of events that are unique to that person's own life history and that are organized temporally and thematically. I use the term *narrative* to refer to a story that is not idiosyncratic to an individual. Thus, a *narrative* is a story that is common among a group of people. A narrative may be shared by the group through social interaction, texts, and other forms of communication, including pictures, performances, and rituals. A group of people with a shared narrative may constitute a community, independent of their physical location. A setting—an organizational or geographic location for a community—however, will often have a clearer narrative, often an archived one, that is preserved and transmitted independently of any individual person. For example, neighborhoods, organizations, or churches (Goldberg, 1985; Hauerwas, 1983; McClendon, 1986; Rappaport & Simkins, 1991) have community narratives about the residents or members, and these are expressed in various ways (often, but not limited to, written documents). These narratives tell the members and others something about themselves, their history, and their future.

Dominant Cultural Narratives:
The Stories Behind Our Stereotypes

Dominant cultural narratives are communicated by mass media or social institutions that touch the lives of most people (e.g., television, newspapers, public schools, religious institutions). These stories about others are often overlearned and evoked by words or symbols that call up from memory a prototype incident (Schank, 1990; Schank & Abelson, 1995). For example, a recent study reported that, in 1994, although only 39% of the violent crimes in Los Angeles County were committed by Blacks, 70% of the time a local television station reported the race of the offender as a minority (Gilliam & Iyengar, 1997). The station was not misreporting particular events, but rather the newscasters were reporting an unrepresentative sample of cases. They were helping perpetuate a dominant cultural narrative about "the dangerous Black man." This narrative, however inaccurate, is easily accessible to most people in the United States. Thus, even when no race was reported in a crime story, 42% of those surveyed falsely recalled a perpetrator, and two thirds of the respondents who did so recalled the person as being Black. This finding held for both Black and White respondents (Gilliam & Iyengar, 1997). These reports of crime may have served as reminders that led to recall of accessible narrative memories (particular stories or scripts), a process familiar to cognitive psychologists, especially those who study social cognition (Wyer, 1995).

A Case of Institutional Racism

Through social network gossip, internal communications, and archival records, universities, like other institutions, transmit many dominant cultural narratives to their students and colleagues. In many cases, the transmission appears to be individually unintentional but deeply embedded in institutional practices and unspoken assumptions or in the university community's own narrative practices. This is sometimes the case in my own setting, as the following example illustrates.

For an entire semester, a high-quality glossy poster was seen on the campus where I work. The same poster was reproduced and circulated several times in mailbox size to advertise each individual talk in a series called "Changing Realities in Academic Research." At this large (35,000 students) state university, such mail is not unusual. We are the state's high-prestige graduate research institution. Founded in 1865, the University of Illinois at Urbana-Champaign now sits between two surprisingly urban cities. As a Big Ten university, it is visible throughout the state and the nation, especially for its sports programs. University staff spend much time and money narrating its official story.

Despite recent local business development, mostly in the retail service industry, the university remains the largest and most visible employer in the area. The twin cities, with a population of just under 100,000 people in a county of 173,000, are surrounded by rural, mostly farming or increasingly "bedroom" communities. According to 1995 estimates, more than 14% of Champaign and more than 11% of Urbana residents are African American. St. Louis is about 180 miles to the south, as is one of the most well-known examples of midwestern urban decay, East St. Louis, which is in Illinois. The University of Illinois sometimes advertises its community outreach program in East St. Louis during football telecasts. The East St. Louis program is run by Champaign-Urbana faculty in the Department of Urban Planning. It does excellent work in community development, albeit far from the local campus.

The twin cities are located about 135 miles directly south of Chicago, along the train route traveled by former sharecroppers looking for work in the North. Quite a few of these migrants settled in Champaign-Urbana, creating a strong, historically Black community (there are about 35 African American churches). This community is in a largely segregated part of the cities, still sometimes referred to, even in polite conversation, as "the North End." In the 1920s, a KKK chapter was active on campus. You can still see pictures of their members if you look through old yearbooks. Until the 1960s, the small number of Black students who came to school here usually found lodging with families in the North End. Not until 1974 did the Psychology Department award a Ph.D. to an African American student.

Physically indistinguishable as Champaign or Urbana, the traditional Black neighborhood today abuts the north side of a wide street in a rundown business district. The edge of the well-groomed University of Illinois campus now reaches just to the opposite side of that street, extending for several blocks along one prominent section. At one time, a baseball field and modest housing were located there. Today, instead, sits what appears from the north, according to many African American residents who live nearby, as an imposing, but uninviting, indeed intimidating, building. That building itself tells a story, and the story it tells was repeated in the poster that was circulating on campus. It is a story about identity, invisibility, and institutional racism. It is not an intentionally told story, but like good projective tests, both the building and the poster are very revealing. They reveal a lot about the university community's narrative about itself and about the personal stories told by the community's neighbors. The building and the poster helped me understand why people benefit from telling their own stories and why one resource for social change is the opportunity to create one's own community narrative.

The widely circulated poster that caught my attention depicts, in what seems to be a realistic photograph, the building that is seen by northside residents as intimidating. It is one of the newest and most celebrated physical facilities on the campus, the Beckman Institute building—a beautiful modern facility where researchers from many departments, primarily in the neurosciences, have new laboratories, offices, a large auditorium, and even a cafeteria. The building was made possible by a $40 million private donation and more than $10 million in state funds. As seen from the north, there are no doors into this building. In addition, the structure is set off by a grassy area, which is itself fenced off from the street that generations of local African Americans have thought of as home. Shortly after it was completed, Alonzo Mitchell, an African American community activist and artist who grew up in the neighborhood, wrote a brief letter in our local newspaper. He said, "if buildings had body language," the Beckman Institute would be telling us what the University of Illinois thinks about the Black Community. Now, years later, the poster tells the same story in starker ways.

As can be seen in Figure 9.1, the apparent photograph of the Beckman Institute is in the center of the poster, sitting on the horizon line. The original poster is in full color, and above and to the sides of the building is a beautiful, sun-filled, blue sky. The foreground, making up the bottom third of the poster, is the green space of cultivated farmland. The building appears to be sitting in the middle of a soybean field, rather

Figure 9.1. Illustration used on posters advertising a series of lectures held on the campus of the University of Illinois (the original is in color). Although the building shown is adjacent to the urban, historically African American community, it is presented here as if it were in a soybean field. Note: Agriculture was not the topic of the series. (Computer-generated composite image courtesy of the Beckman Institute for Advanced Science and Technology, University of Illinois at Urbana-Champaign).

than next to urban North Champaign! In this narrative of the university, the local African American neighborhood does not exist. To the university's Black community neighbors, the narrative says, "You are invisible." This is not a narrative that is beneficial to the African American community! At best, it does not invite their children, who make up about 30% of the students in the local public schools, to become a part of the university community. At worst, it says, "You are of no consequence to us."

Psychology has quite a bit to say about how to understand what this poster signifies and why it is important. There is more here than meets the eye, more than a comment about art and symbolism. Some of the lesson has to do with how a university can inadvertently perpetuate what I call "dominant cultural narratives." It also has to do with how works of art can tell stories and how art and storytelling could be used in the service of identity development and social change.

Figure 9.2. Photograph by the author of a mural (the original is in color) that appears on a wall in the historically African American neighborhood referred to in Figure 9.1. The mural was created by a local community organization.

Writing Our Own Narratives:
An Alternative Example

In the North Champaign neighborhood that was replaced on the Beckman Institute poster by an empty field, a multicolored mural is painted on the side of a building (see Figure 9.2). The mural depicts the theme "united for a healthy community." It illustrates local people of different races and ethnic groups, including a person in a wheelchair, working and socializing in harmony. The story the mural tells is that people who are different from one another can work together for the good of the community and for each other. This is an optimistic narrative. The individuals who appropriate this narrative and make it a part of their own personal life story are not invisible to one another.

For the past 20 years, a community organization in Champaign-Urbana known as the Champaign County Health Care Consumers (CCHCC) has existed. This is a local grassroots, citizen-involvement organization that has created a viable community narrative for many diverse citizens. That narrative provides a positive social identity for its members, many of whom have changed from isolated individuals to people active in the life of their community. The organization involves minority, rural, economically poor, and middle-class citizens and professionals (including university employees) working alongside one another. It provides roles and niches that make it necessary to add new members continuously, because, by design, there are always more roles to be filled than there are people available. This "under-personed" strategy for growth and development is a major factor identified by Barker and Gump (1964) and others (Wicker, 1987) as important in small schools and organizations. It has been found to be a crucial ingredient, together with a clear and convincing community narrative, for the growth and development of empowering voluntary organizations (Luke, Rappaport, & Seidman, 1991; Maton & Salem, 1995; Rappaport, 1993; Zimmerman et al., 1991).

In 1977, the founders of CCHCC documented a lack of consumer involvement in the local health care system. Some 100 citizens first came together to discuss "birth alternatives" for women interested in midwife services. Since then, they have, among their many other activities, forced a local private hospital that had been built with federal funds to open its doors to economically poor people; challenged a policy that had included psychiatric notes in general hospital records, leading the Illinois Human Rights Authority to order a policy of confidentiality; helped increase availability of prenatal care; and worked with senior citizens and the U.S. Office of Civil Rights to obtain a consent decree that promoted a variety of changes in policies that had been detrimental to older people. Just this past year, it assisted a small community that was losing its only medical clinic to find a way to maintain it. These are simply examples taken from a much longer list of CCHCC accomplishments.

The organization's most recent activity involved more than 1,000 volunteers in a countywide campaign to establish a public health district that would serve people in the rural areas of the county. This effort required a county referendum that had twice before failed to win a majority of the voters. With renewed effort and persistence that included both door-to-door canvassing and telephone contacts, the referendum has now passed. Public interest advocate Ralph Nader, looking at the accomplishments of this local organization several years ago, said that the CCHCC "exudes a rare blend of information, a sense of injustice and self-confidence about improving matters. . . . The challenge is to see how this community health group can be replicated in other localities around the nation" (cited in CCHCC, 1987, p. 2).

The CCHCC organization has now grown to more than 7,000 members. It regularly challenges local doctors and hospitals to be responsive to the needs of their community. A quarterly newsletter alerts members to current local issues, problems, and solutions and provides a comprehensive guide to local health care services. The organization operates a health hotline run by trained volunteers who serve as consumer advocates and handle more than 200 calls per month. In the organization's literature, the following identity statement is provided:

> The heart and soul of the CCHCC is a conviction that real improvements in people's lives can be accomplished through collective action. Using consumer task forces to involve those persons most affected by an issue, CCHCC has won its most significant victories through direct action organizing. In the process of these campaigns, the people involved have realized that they personally can take charge of the events that shape their lives. (CCHCC, 1987)

This is a powerful community narrative, available to many of the area's least powerful citizens as a story they can personally join in. The organization does not ask people to be heroes, only to be members of a small group with a clear identity story. Anyone can join a task force and begin to act in concert. Individuals with few resources on their own can benefit from organizing into collectivities with a social identity. No matter how strong or competent one is, sustaining changes in one's life is difficult in the absence of other people who share one's worldview. That is one reason why community narratives are important and why control over the content of the available narratives has social and political consequences.

The Beckman Institute's neighbors have no control over their invisibility to the university unless they find ways to claim and tell their own story. Psychologists interested in social change have a wealth of theoretical, empirical, and practical information that can be of use to ordinary citizens in the service of claiming and giving voice to their own positive identities. One way that psychologists (be they clinical, community, social, or cognitive psychologists) with progressive social values can contribute to social change is to share with local communities information about how to make use of the powerful effects of narratives on human behavior. Another way is to help these grassroots organizations tell their stories.

Stories Can Create Meaning, Emotion, and Collective Identity

People live their life stories, but they also appropriate the stories available to them through their narrative communities. Powerful community stories are told in multimedia ways: They appear in words, in pictures, and in the performances of everyday life. We live and enact our stories, and sometimes we create and adopt new stories. Where do new stories come from? Are they just made up, whole-cloth, out of individual minds? I think not. Rather, new stories are created from the various social contexts in which we live; in turn, some of these stories change our community narratives, enabling and facilitating social change.

Stories are psychologically (and therefore politically) powerful for at least three reasons: (a) They create memory, as suggested in the theoretical analysis described above, (b) they create meaning and emotion, and (c) they create identity.

With respect to meaning and emotion, I offer two examples, one from the laboratory and one from life:

A now-classic series of studies conducted by Lazarus and his colleagues demonstrated that narratives accompanying a filmed event could change the meaning, as well as the emotional and physiological experience, of those events (Lazarus & Alfert, 1964; Lazarus, Speisman, Mordkoff, & Davison, 1962; Speisman, Lazarus, Mordkoff, & Davison, 1964). These researchers showed two groups of observers the same film of tribal circumcision rites. One group listened to a narrator describe the trauma of the procedure. A second group saw the same film accompanied by an "anthropological" sound track in which events were described in a very matter-of-fact way and their local significance was explained. The researchers found that the first group experienced significantly greater physiological and psychological signs of distress. This effect has many counterparts in our day-to-day experiences, including the ways stereotypes serve as powerful indexes to narrative memory, meaning, and even physiological reactions.

Consider the following observation reported in a book by Brent Staples (1994), an African American psychologist. At the time he wrote about it, he was a member of the *New York Times* editorial staff, looking back on his own life experiences. In the mid-1970s, Staples was a new graduate student with a Ford Foundation Fellowship at the University of Chicago. This university community, perhaps more visibly than the one in Champaign-Urbana, has had a tense and long-standing history of separation from, and fear of, its African American neighbors. Staples had grown up in Black neighborhoods and schools in the East, however, with little experience in the White world. Now, exploring his Chicago environment, he discovers with some surprise, during an evening walk in the Hyde Park area where the university is located, that people are afraid of him. On one night, he encounters a White woman walking just ahead of him. She is dressed in a business suit and carries a briefcase. She glances at Staples and begins to run. He wonders what people looking out their window might have thought. What stories would be evoked from their memory? What was this woman thinking?

For some time after that, Staples tries, when encountering White people in similar situations, to look innocent and safe, whistling and avoiding eye contact. Then he describes a change. Staples learns that he can enjoy scaring people by walking toward them rather than avoiding them; he feels his power as they stiffen in fear.

> I held a special contempt for people who cowered in their cars as they waited for the light to change. . . . Thunk! Thunk! Thunk! They hammered down the door lock when I came into view. Once I had hustled across the street, head down, trying to seem harmless. Now I turned brazenly into the headlights and laughed. . . . They'd made me terrifying. Now I'd show them how terrifying I could be. (Staples, 1994, p. 204)

Brent Staples was a graduate student looking for a career. He describes resisting the temptation to go further than he did. His discovery led to a game for him, but it is not difficult to see how other young men with little social power or plans and little to lose might move into making other, more dangerous uses of such knowledge. The point here is that the narrative of the "dangerous Black man" is an accessible cultural story that affects us all, Black and White. That it needs to be challenged is obvious. How to challenge it is something psychologists may have ideas about, if we are willing to use our knowledge to help construct alternative narratives.

Staples goes on to tell us other personal stories, and these need to be heard by both Blacks and Whites. We all need to have accessible narratives that affirm young Black men. Some functional characteristics of such stories should be discernible from research on social cognition. We can collaborate with other community activists to make these stories known and presented in the most effective ways. But ultimately, it will be African American people, making their own collective narrative more public to each other, who will serve as a resource for ordinary citizens. Empowering narratives require believable stories that can be incorporated into the everyday lives of people who seek to work for social change.

Stories are also powerful because they create identity. Identity is a central construct in psychology. The internal sense of "who I am"—not just now, but who I will be, or what Markus and Nurius (1986) call "possible selves"—is influenced by storytelling. This is true, in part, because stories mimic the ways we actually experience the world—as sequential, woven interrelationships experienced in real time. Stories about our people, our community, and our settings are particularly powerful vehicles to influence our possible selves, as ultimately our behavior is propelled by these internalized and appropriated images.

Historical stories have contemporary effects. One of the most well-known narrative accounts of the 20th century's U.S. civil rights movement is the story of Rosa Parks. This story is told in dozens of children's books well-illustrated by artists. It usually presents a canonical picture of the lone heroic individual, just too tired that day to go to the back of the bus, who sparked a spontaneous boycott of the Montgomery, Alabama, bus service. In this sort of account, Rosa Parks is a remarkable individual, the perfect American hero. In fact, as pointed out by Herbert Kohl (1994), in an analysis contrasting the available children's literature with the actual events and with Parks's own autobiography, she was part of a very well-planned and orchestrated community organization. Kohl suggests that the story needs to be "retitled" to include the African American people of Montgomery. The individualized version needs to be rewritten to place Parks "in the context of a coherent community-based social struggle. This does not diminish Parks in any way. It places her, however, in the midst of a consciously planned movement for social change" (p. 140). It opens the possibility for all children to see themselves as activists.

Like the narrative offered by the local health care consumers organization described above, stories can be told in children's books and in public discourse in a way that makes them far more accessible to ordinary children and citizens. Certainly, they should be told this way to our students. In doing so, we help the stories obtain the power to create new possible selves for current generations, who can adopt the community narrative into their own life stories.

Implications for Method and Action

One way that social scientists can be useful to people who have limited access to resources is to serve as amplifiers of their voices. We can listen and write about what they have to say. To act in this way, one must believe that the process is as important as the product. This is not easy for us. We have been trained to tell people what to do, how to live, rather than to listen to their voices and use our resources as servants, trying to facilitate their discoveries and their creativity. In part, this comes from thinking of ourselves as "health care professionals" or "social experimenters" who want to "fix" things, rather than as educators and observers crafting reflections and contexts to facilitate and encourage others. We do not even know much about how to do this for children in our public schools, let alone for adults. The point is not to give up on our own impulses for making things better and for improving social conditions, but rather to have less hubris about our own ideas and more openness to collaboration, led by people who hold a personal stake in the outcomes of such work.

It is possible to help document and disseminate the work of community organizations, the visions of ordinary people, and the strengths and abilities they possess. Community and applied social psychologists would do well to engage in documentation of the social ecology of everyday life as it is experienced by people living and engaging in home, work, neighborhood, and school settings (see, e.g., Wicker, 1992, 1995). This requires an openness to methods of research that are genuinely empowering (see, e.g., Fine, 1994; Lincoln & Guba, 1985; Rappaport, 1990, 1994; Riessman, 1993), rather than distancing. In such work, the collection of data is itself authenticating and respectful, so as to have an empowering effect on the participant. The medium is the message. The process is the outcome.

I recently visited South Africa, where I had the opportunity to meet with activists, scholars, and human services professionals, including college professors. Many of these people had been very active in the anti-apartheid movement. They were now patiently explaining to me, as I visited several townships and saw people living in ways that in the North American context would have been regarded as far worse than the least desirable neighborhoods of our cities, how they had encountered remarkable strengths and powerful abilities among people who had been excluded from even the most modest of physical accommodations, let alone from access to the wealth of the country. Although it would be wrong to romanticize their poverty or their suffering, I also saw many people who did not believe that their identity was equivalent to their lack of adequate housing or their history of oppression.

The Nobel prize-winning South African author Nadine Gordimer (1997) has recently made a similar observation in contrasting race relations for Black citizens of the United States (for whom "the history of the country isn't theirs") with the experience of South African Blacks. Despite more than three centuries of oppression and racist exploitation, she notes,

> black South Africans nevertheless have had *their own earth under their feet.* Despite neglect in official education, their *languages have remained intact as mother tongues.* Their names are *their own ancestral names.* Nothing—neither cruel apartheid denigration nor liberal paternalism— has destroyed their identity. They know who they are. (p. 46)

In South Africa, I also saw people who had created community gardens and used found objects to make sculptures that told positive things about their families and their community. I saw people with a vision.

In Cape Town, I encountered a good deal of the official art that had been and remained prominent in statuary aggrandizing the White authorities. But I also now found, prominently displayed in a museum, a strikingly vivid cardboard sculpture painted in bright acrylics, depicting Nelson Mandela's inauguration. A new and celebratory narrative is taking hold in South Africa. It will not solve all of their problems, but it will be an important part of the solutions.

Hopeful narratives take place in our own backyards as well. But without attention, these new stories will not be known. They will disappear without the chance to be a resource for others—before they can create new possible selves. I do not intend to suggest that such narratives are "all" that is needed. Certainly, more material resources, economic opportunity, and a "fair share" in the social policies of government are required for genuine social change. But the stories and ideas of the people themselves are also a part of the resources that are needed.

Many people in South Africa had collaborated with artists to create "resistance art." In this art, one could often see the stories that were being told by people about their own communities, even in the face of official narratives that had tried to rob them of more than their land—had tried to justify dehumanizing and cruel oppression. Post-apartheid, much of that resistance art may disappear, as new directions will be celebrated by younger artists. Therefore, it is valuable that much of this work (and information about the artists) has been carefully documented by Sue Williamson (1989). Her book includes photographs of paintings and sculptures, murals, peace parks, graffiti, T-shirts, billboards, and ceramics produced by women's collectives. In the foreword to the book, Bishop Desmond Tutu wrote:

> it is important that people know that in being creative they become more than just consumers. They can transcend their often horrendous circumstances and bring something new into being. . . . The Bible says, "Where there is no vision the people perish." This anthology says, "We too have dreams, we too have visions." (p. 7)

One way for community scholars to collaborate with activists is to document their work, their visions.

An exhibition of self-taught art was recently installed at our local museum. The catalog (Flanagan, 1997) presents photographs of both the artists and their works, along with brief biographical materials. A few of these artists are well known, but most are not. As I look at the faces and see beyond them in the photographs, I get a glimpse of their modest homes. I want to know more about their stories. I wish that qualitative researchers had interviewed them, spent time with their families, visited their communities. The visions of these people are verbal as well as visual, social and political as well as aesthetic. These visions need documentation in a social and community psychology concerned with the art of social change, as much as their crafted works need documentation in the art world. This job should be appealing to social scientists who want to understand and help create the future.

Community narratives and the personal stories that follow from individual and collective visions need to be documented. For every Brent Staples (who knows how to do it for himself), there are hundreds, perhaps thousands, of individual citizens with life experiences that would be both enlightening for social scientists and inspirational for other, similarly situated people. Those who have access to storytelling equipment—artists, writers, documenters of social reality (psychologists and other social scientists might be candidates)—can play a part in the creation of new visions for social change. The tools we have, or at least can cultivate, are participant observation, ethnographic recording of the rituals and performances of everyday life, detailed open-ended interviews, textual discourse analysis, and interpretive methods that privilege the perspective of the participants. We can be facilitators in the reciprocity of personal stories and community narratives—the stuff out of which new dreams and new realities are born.

References

Altman, I., & Rogoff, B. (1987). Worldviews in psychology: Trait, interactional, organismic, and transactional perspectives. In D. Stokols, & I. Altman (Eds.), *Handbook of environmental psychology* (pp. 7-40). New York: John Wiley.

Barker, R. G., & Gump, P. V. (1964). *Big school, small school.* Stanford, CA: Stanford University Press.

Bower, G. H., & Clark, M. C. (1969). Narrative stories as mediators for serial learning. *Psychonomic Science, 14,* 181-182.

Bruner, J. (1990). *Acts of meaning.* Cambridge, MA: Harvard University Press.

Champaign County Health Care Consumers (CCHCC). (1987). *Champaign County Health Care Consumers Organization 10-year report.* Champaign, IL: Author.

Cornell University Empowerment Group. (1989, October). *Networking Bulletin, 1*(2).

Deaux, K. (1993). Reconstructing social identity. *Personality and Social Psychology Bulletin, 19,* 4-12.

Fine, M. (1994). Working the hyphens: Reinventing self and other qualitative research. In D. K. Denzin & L. S. Guba (Eds.), *Handbook of qualitative research* (pp. 70-82). Thousand Oaks, CA: Sage.

Flanagan, M. (1997). *Catalogue for the exhibition, "Personal Voice."* Champaign: University of Illinois Krannert Art Museum & Kinkead Pavilion.

Geertz, C. (1973). *Local knowledge.* New York: Basic Books.

Gilliam, D., & Iyengar, S. (1997, March). *Prime suspects: Script-based reasoning about race and crime.* Paper presented at Western Political Science Association meeting, Tucson, AZ.

Goldberg, M. (1985). *Jews and Christians: Getting our stories straight.* Nashville, TN: Abingdon.

Gordimer, N. (1997, June 8). Separate. *New York Times Magazine,* Section 6, 46-48.

Hauerwas, S. (1983). *The peaceable kingdom.* Notre Dame, IN: Notre Dame Press.

Kenny, D. A., & La Voie, L. (1985). Separating individual and group effects. *Journal of Personality and Social Psychology, 48,* 339-348.

Kohl, H. (1994). The politics of children's literature: What's wrong with the Rosa Parks myth. In B. Bigelow, L. Christensen, S. Karp, B. Miner, & B. Peterson (Eds.), *Rethinking our classrooms: Teaching for equity and justice.* Milwaukee, WI: Rethinking Schools Limited.

Lazarus, R. S., & Alfert, E. (1964). Short circuiting of threat by experimentally altering cognitive appraisal. *Journal of Abnormal and Social Psychology, 69,* 195-205.

Lazarus, R. S., Speisman, J. C., Mordkoff, A. M., & Davison, L. A. (1962). A laboratory study of psychological stress produced by a motion picture film. *Psychological Monographs, 76,* 1-35.

Lincoln, Y. S., & Guba, E. G. (1985). *Naturalistic inquiry.* Beverly Hills, CA: Sage.

Luke, D., Rappaport, J., & Seidman, E. (1991). Setting phenotypes in a mutual help organization. *American Journal of Community Psychology, 19,* 147-167.

Mankowski, E., & Rappaport, J. (1995). Stories, identity, and the psychological sense of community. In R. S. Wyer, Jr. (Ed.), *Advances in social cognition* (Vol. 8, pp. 211-226). Mahwah, NJ: Lawrence Erlbaum.

Markus, H., & Nurius, P. (1986). Possible selves. *American Psychologist, 41,* 954-969.

Maton, K. I., & Salem, D. A. (1995). Organizational characteristics of empowering community settings: A multiple case study approach. *American Journal of Community Psychology, 23,* 631-656.

McClendon, J., Jr. (1986). *Systematic theology: Ethics.* Nashville, TN: Abingdon.

Rappaport, J. (1990). Research methods and the empowerment social agenda. In P. Tolan, C. Keys, F. Chertok, & L. Jason (Eds.), *Researching community psychology: Integrating theories and methodologies* (pp. 51-63). Washington, DC: American Psychological Association.

Rappaport, J. (1993). Narrative studies, personal stories, and identity transformation in the mutual help context. *Journal of Applied Behavioral Science, 29,* 239-256.

Rappaport, J. (1994). Empowerment as a guide to doing research: Diversity as a positive value. In E. J. Trickett, R. Watts, & D. Birman (Eds.), *Human diversity: Perspectives on people in context* (pp. 359-382). San Francisco: Jossey-Bass.

Rappaport, J. (1995). Empowerment meets narrative: Listening to stories and creating settings. *American Journal of Community Psychology, 23,* 795-807.

Rappaport, J., & Simkins, R. (1991). Healing and empowering through community narrative. *Prevention in Human Services, 10,* 29-50.

Rappaport, J., & Stewart, E. (1997). A critical look at critical psychology: Elaborating the questions. In D. Fox & I. Prilleltensky (Eds.), *Critical psychology: An introductory handbook* (pp. 301-317). Thousand Oaks, CA: Sage.

Riessman, C. K. (1993). *Narrative analysis.* Newbury Park, CA: Sage.

Salzer, M. S. (1997). *Seeing the pictures in our heads: Toward a narrative conceptualization of stereotypes.* Unpublished manuscript based on a doctoral dissertation, University of Illinois at Urbana-Champaign, Department of Psychology.

Sarbin, T. R. (Ed.). (1986). *Narrative psychology: The storied nature of human conduct.* New York: Praeger.

Schank, R. (1990). *Tell me a story: A new look at real and artificial memory.* New York: Scribner.

Schank, R. C., & Abelson, R. (1995). Knowledge and memory: The real story. In R. Wyer (Ed.), *Advances in social cognition* (Vol. 8). Mahwah, NJ: Lawrence Erlbaum.

Shinn, M. (1990). Mixing and matching: Levels of conceptualization, measurement, and statistical analysis in community research. In P. Tolan, C. Keys, F. Chertok, & L. Jason (Eds.), *Researching community psychology: Integrating theories and methods* (pp. 111-126). Washington, DC: American Psychological Association.

Shweder, R. A., (1990). Cultural psychology: What is it? In J. W. Stigler, R. A. Sweder, & G. Herdt (Eds.), *Cultural psychology: Essays on comparative human development* (pp. 1-43). New York: Cambridge University Press.

Speisman, J. C., Lazarus, R. S., Mordkoff, A., & Davison, L. (1964). Experimental reduction of stress based on ego-defense theory. *Journal of Abnormal and Social Psychology, 68,* 367-380.

Staples, B. (1994). *Parallel time: Growing up in Black and White.* New York: Pantheon.

Stigler, J. W., Shweder, R. A., & Herdt, G. (Eds.). (1990). *Cultural psychology: Essays on comparative human development.* New York: Cambridge University Press.

Thomas, R. E., & Rappaport, J. (1996). Art as community narrative: A resource for social change. In M. B. Lykes, R. Liem, A. Banuazizi, & M. Morris (Eds.), *Myths about the powerless: Contesting social inequalities* (pp. 317-336). Philadelphia: Temple University Press.

Wicker, A. W. (1987). Behavior settings reconsidered: Temporal stages, resources, internal dynamics, context. In D. Stokols & I. Altman (Eds.), *Handbook of environmental psychology* (pp. 613-653). New York: John Wiley.

Wicker, A. W. (1992). Making sense of environments. In W. B. Walsh, K. H. Craik, & R. H. Price (Eds.), *Person environment psychology: Models and perspectives* (pp. 157-192). Mahwah, NJ: Lawrence Erlbaum.

Wicker, A. W. (1995, November). *Work meanings in the Third World: An important consideration for evaluators.* Paper presented at American Evaluation Association and Canadian Evaluation Society joint meeting, Vancouver, BC, Canada.

Williamson, S. (1989). *Resistance art in South Africa.* Capetown: David Phillip.

Wyer, R. S., Jr. (Ed.). (1995). *Advances in social cognition* (Vol. 8). Mahwah, NJ: Lawrence Erlbaum.

Zimmerman, M., Reischl, T., Seidman, E., Rappaport, J., Toro, P., & Salem, D. (1991). Expansion strategies of a mutual help organization. *American Journal of Community Psychology, 19,* 251-279.

Author Index

Subject Index

About the Contributors

Ximena B. Arriaga is Assistant Professor of Psychology at Claremont Graduate University, Claremont, California. She received her Ph.D. in social psychology from the University of North Carolina at Chapel Hill. Her main research interests are in interpersonal relationships, longitudinal research, and interpersonal violence.

Robert D. Caplan is Professor of Psychology and of Psychiatry and Behavioral Sciences at George Washington University, Washington, D.C., where he directs the doctoral program in industrial/organizational psychology. His research is in the area of coping and stress, work-family relationships, and preventive intervention theory. His current work focuses on methods of preventing program failure when organizations adopt prevention-focused interventions. He has authored numerous scientific publications stemming from his research in the United States and abroad.

Jin Nam Choi received his M.A. degree from Seoul National University in Korea. Currently, he is a doctoral candidate in organizational psychology at the University of Michigan and is working as a research associate at the Institute for Social Research. His research interests include organizational processes of innovation diffusion and implementation, organizational change and learning, and the structure of interteam communication networks in organizations.

Stewart I. Donaldson is Associate Professor of Psychology and Director of the Division of Organizational Strategy and Evaluation at Claremont Graduate University, Claremont, California. He is an organizational psychologist who specializes in the changing nature of work, work and well-being, strategic management of human service organizations, and evaluation research. He is the principal investigator of The California Wellness Foundation's Work and Health Initiative Evaluation.

Vangie A. Foshee is Associate Professor in the Department of Health Behavior and Health Education at the University of North Carolina's School of Public Health at Chapel Hill. She received her Ph.D. from the School of Public Health, University of North Carolina at Chapel Hill. Her research concerns are identifying biological, sociological, and psychological determinants of adolescent problem behavior, including cigarette smoking, sexual behavior, and dating violence, and evaluating the effectiveness of prevention programs targeted at adolescents and their families.

Daniel S. Friedland earned his M.A. in organizational psychology at the University of Michigan, where he is currently a doctoral student. His areas of research interest include well-being in relation to social roles and identity, and the implementation of social innovations in organizations. He has coauthored chapters on job-loss, and his dissertation focuses on underemployment and health.

Laura E. Gooler is Associate Director of the Division of Organizational Strategy and Evaluation (DOSE) and Adjunct Assistant Professor at Claremont Graduate University, Claremont, California. In DOSE, she serves as Project Director for the California Wellness Foundation's Work and Health Initiative Evaluation. She received her Ph.D. in industrial/organizational psychology from Baruch College of the City University of New York. She specializes in organizational development, strategy, and evaluation research, and her research interests include the changing nature of work, workforce diversity, work-life balance, teamwork, and workplace health promotion.

James S. Jackson earned his Ph.D. at Wayne State University, Detroit, Michigan, and has been a faculty member at the University of Michigan since 1971. He is the Daniel Katz Distinguished University Professor of Psychology, the Director of the Research Center for Group Dynamics at the Institute for Social Research, and also has appointments in the

School of Public Health, the Center for Afro-American and African Studies, and the Institute of Gerontology. He helped found and continues to direct the African American Mental Health Research Center, funded by the National Institute of Mental Health. In addition, he has a research appointment at the École des Hautes Études en Sciences Sociales in Paris. His research and publication areas include race and ethnic relations, health and mental health, adult development and aging, attitudes and attitude change, and African American politics.

Stuart Oskamp is Professor of Psychology at Claremont Graduate University, Claremont, California. He received his Ph.D. from Stanford University, Stanford, California. His main research interests are in the areas of attitudes and attitude change, environmentally responsible behavior such as recycling and energy conservation, and social issues and public policy. His books include *Attitudes and Opinions* and *Applied Social Psychology.* He has served as President of the American Psychological Association Division of Population and Environmental Psychology and the Society for the Psychological Study of Social Issues (SPSSI) and as editor of *Journal of Social Issues* and *Applied Social Psychology Annual.*

Richard H. Price is Professor of Psychology and Senior Research Scientist at the Institute for Social Research, University of Michigan, Ann Arbor, where he also serves as Director of the Michigan Prevention Research Center. He has written many scientific articles and books on prevention research and has received the Lela Rowland Award for prevention research and the Distinguished Contribution Award from the Society for Community Research and Action. His research interests center on the organization of work, life transitions, and well-being.

Julian Rappaport is Professor of Psychology at the University of Illinois at Urbana-Champaign and a faculty member in the programs in Clinical/Community Psychology and Personality and Social Ecology. He is a recipient of the American Psychological Association's (Division 27) Career Award for Distinguished Contributions to Theory and Research, a past President of the Society for Community Research and Action, and Editor-Emeritus of *American Journal of Community Psychology.*

Karen J. Rowe earned a master's degree in public health from the Department of Health Behavior and Health Education, School of Public Health, University of Michigan. She is currently a Research Coordinator for World Education, working on the Girls' and Women's Education Project in Nepal. She has interests in evaluation research, empowerment, women's health, and international health.

Marybeth Shinn is Professor and Chair of the Psychology Department at New York University. She received her Ph.D. in social and community psychology from the University of Michigan. Her research interests include homelessness, child care, and methods of assessing social contexts. She serves as Associate Editor of *American Journal of Community Psychology* and is a past President of, and recipient of the Award for Distinguished Contributions to Theory and Research from, the Society for Community Research and Action.

Kenneth J. Steinman received his master's degree in public health and is currently a Ph.D. student in the Department of Health Behavior and Health Education, School of Public Health, University of Michigan. His interests include prevention research and evaluation of programs addressing adolescent health, violence, substance abuse, and sexual behavior.

Christine Timko is Associate Director of the Center for Health Care Evaluation, and a Research Health Science Specialist at the Department of Veterans Affairs Health Care System in Palo Alto, California; and is also Consulting Associate Professor in the Department of Psychiatry and Behavioral Sciences at the Stanford University Medical Center, Stanford, California. She received her Ph.D. in social psychology from the University of Massachusetts, Amherst. She conducts program evaluations of psychiatric and substance abuse treatment, and studies the impact of psychiatric and medical problems on the family.

Sam Tsemberis is Founder and Executive Director of Pathways to Housing, Inc., the agency that operates the Consumer Preference Independent Living program described in this volume. He received his Ph.D. from New York University. He has developed and directed several innovative programs for homeless New Yorkers with psychiatric disabilities. He chairs a review committee for federal block grants for the Center for Mental Health Services and is Clinical Assistant Professor in the Department of Psychiatry at New York University Medical Center.

Julie Volckens earned a B.A. from the University of Illinois and then worked for more than 10 years before entering the University of Michigan doctoral program in social psychology, where she has been a NIMH trainee for 4 years. Her research interests include group conflict, racism, dominant-group identity, group-level attributions, and discourse analysis. Before becoming a graduate student, she coauthored a criminal justice article entitled "Women in Small Town Policing: Job Performance and Stress."

Rachel Weiss is a doctoral student in organizational behavior at Claremont Graduate University, Claremont, California. She serves as the Evaluation Project Manager for the Winning New Jobs Program of the California Wellness Foundation's Work and Health Initiative. Her research interests are in the areas of creativity and innovation, qualitative research, and program evaluation.

Marc A. Zimmerman is Associate Professor in the Department of Health Behavior and Health Education in the School of Public Health and in the Combined Program in Education and Psychology at the University of Michigan. He received his Ph.D. in psychology from the University of Illinois. His primary research interests include the application and development of empowerment theory and the study of adolescent health and resiliency.